T5-CQE-226

Darien Cooper's Happy Husband Book

Darien Cooper

coauthor ANNE KRISTIN CARROLL

Two books in one: *You Can Be the Wife of a Happy Husband,* Darien's time-honored bestseller and *We Became the Wives of Happy Husbands* (coauthor, Anne Kristin Carroll), experience stories showing that Darien's biblically-based philosophy really works. A Leader's Guide for use in group studies is available for the first book.

VICTOR BOOKS

a division of SP Publications, Inc.

WHEATON, ILLINOIS 60187

Offices also in Fullerton, California • Whitby, Ontario, Canada • Amersham-on-the-Hill, Bucks, England

Scripture quotations are from *The Amplified Bible,* © 1965, Zondervan Publishing House, Grand Rapids, Mich., in *You Can Be the Wife of a Happy Husband,* unless otherwise noted. In *We Became Wives of Happy Husbands,* Scripture quotations are from the King James Version unless otherwise noted. Other quotations are from *The Living Bible* (LB), © 1971, Tyndale House, Wheaton, Ill.; the *New American Standard Bible* (NASB), © The Lockman Foundation, La Habra, Calif.; 1960, 1962, 1963, 1968, 1971, 1972, 1973; *The New International Version: New Testament* (NIV), © 1973, the New York Bible Society International; *The New Testament in Modern English* (PH), © J. B. Phillips 1958, The Macmillan Company; *The New Berkeley Version in Modern English* (BERK), © 1969 by Zondervan Publishing House, Grand Rapids, Mich.; *The New Testament in the Language of the People* by Charles B. Williams (WMS), © 1966 by Edith S. Williams, Moody Press, Chicago, Ill.; *The New Testament in the Language of Today* by William F. Beck (BECK), © 1963, Concordia Publishing House, St. Louis, Mo. All quotations used by permission.

First paperback editions: *You Can Be the Wife of a Happy Husband,* 1974; *We Became Wives of Happy Husbands,* 1976.

Library of Congress Catalog Card No. 80-51393
ISBN 0-88207-785-6

Printed in the United States of America

VICTOR BOOKS

A division of SP Publications, Inc.
P.O. Box 1825 • Wheaton, Illinois 60187

Foreword

In a day when almost every newspaper in the country gives front page space to the inane, harmful pronouncements of the women's libbers, it is refreshing to hear an attractive, godly woman speak up. Darien Cooper is a real woman—satisfied and fulfilled. It did not take her three or four marriages to discover what it takes to please a man. She discovered that secret the first time around and is practicing what she teaches.

Four men love and admire this young woman: her husband and their three sons. Hundreds of women attend her two weekly Bible classes, where she expounds the principles found in this book. Many troubled wives have been brought into her classes by friends and have gone away transformed by the principles Mrs. Cooper teaches. A number of these women have changed from competitor to partner, much to the amazement of their husbands.

I first met Darien when I went to Atlanta, Ga., to hold a Family Life Seminar. She and her husband, DeWitt, met my wife and me at the Atlanta airport. I was excited when I heard how God was using Darien in the much needed area of developing feminine contentment in the home through teaching biblical principles. But I was even more impressed with the way her husband shared her enthusiasm about her ministry.

Any time I find a man who takes genuine pride in what his wife does outside the home, I know she must be a wise woman. It's natural for a man to feel threatened by his partner's success. Not so with DeWitt. He is thrilled that God is using Darien to help wives experience satisfying relationships with their husbands.

It is about time a woman says some of the things Darien expresses in this book. She has an excellent grasp of the biblical concepts that produce happiness in marriage and states them clearly. She knows that a woman is not some weak, frilly, brainless creature man marries only for erotic pleasure or to display as an ornament. Instead, she sees a woman as an absolute essential to a man's fulfillment in life. But she is vitally aware that a wife must accept her God-given role or she will ruin the partnership.

Darien Cooper has a thorough understanding of the male ego. In this book she discusses the biblical principles every wife needs to know in order to live with that ego. Many family explosions could be avoided if more wives knew these secrets. Hopefully, thousands of women who may never have a chance to hear Darien speak will read this book and find God's help for their marriages.

TIM LAHAYE,
Pastor
Scott Memorial Baptist Church
San Diego, California

Contents

You Can Be the Wife of a Happy Husband

We Became Wives of Happy Husbands

You Can Be the Wife of a Happy Husband

Introduction

You can find your true identity by discovering God's role for you as a woman and a wife. This book is designed to help you make those discoveries.

I believe God has given us women the choice role. Unfortunately, many of us do not realize that being a woman and a wife is a wonderful privilege, so we miss the joy and fulfillment God has in store for us. Though we want happiness, some of us back off after being exposed to the biblical principles and concepts explained in this book. We say, "This is too good to be true," or "It won't work for me," or as I once said, "You've got to be kidding. I don't need help."

At that time I wasn't teachable. Had you asked me if I had any problems personally, I would have replied, "Nothing serious; nothing that needs changing. But my husband—now that's something else!"

I thought I had a good marriage, but as I look back now, I realize I simply had a good man. For 12 years I tried to change DeWitt—the way he did things or didn't do them, or the way he related to me.

I tried direct approaches and subtle ones. I'd cry when he forgot my birthday or our anniversary. I wondered why he wouldn't come and put his arms around me and tell me he was sorry and loved me. But it seemed as if the more I cried, the less attention he gave me.

One day I said, "DeWitt, I've been watching the Joneses next door. Mr. Jones is so thoughtful. He brings his wife candy and flowers. He always kisses her affectionately at the door when he comes home from work. I wonder why you don't do that?"

"Because I don't know her that well," he responded.

I'd listen to what he'd tell me when he came home from work, and give him advice as to what he should or should not have said or done. I couldn't understand why he didn't seem to appreciate my advice and stopped sharing with me.

Then about six years ago, after an intensive study of the Bible, I saw that God had definite solutions to life's problems. And a detailed outline of how a successful marriage should be maintained. I realized that instead of helping DeWitt, I was crushing him—destroying his masculinity. I said, "OK, God, I'm ready for You to show me how to be the kind of wife I should be."

Today, I am enjoying the kind of fulfilling relationship God meant each marriage to be. Life is exciting since I've applied the principles God gave me in the Bible. I've found that I can have complete peace and satisfaction in my marriage, regardless of circumstances.

God is no respecter of persons. His truth is for all who believe and trust Him by obeying His Word. All you need is a teachable attitude—the willingness to let God work in your life. As you trust God and obey His Word, you will find—as I did and as so many other women have—the fulfillment you want.

I have written this book in order to share with as many women as possible the truths that have transformed my life and marriage over the last six years. The only regret I have is that I did not know these principles sooner.

It is important that you read the book in the sequence in which it is written, since each chapter builds on the previous one. Please reserve judgment of any single truth presented until you've read the whole book and have the overall picture. And as you study these principles, remember that they apply whether or not your husband is a believer in Jesus Christ.

As you put these principles into practice and make them

a way of life, you should see changes in your husband as well as yourself. It is exciting to hear and see the reactions of husbands who don't know that their wives are studying God's plan for a happy marriage relationship. Many cannot understand why their wives have suddenly become sweeter or easier to live with.

But changes take time, so be patient and let God do the changing. Rely on Him to build or rebuild your marriage. "Except the Lord builds the house, they labor in vain who build it" (Psalm 127:1).

May I suggest that you begin a personal notebook. As you read this book, jot down in one column attitudes and habits in your life that need to be changed. Ask God to show you creative steps you can take to change each wrong attitude or habit. List these steps in the opposite column. Then, as God leads, try these ideas out. You will be encouraged as you look back later and see the changes God has made in your life.

It is my prayer that through this book, you will discover the full, satisfying life God has for you as a woman and a wife, and that you'll become the wife your husband needs. To put it another way, you will become "the wife of a happy husband."

I want to express deep appreciation to the many people whose dedicated help has made this book possible: My husband DeWitt and three sons, Craig, Brian, and Ken, made writing easier because of their enthusiastic cooperation. Mrs. Willis Horton patiently taught me many of these truths. Phyllis Ott typed the manuscript and gave helpful suggestions. Anna Stanley gave me the idea of writing this book. And, finally, I appreciate the scores of women who have permitted me to tell their experiences as illustrations—disguised, of course, to conceal identities.

1
The Perfect Plan

Anne Carroll was desperate. She picked up the telephone directory and found the list of agencies offering to help a person in an emotional crisis. She dialed one number after another, sharing her problems with several different persons, then sat back in her chair and groaned.

"I've tried all those ideas before. They're only temporary help. They only touch the surface. I need a permanent solution to my problems—I need it now— right now!"

Completely frustrated, Anne decided suicide was the only answer. She went to bed that night wondering just how she'd kill herself. She loved her husband and boys and didn't want to cause them shame. She would like to simply disappear.

No one would have thought that sensitive, lovable, beautiful Anne Carroll was considering suicide. She had grown up in a wealthy home and radiated an air of sophistication. She was vivacious and well educated. Friends figured she "had the world on a string."

Early in her search for answers, Anne had attended a Bible college. She had copied the life-style of students who had the quality of life she wanted. But faking it was not the answer to her need. She left school.

Soon afterward, her teen marriage ended in divorce. Nothing traumatic, just the quiet dissolving of a nonfulfilling relationship.

Six weeks after her divorce was final she married a man who was the direct opposite of her first husband. Her new marriage, though in some ways exciting, seemed empty. So she tried careers: work in publishing, as a model, a legal secretary, a travel representative. But success in these areas was only a temporary diversion.

When her father died, she got caught up in the occult through trying to reach him. At first, spiritualism (spiritism) seemed to give her what she had been looking for but hadn't found in her study of Christianity. However, Satan's imitation of Christianity failed to satisfy her too. She became more and more depressed and overwhelmed by the evil power with which she was experimenting. She realized that spiritualism was not the answer to her needs and gave it up.

During a period of separation from her husband, she tried drugs. Her doctor prescribed whatever she wanted—barbiturates, tranquilizers, amphetamines. Pep pills when awake and downers to sleep. One day, while reading the newspaper, she discovered she was taking the amount of drugs used to treat schizophrenic patients in mental hospitals. Through sheer willpower she broke herself of the drug habit.

It was after returning to her husband that Anne decided on suicide. She was completely frustrated—unhappy with her husband and unhappy without him. In this desperate state, she reluctantly agreed to attend a women's neighborhood Bible study.

Her first reaction to the study was, "These ideas may help women whose problems are minor, but they can't help me with mine."

At the second meeting, however, she clearly saw her need for Jesus Christ. She realized for the first time that He loved her personally, died for her personally, and was ready and available to answer personally all the problems and frustrations of her life.

But after receiving Jesus Christ as her Saviour, Anne did not know how to apply her newfound faith to her marriage, and it ended in divorce.

Through the next year, Anne learned about God's principles for a happy marriage. Much to her surprise she discovered that she had been the major factor contributing to her husband's drinking and unfaithfulness. As she applied the principles she'd learned, her attitudes and actions began to change. Within a year, Anne and Jim were remarried.

Today, their marriage is a success. It is not completely without problems, of course. Jesus Christ never promised that. But now two people who became one flesh are enjoying the happiness that marriage was designed to give.

Many women can identify with Anne in her search for personal and marital fulfillment. The United States divorce rate for 1971 indicates that a great many women are not happy in their marital relationships. There was one divorce for every three marriages that year. Such heartache and disappointment is not necessary. There is a better way, not only for Anne, but for you, too, if you are willing to accept it.

A Satisfying Life

God did not create you and put you on this earth to live an apathetic, frustrated, defeated, or discouraged life. He meant you to be happier than you ever dreamed possible. "Now glory be to God who by His mighty power at work within us is able to do far more than we would ever dare to ask or even dream of—infinitely beyond our highest prayers, desires, thoughts, or hopes" (Ephesians 3:20, LB). Jesus Christ said that He came to provide a satisfying, complete life for you. "I came that they may have and enjoy life, and have it in abundance—to the full, till it overflows" (John 10:10).

This life is available to you regardless of your background, education, nationality, or present circumstances. There is no problem too large or too small for Christ to work out in your life. All that He requires from you is a willing heart and obedience to His plan. "If you are willing and obedient, you shall eat the good of the land" (Isaiah 1:19). The "good of the land" can be compared to an abundant life for you.

A Personalized Plan

God loves you so much that He has worked out a personal plan for you to experience growth, development, and fulfillment. You should think of your life as a divine prescription from the hand of God. "You made all the delicate, inner parts of my body, and knit them together in my mother's womb. Thank You for making me so wonderfully complex! It is amazing to think about.

"Your workmanship is marvelous—and how well I know it. You were there while I was being formed in utter seclusion! You saw me before I was born and scheduled each day of my life before I began to breathe. Every day was recorded in Your Book! How precious it is, Lord, to realize that You are thinking about me constantly! I can't even count how many times a day Your thoughts turn towards me. And when I waken in the morning, You are still thinking of me!" (Psalm 139:13-18, LB)

God cares so much for you that He is always thinking about you and watching everything that concerns you. No accidents occur in the lives of God's children. He desires to use your personality, your physical makeup, and your background to your advantage.

If you trust Him, He can take all of the things in your life that you would like to change and work them out for your good. "We are assured and know that (God being a partner in their labor), all things work together and are (fitting into a plan) for good to those who love God and are called according to (His) design and purpose" (Romans 8:28). Notice that He did not say that all things *are good,* but that He would *work all things out for your good.* Only God can perform such miracles.

Do not question what God is doing; simply trust Him to know what is best for you. "But who are you, a mere man, to criticize and contradict and answer back to God? Will what is formed say to Him that formed it, 'Why have You made me thus?' " (Romans 9:20) This means that you are not to question why you are the way you are or why your husband is as he is. Rather, you are to discover and accept God's plan for your life so that He can work out all things to your advantage.

Marriage—A Fulfilling Relationship

Everything God has designed for you is for your benefit. Thus, marriage was designed by God to give you the greatest human happiness possible. This relationship is described in Ephesians 5:21-33: "Be subject to one another out of reverence for Christ, the Messiah, the Anointed One. Wives, be subject—be submissive and adapt yourselves—to your own husbands as [a service] to the Lord. For the husband is head of the wife as Christ is the Head of the Church, Himself the Saviour of [His] body. As the Church is subject to Christ, so let wives also be subject in everything to their husbands.

"Husbands, love your wives, as Christ loved the Church and gave Himself up for her. . . . Even so husbands should love their wives as [being in a sense] their own bodies. He who loves his own wife loves himself. For no man ever hated his own flesh, but nourishes and carefully protects and cherishes it, as Christ does the Church. . . . For this reason a man shall leave his father and his mother and shall be joined to his wife, and the two shall become one flesh. . . . However, let each man of you (without exception) love his wife as [being in a sense] his very own self; and let the wife see that she respects and reverences her husband."

I believe the role of the wife in the marital relationship is the choice role. She is to be loved, protected, and cherished by her husband in the same way that Christ gave Himself for the Church (believers). The words "be subject" or "be submissive" describe the way you are to relate to your husband. Another way of saying it is that you are to be a *responder* to your husband's love, protection, and leadership. Submission never means that your personality, abilities, talents, or individuality are buried, but that they will be channeled to operate to the maximum.

Someone said, "Woman was created from man, not from his head to be commanded by him, nor from his feet to be his slave. Rather, she was taken from his side to complement him, near his arms to be protected by him, and close to his heart to be loved." Submission never imprisons you. It liberates you, giving you the freedom to be creative under the protection of divinely appointed authority.

Wasn't your relationship before marriage one of your responding to his love and leadership? He expressed his love and leadership by being thoughtful, complimenting you, and bringing you gifts. You responded to this love by making yourself attractive to please him or by going places with him that you may not have really cared about simply because you enjoyed his company.

Then, after marriage things began to change. What happened? Could it be that you gradually left your role of responder by no longer taking time to look your best for your husband or refusing to share his interests? Yes, it is easy to stop responding to your husband without even realizing it.

A wise woman knows that she cannot take her role lightly but must seriously work at building a lasting, fulfilling relationship. "Every wise woman builds her house, but the foolish one tears it down with her own hands" (Proverbs 14:1). A woman can act foolishly and destroy her marriage, yet not be aware that she is violating principles that build a successful marriage. That is the reason women must be taught "to love their husbands and their children; to be self-controlled, chaste, homemakers, good-natured (kindhearted), adapting and subordinating themselves to their husbands, that the Word of God may not be exposed to reproach—blasphemed or discredited" (Titus 2:4-5).

Because the world has done an effective job of distorting the marriage relationship and its respective roles, the foolish woman often feels unfulfilled. She is convinced that her unhappiness is caused by her homemaking and child care responsibilities. She seeks fulfillment in trying to change her role through such means as the women's liberation movement. Actually, though, her unhappiness is not a result of her role but of her failure to understand and fulfill the role God designed for her.

The wise woman recognizes God's principles for building a successful marriage and applies them. She realizes that a successful marriage requires planning in the same way any successful venture does. For instance, in baking a light, delicious cake, she must put in the right ingredients at the right time, in the proper proportions. The same is true of a marriage. In order to develop a happy marriage the wise woman will use the proper principles, at the right time, with a divine balance. A good marriage does not just happen. It is deliberately built.

The Book of Esther gives examples of both the foolish and wise woman. Queen Vashti, the foolish woman, did not respond to her husband's leadership when he requested that she join the party he was giving and show his guests her beauty. As a result, she was banished from the king's presence, and he chose Esther to be his queen.*

Esther, a wise woman, responded to King Ahasuerus' leadership and the results were fantastic! During a period of crisis when she could have lost her life, her submissive attitude and wise actions caused the king to say, "Now tell me what you really want, and I will give it to you, even if it is half of the kingdom!" (Esther 5:6, LB) The crisis was over. Esther's life and the lives of her people were saved because of right and wise actions on her part.

A wise woman will build a successful marriage by meeting her husband's needs in the manner described in Proverbs 31:12: "She will comfort, encourage and do him only good as long as there is life within her."

Use this verse as a measuring stick to determine your own attitudes or actions. Ask yourself, "How can I comfort, encourage, or do my husband good?" Sometimes this may mean comforting him when his boss has given him a hard day at work or encouraging him when he begins to doubt his ability to provide for his family. As you act wisely, you will see a miraculous blossoming of your marriage relationship.

---

* Even though some Christians believe that Queen Vashti was asked to perform some lewd act and was therefore justified in her disobedience, there is nothing in the Hebrew text or the customs of the Persians to indicate that she was asked to commit a sin.

2 Your Relationship with the Designer

The need for a woman was evident in the life of the first man. Adam was created perfect by the Lord and placed in a perfect environment, the Garden of Eden. There, he had fellowship with God and an interesting occupation. Yet he needed a counterpart—someone who could meet his human needs.

So God provided the woman. "Now the Lord God said, 'It is not good [sufficient, satisfactory] that the man should be alone; I will make him a helper meet (suitable, adapted, completing) for him.' Then Adam said, 'This [creature] is now bone of my bones, and flesh of my flesh. She shall be called Woman, because she was taken out of a man' " (Genesis 2:18, 23).

Because God made woman, she was perfect. Her beauty must have been beyond anything we can imagine. Adam took one look at her and saw immediately that she was different from him, yet was his counterpart.

The New Testament echoes man's need for the woman and God's purpose in making her. "The man wasn't made from the woman but the woman from man, and the man wasn't made for the woman but the woman for the man" (1 Corinthians 11:8-9, BECK). One beautiful aspect of God's plan is that the woman will find happiness herself as she meets her husband's needs.

A woman can also have tremendous influence on her husband because of her special abilities to meet those needs.

When the first woman left her role of responding to her husband's leadership, she made a grave mistake which affected all mankind (see Genesis 3:1-6). Eve allowed Satan's subtle conversation and deceit to influence her thinking and cause her to doubt that God's plan was for her good. Once she doubted God's complete love and provision, it was not long before she sinned—acted independently of God and His plan for her life.

Having made the mistake herself, Eve used her influence to draw her husband into the same mistake. "And she gave some also to her husband, and he ate" (Genesis 3:6). She gave and he ate! According to 1 Timothy 2:13-14, Adam was not deceived. He knew what he was doing. He had a choice between continuing in perfect fellowship with the Lord or joining his beloved wife in her fallen state. Knowing the consequences, he chose a fallen state with Eve rather than be without her. Yes, the influence of a woman is tremendous.

If you aren't trusting God for guidance, you may influence your husband in the wrong way. An account is given in Genesis 16 of Sarai (later called Sarah), a godly woman, who left her role of responding to her husband's leadership and influenced him in a way she later regretted. Many years had passed since God had promised them a son. Sarai became impatient and tried to help God fulfill His promise by giving her maid to her husband so the maid might bear them a son.

Sarai stepped out of the role God had designed for her and took matters into her own hands, thus influencing her husband to sin. This sin is causing and has caused pain for many people through the centuries as the children of Hagar and Sarai have warred against each other. Woman's role is a big responsibility as well as a wonderful privilege.

Woman's Need

Before the fall of man (see Genesis 3), woman was complete in body, soul, and spirit. Each day she enjoyed fellowship with the Lord and her husband. When she disobeyed God and ate the fruit of the tree of the knowledge of good and evil, she died as God had said she would. She did not die physically for several hundred years, but she died spiritually at once. Her human spirit, the part of her that could understand God's truths and enjoy His fellowship, died then. Immediately, there was an emptiness in her life that could be filled only by regaining a personal relationship with God Himself.

It has been said that "there is a God-shaped vacuum in the heart of each person which cannot be filled by anything or anyone but God, the Creator, made known through Jesus Christ." Each member of the human race comes into this world in the same fallen state in which Eve found herself immediately after her sin. The old sin nature has been transmitted to each of us through Adam. "Therefore as sin came into the world through one man and death as the result of sin, so death spread to all men, [no one being able to stop it or to escape its power] because all men sinned" (Romans 5:12).

Figure A in the following drawings illustrates our condition when we come into the world. Each of us has a control center in her life. Without Christ in our lives, the old sin nature (self—I—flesh—old man—or whatever term you use) is controlling us. This sin nature shows up clearly in children. We don't have to teach them to be selfish or to demand their own way. They do that naturally. The old sin nature is selfish and demanding.

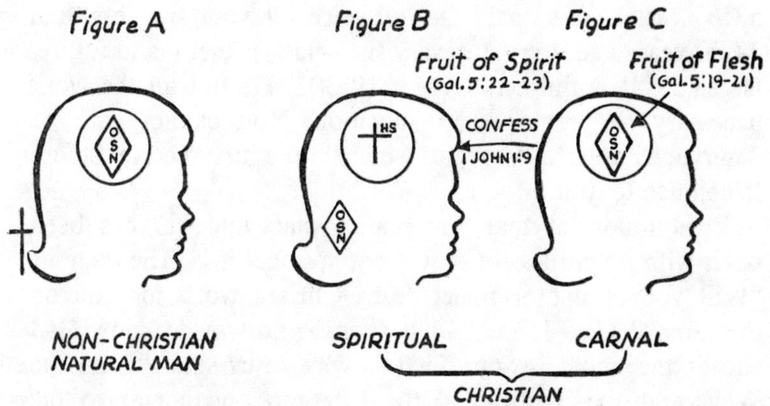

OSN = Old Sin Nature, "I", or Self controlling the life

✝HS = Christ indwelling the believer through the power of the Holy Spirit

◯ = Control center of your life

✝ = Christ outside the life of the non-Christian

God loved you so much He designed a plan whereby you could be restored to fellowship with Him without compromising His own perfect character. (The barrier of sin between you and God had to be removed before God could express His love for you since His righteousness could not tolerate contact with sin. God, being perfectly just, could not overlook your sin but required that the penalty—death—be paid.) Jesus, who is God's Son, accomplished the Father's plan by leaving the glories of heaven to come to earth. He was born into the human race, adding humanity to His deity. By living a perfect life and willingly dying on the cross to pay the penalty for our sins, He provided for our salvation. "He made Him who knew no sin to be sin on our behalf, that we might become the righteousness of God in Him" (2 Corinthians 5:21, NASB).

While Jesus hung there on the cross for three hours, the Father "caused the iniquity of us all to fall on Him" (Isaiah

53:6, NASB). Jesus paid the full price for your sins less than 2,000 years ago, for your every sin—past, present, and future. He said, "It is finished" (John 19:30). He did all the work necessary to provide your salvation. You cannot earn or deserve it. It is a free gift which you must receive before it belongs to you.

It is important that you realize that your sin has been dealt with, regardless of how great you feel it is. The issue is, "Will you accept or reject Jesus Christ's work for you on the cross?" (See John 3:18.) There is no way to know God except through His Son. That is why Jesus said, "I am the Way, and the Truth, and the Life; no one comes to the Father, but through Me" (John 14:6, NASB). When you accept His work on the cross for you, personally, you become God's child.

If you're not sure right now that you are God's child, a member of His forever family, why don't you make sure? The Bible says that you can *know* you are God's child once you have received His Son. "God has given us eternal life, and this life is in His Son. He who has the Son has the life; he who does not have the Son of God does not have the life. These things I have written to you who believe in the name of the Son of God, in order that you may *know that you have eternal life*" (1 John 5:11-13, NASB).

Right now, in the silence of your own heart, you can tell the Father that you do accept His perfect gift of salvation by receiving His Son as your personal Saviour. You can know that you are His child on the basis of His Word, not by what you do or feel.

When you, whether just now or in the past, trusted Jesus Christ to come into your life, you moved to the condition represented by Figure B (p. 23). Jesus Christ came into your life through the renewing power of the Holy Spirit, and you became a child of God. At that moment the Holy Spirit came to live in you so you could live a Christian life (see Romans 8:9). Just as you could not die to pay for your own sins, neither can you, yourself, live the Christian life. Jesus Christ wants to relive His life in you and through you, moment by moment, if you will allow Him. As you trust in His victory over sin for you at the cross, the old sin nature in you is rendered helpless or inactive.

Because of Christ's victory over sin, you no longer have to panic when things go wrong. You know those days when Johnny and Jim begin a fight and, just as you are trying to settle it, the phone rings, then something boils over on the stove? You can have real control and peace through such times by drawing on Jesus' strength instead of your own. He promises to be sufficient (see 2 Corinthians 9:8). Not only that, He says He will use just such irritations as these to shape or mold you into the image of His Son Jesus Christ (see Romans 8:29).

It is as if you are a diamond in the rough being made into the image of Jesus Christ by the Master Craftsman. Each day can become an adventure if you think of its joys and trials as part of God's process of shaping you into a divine original. You can relax, trusting His skilled craftsmanship. "He has made us what we are, because He has created us through our union with Christ Jesus for doing good deeds" (Ephesians 2:10, WMS).

Even though you are God's child, it is possible for you to again take control of your life and feel frustrated and dissatisfied. Figure C (p. 23) pictures this condition. Paul describes it as follows: "I don't understand myself at all, for I really want to do what is right, but I can't. I do what I don't want to—what I hate. I know perfectly well that what I am doing is wrong, and my bad conscience proves that I agree with these laws I am breaking. But I can't help myself, because I'm no longer doing it. It is sin inside me that is stronger than

I am that makes me do these evil things.

"I know I am rotten through and through so far as my old sinful nature [OSN] is concerned. No matter which way I turn I can't make myself do right. I want to, but I can't. When I want to do good, I don't; and when I try not to do wrong, I do it anyway. Now if I am doing what I don't want to, it is plain where the trouble is: sin still has me in its evil grasp. . . . So you see how it is: my new life tells me to do right, but the old nature that is still inside me loves to sin.

"Oh, what a terrible predicament I'm in! Who will free me from my slavery to this deadly lower nature? Thank God! It has been done by Jesus Christ, our Lord. He has set me free" (Romans 7:15-25, LB).

Worry, jealousy, discouragement, a critical attitude, and bitterness are symptoms that you are controlling your own life. Recognize these symptoms as sin and claim the promise in 1 John 1:9 (KJV): "If we confess our sins, He is faithful and just to forgive us our sins, and to cleanse us from all unrighteousness." Then by faith, know you are filled and controlled by the Holy Spirit and back in the condition described in Figure B. (See Colossians 2:6 and Ephesians 5:18.)

Remember that Jesus Christ is a Gentleman. He will not come into your life against your will, nor does He take control of your life without your permission. However, once you've invited Him into your life, He promises never to leave you (see Hebrews 13:5).

Both Christianity and marriage involve a deliberate choice. You choose to commit your total person—intellect, emotions, and will to another. When I met DeWitt, intellectually I liked what I saw—looks, personality, and many other qualities. Yet there is more to marriage than respect and admiration. As we became better acquainted, cupid found his mark. But our loving each other didn't make us married. We became engaged and the wedding day arrived. Intellectually, I believed that he was the most wonderful man in all of the world. Emotionally, my heart beat twice as fast when we were together. But something more took place. In exchanging our vows before the minister, we committed our wills to each other. It was this act of committing our entire selves—intellect, emotions, and will—to each other that made us truly married. The same is true in Christianity. Through a deliberate committing of your will, you become a member of God's family. Both commitments are designed to enable you to be a complete, fulfilled woman.

As Christ meets your personal needs, you can, in turn, meet your husband's needs by following the pattern given in 1 Corinthians 7:34: "But the married woman has her cares [centered] in earthly affairs, how she may please her husband." Begin doing the things for your husband that you know will please him. Sew on that button he has been talking about for so long. Have supper on time. Enjoy a ball game with him. Bake the pie he loves, or train the children to remove their bicycles from the driveway before he comes home. Make it a point to fulfill your husband's desires for you and the children. As you do, you will find that your marriage relationship will take on new meaning.

3
Accepting Your Husband as He Is

The most important gift from God is a personal relationship with Jesus Christ. For the married woman, His next most important gift is her marriage. It is a relationship God created and honors. As she responds to her husband in the way God means her to, she can expect God to bless her.

Marriage—Wonderful Gift or Surprise Package

You may have thought when you received your "gift" that it was perfect. But after the exchange of "I do's," when you began to unwrap your package, the gift turned out to be a surprise. You may have even decided that you had the wrong husband. It's important to realize that, even though you did not know exactly what you were getting, God did.

One wonderful thing about God is that He does not fail. If you trust Him, He will take all things and work them out for your good (see Romans 8:28). He can use the very thing in your husband that you dislike most to mold you into the image of Christ. He wants you to settle down to a lifetime of enjoying the gift you promised to honor and cherish.

What Acceptance Involves

You learn to accept others, including your husband, by noticing how Christ accepts you: "While we were yet sinners, Christ died for us" (Romans 5:8, KJV). God loves and accepts you unconditionally. You are not on probation with Him. Unconditional love and acceptance, then, should be the basis of your marriage.

At times, you may feel that it is asking too much of you to accept your husband as he is. But I guarantee that as you begin to accept him, you will develop a more meaningful relationship with him because both of you will have the freedom you need to mature.

When you accept your husband the way he is, you will give him the freedom to be the man he wants to be. He will have freedom to come and go as he pleases and to make his own decisions. In other words, true love is letting go! Your husband will love you freely as he did when he chose to marry you unless you stifle that love with your possessiveness.

A plant needs water, sun, and fresh air, with room to spread its roots in order to grow and be healthy. Even so, a man needs unconditional love, freedom, and acceptance in order to love and cherish you as God meant him to. As you love your husband unconditionally—without demands and ultimatums—you will see him drawn to you like steel to a magnet.

True love is beautifully described in 1 Corinthians 13:4-7: "Love endures long and is patient and kind; love never is envious nor boils over with jealousy; is not boastful or vainglorious, does not display itself haughtily. It is not conceited—arrogant and inflated with pride; it is not rude (unmannerly), and does not act unbecomingly.

"Love [God's love in us] does not insist on its own rights or its own way, for it is not self-seeking; it is not touchy or fretful or resentful; it takes no account of the evil done to it—pays no attention to a suffered wrong. It does not rejoice at injustice and unrighteousness, but rejoices when right and truth prevail.

"Love bears up under anything and everything that comes, is ever ready to believe the best of every person, its hopes are fadeless under all circumstances and it endures everything [without weakening]."

Remember, you do not have the power to love like that, but Jesus Christ can love through you, if you allow Him to.

Giving Your Expectations to God

The basis for your discontentment and inability to accept your husband lies in your expectations of him and his failure to meet your goals. When he fails to live up to your expectations, you may be hurt, irritated, and disappointed. You and your husband will only be contented and free when you quit setting goals and stop expecting him to be who he is not.

Mary was a virtual prisoner of her own preconceived ideas of how her husband should act. She was raised in a home where proper table manners were expected. When her husband Don first came to the table in his undershirt and then put his elbows on the table, she was shocked. As time went on, she found that he had other habits she considered uncouth. She tried to correct him, but instead of changing Don, her efforts only put a strain on their relationship.

When Mary finally committed her expectations to God, the tension between her and Don disappeared. After that when her husband came to the table properly dressed, she was grateful. When his manners didn't come up to her expectations, she wasn't disappointed. In the climate of her acceptance, Don began to choose better etiquette himself.

If, like Mary, you are disappointed in your husband, you may be trying to make him meet the need in your life that only Christ can meet. "He who believes in Him [Christ]—who adheres to, trusts in and relies on Him—shall never be disappointed or put to shame" (1 Peter 2:6). Let your disappointment be a signal to worship only Christ.

Changing Your Husband

It may seem only right to help your husband change attitudes, traits, and actions that are making him unhappy. But your well-meaning efforts will communicate to him, "I don't love you as you are. I want you to be different." A man wants his wife to be proud, not ashamed of him. When she is not, he becomes discouraged. The masculine abilities God has given him to cope with life are crushed instead of liberated. He cannot live a healthy, satisfying life when constantly on trial. Your intentions may be sincere but can lead to disaster. God says, "There is a way that seemeth right unto a man, but the end thereof are the ways of death" (Proverbs 16:25, KJV).

God did not give you the job of convicting your husband of sin or error. That is the work of the Holy Spirit (see John 16:8-11). When you take on that job, you only get in God's way and slow down His work. Neither are you to be your husband's mother—correcting and training him. Having good intentions for his future is not enough. You must act upon the principles set forth in God's Word.

Communication breaks down in an atmosphere of nonacceptance. When your husband tells you what he has said or done, don't criticize, point out where he was wrong, or tell him what he should have done. If you do, he may decide it is less painful to keep his thoughts to himself and stop confiding in you. Only when he is sure of your total acceptance will he confide in you. If you hold his confidences sacred, he'll know he can trust you not to ridicule or belittle him. If you must tell his secrets to someone, tell them to Jesus Christ.

You, the Critic

Are you aware that unasked-for advice is really veiled criticism? Yes, giving unasked-for advice is just another way of attempting to change your man. A friend of mine, Tammy, had stopped her obvious methods of correcting her husband Jack. Yet Jack was not confiding in her freely, and Tammy could not understand why.

One day as they were driving along, he started telling her about one of his business transactions. Tammy began to respond in her usual way with "I would have done so and so" and "Why didn't you handle it this way?"

Jack suddenly stopped talking. When she finally got him to tell her what was wrong, he said, "You never approve or agree with anything I do. I shouldn't have tried to share this with you."

Tammy had not realized that her unasked-for advice was actually criticism of him. She honestly had not intended to put him down. Sadly, she realized that her advice or veiled criticism told Jack that she did not accept him as he was.

Let's see what Jesus had to say about criticism. "Don't criticize and then you won't be criticized! For others will treat you as you treat them. And why worry about a speck in the eye of a brother when you have a board in your own? Should you say, 'Friend, let me help you get that speck out of your eye,' when you can't even see because of the board in your own? Hypocrite! First get rid of the board. Then you can see to help your brother" (Matthew 7:1-5, LB).

When you criticize your husband or anyone else, you are assuming an "I'm better than you are," attitude. Wouldn't it be wiser to ask God to show you your failures and let Him deal with your husband as He sees best? Make it a habit, when you have the desire to change something about your husband, to ask Christ to show you your own faults. If you follow Jesus' advice to "be humble, thinking of others as better than yourself" (Philippians 2:3, LB), your critical, self-righteous, or martyr attitude will disappear.

Don't try to change your husband by demanding your own way. Though you may feel you have succeeded in some area when he gives in, he may just want to keep peace in the household. Over a period of time, your domineering attitude may develop a coolness in your man and eventually destroy his love for you. You may win a few battles, but you will lose the war. Forfeiting a beautiful, fulfilling marital relationship is not worth the temporary "success."

Your Neighbor's Model Husband

Trying to change your husband by using other men as shining examples does not work either. Refrain from pointing out the neighbor who keeps his yard well-manicured when you want your husband to work in yours. If you remind him of the expensive wardrobe Bill bought Jane, or about your dad's success in handling a situation, you are shouting loud and clear, "I am not pleased with you as you are." Manipulation won't encourage your husband to love and cherish you.

When you do not accept your husband the way he is, he may rebel, as the writer of Proverbs suggests. "The north wind brings forth rain; so does a backbiting tongue [of a wife] bring forth an angry countenance [in her husband]. It is better to dwell in the corner of the housetop than to share a house with a disagreeing, quarrelsome, and scolding woman" (Proverbs 25:23-24). Naturally, a man rebels. He is struggling to maintain his freedom to become the man God meant him to be.

You may not feel that your actions classify you as disagreeable, quarrelsome, or scolding though your husband has been acting angry and rebellious. Ask God to show you how you may unknowingly be the cause of his bad temper. If Christ does point out some wrong thing in your behavior, confess it as sin and trust Him to live through you and change you. Realize that He can cause your mistakes to work together for your good as you turn to Him for guidance. God promises His children, "I will restore or replace for you the years that the locust has eaten. . . . And my people shall never be put to shame" (Joel 2:25-26).

God's Formula for Accepting Your Husband

God has a plan through which you can learn to accept your husband. It is clearly outlined in Philippians 4:4, 6-8 (BECK): "Be happy in the Lord always! . . . Don't worry about anything, but in everything go to God, and pray to let Him know what you want, and give thanks. Then God's peace, better than our thinking, will guard your hearts and minds in Christ Jesus. . . . Keep your minds on all that is true or noble, right or pure, lovely or appealing, on anything that is excellent or that deserves praise."

The first step in God's plan is to commit all of your problems to Him. Regardless of what has worried, upset, or irritated you, Christ says you should tell Him about it. Then let Him work it out. Resist the impulse to return to the problem because you've "thought of something else that might work." Trust Him for the solution. If you don't, you're saying in effect, "God, You are not able to handle my problem."

Don't be like the man who was walking along the road with a heavy load on his back. A farmer stopped to give him a ride. The man climbed onto the farmer's truck but left the load on his back. "Why don't you put your load down on the truck?" the farmer called out to him.

"It was so kind of you to give me a ride," the man answered, "I don't want to ask you to carry my load too."

How foolish! But that is what you do when you do not let Jesus Christ carry all of your burdens. He died for you and paid for your sins. He offers you victory over each problem and is pleased when you claim it (see 1 Corinthians 10:13).

How do you commit your burdens or problems to God? By talking to Him about them. That's prayer—simply opening up to God, knowing He understands perfectly. God will not force His solutions on you even though He is God of the universe. Instead, He waits for you to come to Him and share with Him and ask for His help.

Since He sees things from a different viewpoint and knows what's best for you, don't limit Him by telling Him when and how to answer your prayers. Let Him work out your problems according to His timing and plan. Then thank Him for answering, trusting Him to do what is best.

After giving your problems to God and thanking Him for taking care of them, fix your mind on whatever pure, honorable, and praiseworthy qualities your husband has (if your problem involves him). Does he get up each morning, regardless of how he feels, and go to work? Thank God. Is he kind and gentle to the children? Thank the Lord. Is he a sociable guy? Be grateful.

If you have a hard time thinking of some positive traits, think back to the qualities that drew you to him before marriage. Those traits are still in him but may have been buried during the years of your marriage. Concentrate on his positive traits and his weaknesses will diminish. This idea is different from a "self-improvement" plan because you're trusting God to improve you and your husband as you follow His formula.

It might be comforting to realize that negative traits are distorted positive traits. If negative traits can be modified or channeled in the right direction, they can become strengths. Stubbornness can become perseverance. Cowardice can be turned to gentleness. Tactlessness can be turned to frankness. If you trust Jesus Christ to take care of your husband's problems, and fix your mind on his assets, you can help him turn bad traits into good ones.

The results you can expect are described in Philippians 4:8. You will experience God's peace which is more wonderful than the human mind can understand. It is a deep, inner quietness that depends not on circumstances, but on your relationship with Jesus Christ.

The formula can be stated in this way: Problems transferred to Christ, plus focusing on the positive, equals peace.

Application

Now that you know you should accept your husband as he is, try to apply the principle in your own marriage relationship. Look for opportunities to tell your husband that you are glad he is the kind of man he is. Tell him you know you have made many mistakes and are willing to correct them. Explain that you realize you have not been the loving, understanding, submissive wife you should have been.

Do not confess past immorality. You may relieve your own guilt but hurt your husband. If you have made such mistakes, simply confess them to Jesus Christ and accept His forgiveness. He forgives and forgets and so should you. Show your husband through your actions as well as your words that you accept him as he is. Both of you will begin to experience the sheer joy and freedom that comes from following God's principles.

4
Helping Your Husband Love Himself

The key to fulfillment and contentment in your life is described by Jesus: " 'You must love the Lord your God with your whole heart, your whole soul, and your whole mind.' This is the greatest command, and is first in importance. The second is like it: 'You must love your neighbor as you do yourself' " (Matthew 22:37-39, WMS). When the first commandment is true in your life, the second can become a reality. Furthermore, you cannot love someone else until you first love yourself. And you can love yourself only when you see yourself from God's viewpoint. In the Bible you will discover:

1. You are a person of *worth* and *value*—so valuable, that Jesus Christ was willing to leave the glories of heaven, become the God-Man, live a sinless life, and die to pay for your sins. If you were the only person to ever live, He still would have died for only you (see 1 Peter 1:18-22).
2. You *belong* to the Royal Family and have the greatest heritage possible. As a member of God's family, you need never feel inferior.

3. If you're a Christian, God accepts you as you are.
4. He loves you unconditionally.
5. If you're a Christian, God promises to provide all of your needs. "My God will amply supply your every need, through Christ Jesus, from His riches in glory" (Philippians 4:19, WMS). When you realize who you are in Christ, you can be free of feelings of guilt or inferiority and begin to love yourself. Once you love yourself, you can genuinely love your husband and meet the needs of his life that God has meant you to meet.

One of those needs is described in Ephesians 5:33: "Let the wife see that she respects and reverences her husband—that she notices him, regards him, honors him, prefers him, venerates and esteems him; and that she defers to him, praises him, and loves and admires him exceedingly." Your man has a strong need to know you are proud of him, pleased with him, and admire him.

Nothing will be too big for him if he has your loving support and admiration. You see, a compliment acts as a stimulus and is a source of encouragement; whereas, a complaint acts as a depressant and is a source of discouragement.

As you fulfill your husband's need for admiration, you will help him love himself. He, in turn, then will be able to nourish, protect, and cherish you as described in Ephesians 5:28-29: "Even so husbands should love their wives as [being in a sense] their own bodies. He who loves his own wife loves himself. For no man ever hated his own flesh, but nourishes and carefully protects and cherishes it, as Christ does the Church."

Knowing that God made you and your husband different so you would complement each other should give you an incentive to meet his need for praise and admiration. Remember, each of you is unfulfilled alone, but together, you make a whole. Your husband's need for admiration is fulfilled through your genuine praise. His love and strength in turn should meet your need for tenderness and protection. Your intuition complements his wisdom. Your loyal support undergirds his initiative. When you and your husband use these abilities to strengthen each other, you will develop a lasting marriage.

You'll find further motivation in understanding your role in marriage as described in 1 Corinthians 11:7, KJV: "For a man . . . is the image and glory of God; but the woman is the glory of the man." As man allows Jesus Christ to control his life by the power of the Holy Spirit, Christ's qualities are manifested through him and he reflects God's glory. His wife, however, is to reflect her husband's glory. She does this by bringing attention to his commendable qualities, by praising him, honoring him, and giving him proper distinction.

As you sincerely praise your husband, you may need help in uncovering traits, interests, or strengths that you can honestly admire. Discovering things about him that you may have overlooked for years will be exciting. How do you go about detecting these hidden qualities?

1. Watch your husband

If you want a manly man, praise him for his physical strength and the ease with which he does manly or difficult things such as opening tight jars, moving furniture, mowing the lawn, and handling heavy equipment rather than praising him for doing easier tasks usually thought of as women's work, such as dishes and dusting. Express appreciation whenever he does any of the usual chores around the house instead of saying, "Well, it's about time."

Your appreciation and gratitude should gradually encourage him to do things around the house if he has been unwilling to do them before. But don't be discouraged if his first reaction to "Wow, you sure have strong arms!" is "Yours would be strong, too, if you ever used them." He may have built a wall around himself because he's missed your appreciation in the past. Give him time.

Compliment him on his broad shoulders, deep voice, strong hands, and yes, even on his beard—though you may feel like saying, "I wish you'd shave that thing off!"

Praise or show appreciation for his courage, honor, determination, cleverness, intellectual ability, achievements, skills, leadership, aspirations, and/or ideals. Have you thanked him lately for the many hours he spends earning a living for your family? His faithfulness in providing for you demonstrates praiseworthy qualities of dependability and responsibility.

Praise him for the way in which he stands behind his convictions as he directs your home and household. You may not always agree with his decisions, but you can compliment him for his courage in standing by them. Approve and compliment his determination when he accomplishes his goals. You may have been calling his determination stubbornness. If you see it as a worthy trait, God can use you to turn it to His use. (Be sure to ask God to show you ways you can apply this principle of admiration.)

These are just a few suggestions to get you started. Now a word of caution: Start off gently, trusting Christ to point out things in your husband you can sincerely praise. If you come on too strong at first, you may appear phony.

If you have a son, be sure to praise him for masculine qualities and traits too. Your wisely given encouragement will help him develop into a stronger man, one with a better understanding of himself and God's role for him.

Be sure that your motives are right when you praise your men. If you do it so you can change or manipulate them, they'll think you're flattering them or "buttering them up." Ask God to give you pure motives and then, in faith, believe He will.

2. Listen to him

Even if your husband is talking about something you don't understand or feel interested in, give him your undivided attention. You'll learn a lot about him. You will begin to detect how he feels about people and situations. You will even discover noble, mature dimensions in his character that you never knew were there.

Many of us wives don't know our husbands because we never quit talking long enough to listen to them. Scripture says, "Let a woman learn in quietness in entire submissiveness" (1 Timothy 2:11).

3. Develop an interest in things he likes

If you are married to a sportsman, learn enough about his favorite sports so he can talk to you about them. But don't become an expert. He will enjoy teaching you some things himself if you show an interest. You may not believe it now, but after you learn something about his interests, whether they be sports or hobbies, you will most likely find that you enjoy them too.

Don't Get Discouraged

At first you may feel utterly foolish praising your husband. But if you remind yourself of his need, and continue by faith, you will find that words of praise come more and more easily. As a matter of fact, you will probably find that you like to give praise as much as he enjoys receiving it.

Many women feel that their husbands are already too egocentric and are afraid that if they openly express admiration, their husbands will become more boastful. Actually, the opposite will probably occur. The man who constantly brags about himself usually feels insecure and is trying to convince himself and you that he's great.

"Showing off" is his attempt to bolster his ego. Give him

your attention and praise, and soon he will begin to believe in himself and no longer feel the need to boast. Should he be truly egocentric, your job is not to correct his weakness, but to support and encourage him. As you pray for him, trust God to deal with his problem.

After applying these principles of admiration, Carol said excitedly, "I can't get over how my husband is 'eating this up!' Yesterday he stayed home for lunch about an hour and a half instead of his usual 30 minutes. I thought he would never go back to work." Laughingly, she continued, "If he keeps this up, I'll never get any work done." Of course, she was enjoying his attentiveness as much as he was relishing her admiration.

As you trust Jesus Christ to help you understand your husband, you will be pleasantly surprised to discover what a wonderful man you married. For the first time, you may see that he has been expressing his love for you all along. Because he did not always show it in a tender, sensitive way, you hadn't recognized it as love.

Perhaps he straightened up the kitchen after an argument, or teases you constantly, or made you that special cabinet you've wanted, or even dug up the ground by the garage so you could plant roses. Don't force your husband to express his love the way you do. Accept these loving gestures, even his constant teasing, as his way of saying he loves you.

If you have a hard time finding admirable qualities in your man, believe, by faith, that they do exist although they may be dormant. "Love bears up under anything and everything that comes, is ever ready to believe the best of every person, its hopes are fadeless under all circumstances and it endures everything [without weakening]" (1 Corinthians 13:7). Your unwavering belief in him will begin to reveal his positive traits. Don't push him—just believe in him, and you will begin to experience a deeper, closer relationship with your man.

Your Reward

Do you feel this marriage relationship is all one-sided, that your husband receives all the benefits? Well, cheer up. When you follow God's plan for your life, you will be rewarded threefold. First, as your husband begins to respond to your loving admiration, one of your rewards will be his own expression of appreciation and love for you. God's Word teaches, "For whatsoever a man soweth, that shall he also reap" (Galatians 6:7, KJV). Your loving patience and kindness to your husband will encourage the highest and best in him. That is worth working toward.

Every man is different, of course. One will quickly and lovingly react to his wife's overtures. Another will neither react quickly nor easily. It is your job to patiently respond to God and your husband in loving submission. It is God's place to work in your husband's life. Trust God to repair any damage done to your marriage relationship because you have not let Jesus Christ control your life. If you have sown seeds of bitterness, jealousy, or selfishness for years, it may take some time for God to get rid of the weeds.

However, do try to be honest and objective. Do not assume responsibilities that are your husband's alone. Realize that there are needs in his life that you cannot meet, such as his need to make Christ Lord in his life or his need for acceptance and approval by others in business and society. Your main job is to comfort, encourage, and support your man when he is with you.

Second, Jesus Christ will give you inner peace and stability when you live to please and obey Him and not yourself (see Romans 8:6-7). If you accept your husband as he is, admire him, and care for your household because Christ instructs you to, you will not be "puffed up" when your husband praises you for your efforts. Nor will you be discouraged when he fails to praise you for a job well done. You will realize that what follows as a result of your obedience to Christ is His responsibility. "I am convinced and sure of this very thing, that He who began a good work in you will continue until the day of Jesus Christ—right up to the time of His return—developing [that good work] and perfecting and bringing it to full completion in you" (Philippians 1:6).

If, for instance, you cleaned your house just to receive your husband's praise, only to have him say, "Hey, you missed that cobweb in the corner," your day would be spoiled. But if you cleaned the house first of all to please the Lord, you would not be so hurt.

Third, you will receive rewards in eternity as you trust and obey Christ for every need. "Whatever you do, do your work heartily, as for the Lord rather than for men; knowing that from the Lord you will receive the reward of your inheritance. It is the Lord Christ whom you serve" (Colossians 3:23-24, NASB).

When you are tempted to "throw in the towel," remember that if you faithfully trust Christ, you will receive both earthly and eternal rewards. "If any man's work . . . remains, he shall receive a reward" (1 Corinthians 3:14, NASB).

It took this very principle of eternal rewards to jolt me into confessing a sin in my life one day. I was very angry with a certain individual and was verbally tearing her apart—and enjoying it. I knew I was wrong and could expect discipline from Christ if I didn't confess my sin (see Hebrews 12:6). But my attitude was, "I have a few more things I want to say first."

After some time, God brought the principle of eternal rewards to my mind, reminding me that my sinful attitude would cause misery for me now and I would lose my eternal rewards (see 1 Corinthians 3:11-15). That's all the reminder I needed to help me realize that I did not want to pay the high price of sin.

You will not regret trusting Jesus Christ. Under His plan, you can expect maximum benefits, both for you and for your husband.

5 Not Second Best

In order to fulfill your role as a wife adequately, you must understand the place God expects your husband to occupy in your life. When we examine Ephesians 5:24, we see that the husband-wife relationship parallels Christ's relationship with the Church (all believers). "As the Church is subject to Christ, so let wives also be subject in everything to their husbands." You, as a believer, are to depend totally on Jesus Christ for your very existence. When Jesus is first in your inner spiritual life, He will enable you to put your husband first in your human relationships and activities.

When your husband has the assurance that he is first in your life, his self-confidence will be strengthened; he will be more able to face the world. The fact that he may have been cut down by his business opponents will be less painful if he can return to the haven of his home where you accept, admire, and support him.

However, remember that it is your support, not your protection that your husband needs. He will develop traits of independence, courage, and confidence only as he faces and tackles his problems—with your support, not your protection or smothering. If you're tempted to feel sorry for him, remember that most men thrive on the challenge of caring for and protecting their families, not on being cared for and protected.

At the time of marriage, you and your husband became one or "one flesh" (see Genesis 2:24). Now, no normal person will ever intentionally harm himself. Yet wives often unintentionally hurt their husbands—their own flesh. As you give Jesus Christ more and more freedom to control you, He will enable you to begin to love your husband as you love yourself and you will not want to hurt him in any way.

As you search God's Word, as you study the principles we're discussing, and as you allow Christ to control your life, He will enable you to love your husband as yourself. He'll show you ways in which you may be hurting your man. Trust God to help you correct any harmful attitudes. Then you will become the blessing to your husband that God describes in Proverbs 18:22 (LB): "The man who finds a wife finds a good thing; she is a blessing to him from the Lord." What a privilege we have to be able to meet our husbands' needs!

Attitudes and Actions to Avoid

Disloyalty: As you study your Bible, you will discover that certain attitudes and actions are not in harmony with God's plan for you as a responder. *Disloyalty* to your man is one. If you love your husband as yourself, you will protect him and be loyal to him in his presence or absence. "[Love] doesn't plan to hurt anyone. It doesn't delight in evil but is happy with the truth. It bears everything, believes everything, hopes for everything, endures everything. Love never dies" (1 Corinthians 13:5-7, BECK).

Being loyal means that you will confess as sin and give up any critical attitude you may have toward your husband. Trust Jesus Christ to show you good, positive things to say about him, rather than negative things. Your criticism of or uncomplimentary attitude toward your husband, especially in front of others, can hurt him as much as a slap in the face.

Even criticism directed toward someone other than your husband may cost you his respect and trust. He will think, and no doubt justly, that your critical attitude does not stop with certain people but influences all your relationships.

It may help you to realize that the very faults that irritate you in others are usually the ones you have trouble with yourself. That is why they irritate you. Christ said, "Don't judge, so that you will not be judged. . . . Why do you look at the speck in your brother's eye and don't notice the log in your own eye?" (Matthew 7:1, 3, BECK)

"Therefore you have no excuse or defense or justification, O man, whoever you are who judges and condemns another. For in posing as judge and passing sentence on another you condemn yourself, because you who judge are habitually practicing the very same things [that you censure and denounce]" (Romans 2:1).

Selfishness: Be sure you aren't giving your husband the feeling that he rates last. After spending hours washing, cleaning, and cooking for him, you may think you are the epitome of unselfishness. But whose desires do you consider when you accept or reject a dinner engagement? Whose likes and dislikes do you consider when planning a meal? Whose errands do you run first? When you buy your husband something to wear, do you buy what you want or what you know he likes best?

Do you plan your activities so you can stop and visit with him if he should need to talk when he gets home from work? Remember, he can easily tell if he does not have your complete attention when he talks to you. The uninterested look on your face, glancing at the clock or out of the window, or yawning will give you away. Your interest must be sincere.

Jealousy: You'll also have to beware of jealousy if you are to love your husband as yourself. Jealousy tells your husband that you love yourself more than you love him because you want what makes *you* happy rather than what makes *him* happy. Jealousy is simply denying another person pleasures that may draw him away from you. You may resent his "night out with the boys," his time-consuming career, or some other activity or person. Yet if you love him as you love yourself, you will give him liberty to have any pleasure that makes him happy.

"What if I lose him?" you may ask. That's a normal concern. But do remember that you belong to Jesus Christ. Trust Him with your fears, and He will protect your interests. "Then you will lie down in peace and safety, unafraid; and I will bind you to Me forever with chains of righteousness and justice and love and mercy. I will betroth you to Me in faithfulness, and love, and you will really know Me then as you never have before" (Hosea 2:18-20, LB). If you ask God to take away your jealousy, and trust Him to help you win rather than lose your husband's love.

However, if you continue to check up on your husband, you can expect strained relations with him. "Jealousy makes [the wronged] man furious; therefore, he will not spare in the day of vengeance [upon the detected ones]" (Proverbs 6:34).

The secret of healthy lives for both husband and wife is found in Proverbs 14:30: "A calm and undisturbed mind and heart are the life and health of the body, but envy, jealousy, and wrath are as rottenness of the bones."

After hearing these principles about jealousy, Sarah realized that her jealousy was one of the main factors in causing her husband to leave her and ask for a divorce. Right away she set about getting her relationship with the Lord straightened out by confessing to Him, as sin, her jealousy, bitterness, resentfulness, and desire for revenge. Even though her husband had been stepping out on her, she committed the situation to the Lord, trusting Him to look after her interests.

As she trusted God, moment by moment, her life began to take on a new stability, expressed in a calm and gentle spirit. During the rare occasions when her husband was home, she began to show him that she accepted him as he was. She admired him instead of criticizing him and gave him the freedom to do what he wanted to do and to be the man he wanted to be. In other words, she made the time they spent together enjoyable for both of them.

Within a few weeks he moved back home. As time went on, he began staying home all day on his day off—quite a victory. Then one day as they sat by their backyard pool talking, he commented, "It is just great spending time with you."

Bossiness: Finally, don't tell your husband how to run his life. When he shares his problems with you, avoid responding to him as you like him to respond to you. Generally, when we women have problems, we want solutions from our men. We are comforted when they either remove or solve our problems. (By the way, do not ask your husband for help with a problem unless you are ready to accept his advice or solution.)

On the other hand, when your man has a problem, he doesn't need your solutions. He needs you to listen, to be sympathetic, and to restore his self-esteem by encouraging him to make his own decision. In other words, you need to reinforce his faith in himself so he will be free to use his God-given, masculine ability to conquer the situation.

Areas of Potential Imbalance

When you center your activities around your husband, you will have a happy man and a balanced life yourself. In other words, you will be the satisfied, complete woman you want to be. As you give your man his right place, you will find him more willing to give you freedom to enjoy other interests and activities as long as they don't become a threat to his role or position. Many men act possessive and domineering because they feel that their masculine role or position in their wives' affections is insecure.

This diagram explains the proper balance:

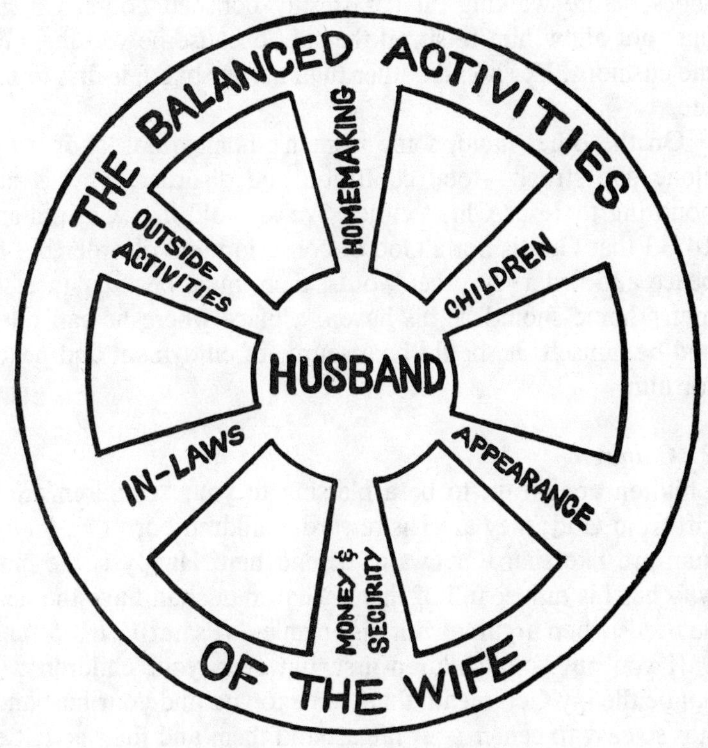

When the husband is at the hub of your activities, and the spokes (other elements) of your life are in correct proportion, the wheel (your life) will roll smoothly. If the spokes get out of adjustment, the wheel will wobble or even crash in its course. It is imbalance of the spokes that causes the problem, not necessarily any spoke or activity itself.

1. Homemaking

While a good thing in itself, homemaking can easily get out of balance and dominate your life. A woman who likes to keep an immaculate house may insist that her husband remove his shoes before walking on her freshly polished floors. Or she may not allow him to sit on the sofa because he will mess up the cushions. Her home, rather than her husband, is first in her life.

On the other hand, some women's homes look as if a cyclone had struck—total confusion and disorder. This is not honoring to Jesus Christ either. We are told in 1 Corinthians 14:33 that God is not a God of confusion and disorder but of peace and order. In other words, there must be a balance. A man's home should be his haven, a place where he can relax and be himself. It should be a source of enjoyment and peace for him.

2. Children

Children are meant to be a blessing to you. "Children are a gift from God; they are His reward. Children born to a young man are like sharp arrows to defend him. Happy is the man who has his quiver full of them. That man shall have the help he needs when arguing with his enemies" (Psalm 127:3-5, LB).

If you put your children first, however, your children will not be the joy God meant them to be to you and your husband. It is so easy to center your life around them and their activities and needs and neglect your husband. You tend to think, "Well, he is an adult and can look after himself. My children are young and need me so desperately." Remember, God made woman because man needed her. The relationship between you and your husband is meant to continue until death. Your children will be with you only a short time.

Not that you should neglect your children. When your priorities are in order, you will find you have adequate time for both. The family will be a closer unit. Your children will feel secure with parents who love each other, and your husband won't be likely to resent the children for taking his place in your life. You give your best to your children when your husband is the hub of your life.

3. Appearance

Your appearance is another area that communicates to your husband his importance in your life. Remember, he may be exposed to stimulating, well-groomed women in the business world, and they remind him of his need for a woman. He rushes home to be with his wife, eagerly opens the door—and there you are!

His anticipations are either fulfilled or disappointed. Even though you may have four preschoolers and mountains of diapers and dishes to manage, you should arrange, whenever possible, to spend a few minutes before his arrival freshening up. Your husband does not want to be taken for granted any more than you do. So be sure you don't spend all your time shopping, grooming, and sewing to look nice for others rather than for him. Give him your best and you will reap the dividends.

Of course you can overdo in the area of grooming, spending so much time and money on yourself and your own looks that your husband may wonder if you are dressing to please him or attract other men. Grooming can become a very self-centered activity. Like other areas of your life, this one needs to be balanced.

4. Money and Security

It is very easy for the area or "spoke" of money and security to dominate your life. Poor handling of money or the lack of money can be a constant source of friction between you and your husband.

Books have been written on the subject of money management so we won't discuss the subject here except to point out that you and your husband should plan the handling of your income early in your marriage. Here again, you may offer advice but your husband should manage the money and keep the books unless he specifically asks you to do this job for him.

Interestingly, the Bible speaks about a happy man being able to trust his wife in buying and selling, so it is quite biblical for a man to commit his household and money matters into his wife's hands if she is wise in those matters. "Her husband can trust her, and she will richly satisfy his needs. She goes out to inspect a field, and buys it; with her own hands she plants a vineyard. She makes belted linen garments to sell to the merchants" (Proverbs 31:11, 16, 24, LB).

When money is in short supply, your attitude toward the situation and your husband's struggle to bring in enough can either make or break him. Possibly more than at any other time, your husband needs your support and encouragement then. Men feel as if they've failed if they can't supply the family income. Without proper support from their wives, men have turned to alcohol, other women, and even suicide during times of financial crisis. If you scold, nag, or fret, you will only increase your husband's sense of failure.

Beware that the need for security doesn't kill your husband's incentive at work. You may resist his taking a promotion. You don't want to move, or you feel that your way of life will be threatened. If you take that attitude, you may see your husband's interest in you and his work and life itself begin to wane.

Put your trust in God, rather than your situation and finances, and you'll be able to face changes in your husband's career gracefully. God warns against trying to gain security from possessions. "He who leans on, trusts and is confident in his riches shall fall, but the [uncompromisingly] righteous shall flourish like a green bough" (Proverbs 11:28). A man can be a greater success financially if he is not distracted by an unfulfilled wife but has her support and encouragement.

5. In-laws

Another area that can be turned from a blessing to a curse when out of balance is the relationship of you and your husband to your parents. The Lord made provision for the in-law problem before it was a reality. He told Adam and Eve, "A man shall leave his father and mother and shall become united and cleave to his wife, and they shall become one flesh" (Genesis 2:24).

Once you and your husband become one flesh in marriage, your husband, not your parents, is to be the center of your life. Of course, you are to continue to honor and respect your parents and his. Call or write them occasionally and share some bit of family news: a child's good report card, some cute thing a young child has said or done, your husband's promotion. "Honor (esteem and value as precious) your father and your mother; this is the first commandment with a promise: that all may be well with you and that you may live long on the earth" (Ephesians 6:2-3). You can benefit from their maturity and experience as they give you words of counsel.

However, problems arise when you honor your parents' wishes and desires above your husband's. Do not make your husband feel that he must compete with your parents—or with his. When he knows he is first in your life, he will appreciate the parents who gave him such a wonderful wife.

6. Outside activities

The last "spoke" we'll discuss is that of outside activities: social life, church work, clubs, and so forth. "Surely my husband knows he is more important than my outside interests," you may say. How is he to know it? He must judge by what he sees and hears. If you spend most of your time directing the women's missionary group at church or a Girl Scout troop, what conclusion can he reach other than that those activities are more important to you than he is?

Even though activities are good in themselves they can take so much of your time and attention that your husband feels he is less important to you than they are. As a matter of fact, if you talk too much about Jesus Christ or are habitually reading your Bible in front of him or are always going to Gospel meetings, your husband could begin to feel about Christ the same way he would feel about a man with whom you were having an affair. This may sound ridiculous, but perhaps all he knows is that someone besides himself has priority in your life.

A non-Christian does not grasp spiritual truths. "But the man who isn't a Christian can't understand and can't accept these thoughts from God which the Holy Spirit teaches us. They sound foolish to him, because only those who have the Holy Spirit within them can understand what the Holy Spirit means. Others just can't take it in" (1 Corinthians 2:14, LB). A Christian husband can also be "turned off" to spiritual truth by an overenthusiastic Christian wife who is constantly talking about spiritual truths she has just discovered.

You win your husband to spiritual values by incorporating them into your life, thereby becoming the wife he wants you to be. "In like manner, you married women, he submissive to your own husbands—subordinate yourselves as being secondary to and dependent on them, and adapt yourselves to them. So that even if any do not obey the Word [of God], they may be won over not by discussion but by the [godly] lives of their wives, when they observe the pure and modest way in which you conduct yourselves, together with your reverence" (1

Peter 3:1-2). This does not mean living by some group's "do's or don'ts," however.

Suppose you and your husband are enjoying certain activities together when suddenly you become a Christian and start changing your way of life. He finds himself spending time alone because you are either at church or refuse to go certain places with him that you once enjoyed together. Your husband may feel threatened by the sudden changes in you because he sees your relationship being destroyed.

I am sure you have heard that the Word of God divides people. "Do not think that I have come to bring peace upon the earth; I have not come to bring peace but a sword. For I have come to part asunder a man from his father, and a daughter from her mother, and a newly married wife from her mother-in-law; and a man's foes will be they of his own household" (Matthew 10:34-36). Notice that every family relationship is mentioned here *except the marital relationship.* Might this omission not be significant? The fact that the marital relationship is not mentioned suggests that God does not divide a married couple. He does not divide what He has united into one flesh. Rather, His Word properly applied will produce a precious marriage relationship.

You may say, "Then why the verses in 1 Corinthians 7:13-16 about letting an unsaved husband leave you if he chooses?" God gives these directions so that a Christian can peacefully deal with any marital problems that may arise. Division in the home comes from sin in the life of husband or wife, not from God.

Usually, as a woman trusts Jesus Christ, her life will demonstrate a stability and inner happiness that will help draw her husband to Christ. But not always. "For how do you know, O wife, whether you will save your husband? Or how do you know, O husband, whether you will save your wife?" (1 Corinthians 7:16, NASB)

Regardless of the spiritual status of your husband, however, your role, your way of relating to him should be the same. If he is a Christian, or when he becomes one, you will share spiritual truths together as he takes the lead or initiates the conversation. Generally speaking, the spiritual truths you learn are for your own edification, not for you to teach to your husband. When you have the strong desire to share these things, pray for your husband instead.

Margaret applied these principles. When James asked how she had become such a wonderful wife, she gently explained, "Jesus Christ is the source of my inner peace; He gives me the power to be the wife I should be." In responding to her husband as she did, Margaret did not make him feel that she no longer needed him. Christ had enabled her to willingly be dependent on her husband.

When a man is the center of his wife's life, he will rarely seek out another woman. Sex is seldom the primary reason for a man's promiscuity. He is usually looking for a woman who will accept him as he is, admire him, need him, and give him first place in her life.

Reconstruction Program

Do you feel that making your husband the true center of your life is too big an order for you to fill? I hope so, because then you will see your need to let Jesus Christ take over and do it for you. Your order is not too big for Him to fill. He is the only One who can make you the real woman you want to be. "A wise, understanding and prudent wife is from the Lord" (Proverbs 19:14).

Jesus Christ can use the laboratory of marriage to make you a godly woman. "A capable, intelligent, and virtuous woman, who is he who can find her? She is far more precious than jewels, and her value is far above rubies or pearls" (Proverbs 31:10). I think it is significant that a pearl is mentioned here.

A pearl is formed under water through suffering. Frequently God uses difficult circumstances, even marriage problems, to make you His pearl.

Marriage reveals the real you. It brings out your habit patterns and exposes you for what you really are. Your husband does not make you what you are; he simply acts as a stimulus to bring out what is on the inside. "Keep your heart with all vigilance and above all that you guard, for out of it flow the springs of life" (Proverbs 4:23).

True, you will always have the Old Sin Nature (OSN) until Christ takes you to be with Him, but you do not have to be under its control. If Jesus Christ is the source of power in your life, He will enable you to form new response patterns to life situations. You will not need to be a slave to the Old Sin Nature. He will enable you to break the hold of the OSN and its habit patterns (see Romans 8:1-4). Each time you feel the pull of the OSN, as it tries to control you, simply turn to God and ask for His deliverance from the temptation to respond in the old sinful pattern.

Do understand that temptation itself or an evil thought in itself is not sin. It is what you do with that thought or temptation that determines whether or not it becomes sin. "But every person is tempted when he is drawn away, enticed and baited by his own desire (lust, passions). Then, his own evil desire when it has conceived gives birth to sin, and sin when it is fully matured brings forth death" (James 1:14-15).

The following diagram of a phonograph shows the choice we have. We may play the record of old habit patterns formed by the OSN. Or we may push the reject button on the old record and drop into place the new record of life in the Spirit.

The choice is yours. You will discover that as you trust Christ to control you, all areas of your life will begin to fall into line with God's plan for you. When Christ is first in your inner spiritual life, He will direct you to put your husband

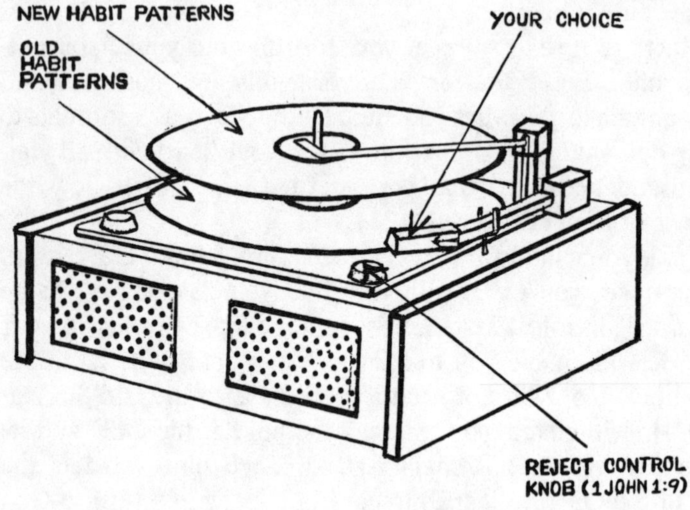

first in your human relationships and activities because this is His plan for you as a wife.

6
Follow the Leader

Someone must assume major responsibilities, make decisions, and direct activities in any functioning unit to prevent disorder and chaos. Any successful business or organization recognizes this need. Yet frequently families ignore the principle of leadership and therefore do not experience the harmony and peace God meant them to enjoy. Since the family is the basic unit of society, its stability will determine not only the security and happiness of its members but also the strength of the nation. Stability for both home and nation depends on recognizing the man as head of the family.

The Divine Order

God designated the man as the undisputed head of the family when He said to Eve, "Your desire and craving shall be for your husband, and he shall rule over you" (Genesis 3:16). This same principle is reaffirmed in the New Testament in Ephesians 5:22-23 (LB): "You wives must submit to your husbands' leadership in the same way you submit to the Lord. For a husband is in charge of his wife in the same way Christ is in charge of His body the Church. (He gave His very life to take care of it and be its Saviour!) So you wives must willingly obey your husbands in everything, just as the Church obeys Christ." *Society* did not assign the position of leadership to man; he was *divinely* appointed "head of the family."

A home with two heads or with the wife as the head could be called a monstrosity because the order of the man's and woman's roles has been distorted, thereby creating an abnormal condition. As homes have become more wife-dominated, there has been a rise in juvenile delinquency, rebellion, homosexuality, the divorce rate, and the number of frustrated women, because the home was designed by God to run efficiently with the man as the leader. Ignoring this principle of his leadership or devising substitutes creates untold problems.

God's order for the home is that the husband be the head of the wife as Christ is the head of the man. "Christ is the head of every man, the head of a woman is her husband, and the Head of Christ is God" (1 Corinthians 11:3). God the Father designed, for our benefit, this order of authority which can be described as "God's umbrella of protection." (See the illustration on the next page.) God's order is as follows:

God the Father
Christ
Man
Woman
Children

Christ, who is God and *equal* with the Father, is subject to the Father. The man is subject to those in authority over him: God, and others such as government officials, police, and employer (though all men are equals). The wife is subject to her husband, though she is his equal. The children are subject to their parents' authority, though they are not inferior beings. God uses this order of authority in the human race to protect and provide us with maximum happiness.

GOD'S UMBRELLA OF PROTECTION

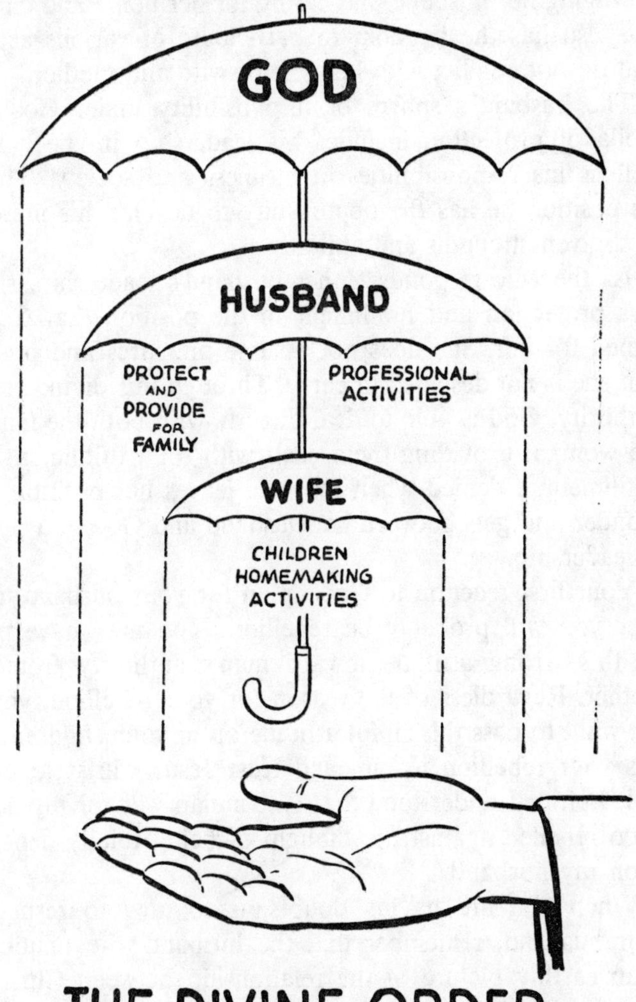

THE DIVINE ORDER

The woman, operating under God's prescribed umbrella of protection for her, assumes her role of supporting and encouraging her husband and caring for her home and children. She also has the freedom to participate in various activities that do not conflict with her role of wife and mother.

The husband's sphere of responsibility under God's umbrella of protection includes his leadership in the home as well as his responsibilities in business and society. Through his position he has the opportunity to develop his masculine God-given strengths and abilities.

As the wife responds to her husband's leadership, she enjoys protection and fulfillment in the position that God designed for her. She does not assume pressures and problems that she is not designed to carry. Through this divine order of authority, God is able to deal directly with both the man and the woman, providing them each with total fulfillment. This fulfillment is denied when the wife leaves her position of responder and gets between her husband and God in a position of leadership.

Your first reaction to God's plan for your husband to rule over you will probably be rebellion. You may have picked up this wrong attitude toward man's authority from your mother. Regardless of the reason for your rebellion, you will not want to pass this sinful attitude on to your children. Confess your rebellion as sin, and trust Jesus Christ to change you. Before I understood that God's plan was for my benefit, I too rebelled against the thought of being totally dependent upon my husband.

When you are having doubts as to how to respond to your husband, remember that the husband-wife relationship is an earthly picture of the relationship between Christ and the Church (believers). Just as the Church is totally dependent on Jesus Christ, so you as a wife are to be totally dependent on your husband. In this atmosphere, you are protected and fulfilled; your husband is inspired to be the man God created him to be; and your children are provided with an ideal atmosphere in which to develop and mature. God's plan is all-inclusive—total provision for everyone. You are totally surrounded by His loving protection, His umbrella (divine order) above and His loving hand underneath. "Though he [the righteous] fall, he shall not be utterly cast down, for the Lord grasps his hand in support and upholds him" (Psalm 37:24).

Roles of the Husband and Wife

Some people think marriage is a 50-50 deal, but it is not. It requires 100% from each partner. Each partner has a role that demands his all. Each role is equal in importance to the other but carries with it different responses and responsibilities. The fact that the roles are different does not mean that one is inferior to the other. Each role is judged in terms of its function and cannot operate efficiently without the other. A husband and wife complement each other in much the same way as a lock and key go together. Either is incomplete without the other.

Our position in God's divine order has nothing to do with our individual worth or importance. Individual worth and *not* respective roles is in view in Galatians 3:28. "There is [now no distinction], neither Jew nor Greek, there is neither slave nor free, there is not male and female; for you are all one in Christ Jesus." A woman tends to differ from a man in her interests, thinking, and abilities, as well as in her body. These distinctions make her the husband's complement, but they do not make her inferior. Neither man nor woman has cause for boasting. Neither needs to fret about having an inferior position.

The roles of the husband and wife could be compared to the offices of president and vice president of an organization. Each party understands, on acceptance of the position, that each office carries with it heavy responsibilities. Since the policies are clearly established, there is never any doubt about who is the president. However, the president's success depends on the vice president's help in carrying out the policies. When new decisions have to be made, the president may consult the vice president for advice, but he assumes responsibility for the final decision.

Once a policy is decided, they work together as a team to carry it out. The president may, if he chooses, delegate some of his authority to the vice president. When the president is gone, he can trust the vice president to carry on as if he himself were there. In this relationship, they share a oneness, good communication, emotional peace, and security, provided the vice president is not struggling to gain control of the organization!

God meant the man's and woman's roles to be different. After all He made them male and female (Genesis 1:27), not unisex. This difference is not only physical but also emotional and temperamental. Masculine traits include the ability to see the overall picture in a situation and to be firm and decisive when solving problems. Womanly traits include the ability to see details of a situation and to contribute valuable insights based on a compassionate, sensitive nature. For instance, as you prepare for a business party, you may be caught up in the details of the party preparation or how to prevent Mrs. X from offending Mrs. Y. Your husband may be thinking in terms of how the party will contribute to his business success for the coming year. By using your respective natural traits, you will be able to work together as a team.

If you do not recognize that God designed you and your husband to complement each other, you may try to force your husband to act and respond to life as you do. Should you succeed, he would have to switch to the feminine role of being the responder, abandoning his masculine responsibilities. If you recognize, however, that by nature your roles are different, you can develop your feminine traits and become a truly feminine woman.

Does My Advice or Opinion Count?

A woman's advice and insights are valuable assets to a man. However, there are some things to consider if your advice is to be effective.

A man will value your advice more highly if he asks for it, which he probably will if you are being a loving, submissive wife. When he asks your opinion, answer him objectively, sticking to the issue and the facts involved. Remember, men tend to use speech to express ideas and communicate factual information, while women have a tendency to use speech to express feelings or vent their emotions. As you give your opinion, try not to express your emotions, but briefly share, on the basis of facts, your thoughts concerning the situation.

Do I have to wait until I am asked to share my opinion? Only if you know your husband does not want unasked-for advice. The judgment, wisdom, and opinion of a loving wife are great assets to a man. To withhold these insights is doing your husband a great injustice. Being submissive does not mean saying nothing; it means putting yourself completely at the disposal of the person who is over you.

Many times a man needs insights or information in order to make a wise decision or to formulate a correct viewpoint. For instance, you are usually more closely involved with your children's activities and friends than your husband is. To aid him in making decisions and establishing policies regarding the children and their activities, you may need to contribute information. Also, you may be able to share insights based on God's Word that will help him avoid or correct a wrong and destructive viewpoint. "The heart of her husband doth safely trust in her [the virtuous woman] . . . She openeth her mouth with wisdom" (Proverbs 31:11, 26, KJV).

The Bible gives an example of a wife who helped her husband correct his point of view. Manoah and his wife had no children. The Angel of the Lord appeared to Mrs. Manoah and told her she would bear a son. This son, Samson, would begin to rescue Israel from the Philistines.

After Manoah's wife told him about the Angel's visit, he prayed that God would send the Angel again to give them more instructions about caring for the child. When the Angel of the Lord did come, Manoah did not recognize Him until He had ascended into heaven. "And Manoah said to his wife, 'We shall surely die, because we have seen God.' But his [sensible] wife said to him, 'If the Lord were pleased to kill us, He would not have received a burnt offering and a cereal offering at our hands, or have shown us all these things, or now have announced such things as these' " (Judges 13:22-23).

A wife can be a great help to her husband by sharing her insights in the proper way. True, she must give him advice in a feminine manner as described in Proverbs 31:26: "She opens her mouth with skillful and godly wisdom, and in her tongue is the law of kindness—giving counsel and instruction."

Ask yourself, "How will my words or actions affect my husband? Will what I say or do in a certain situation jeopardize his position as my leader?" If you consider these questions before you speak or act, you will be more apt to obey the "law of kindness" and will not run the risk of undermining his role as leader.

Never attempt to force your point of view on your husband. Simply say, "I feel this way," or "I believe such and such."

Leave him free to use or not use your advice as he sees best. Your job is to enhance his role as leader, so don't give your advice on a man-to-man basis or with an attitude of authority, superiority, or motherliness. Express your thoughts lovingly, leaving the final decision to your husband, assuring him of your support.

If you feel he is making the wrong decision, you may appeal your case to a higher court (talk to Christ about the situation in prayer and trust Christ for the ultimate outcome). Contributing your advice in this feminine way will relieve you of the burdensome responsibility of the final decision and will give support and encouragement to your husband.

7
Protection for Your Benefit

Under God's umbrella of protection, the husband is God's earthly agent through whom He protects the woman physically, psychologically, and spiritually. His provision is complete.

In what way do you need physical protection? You need protection from laborious tasks as well as from physical attack. Let's face it! It is not likely that you are as strong, muscularly, as a man. "In the same way you married men should live considerately with [your wives], with an intelligent recognition [of the marriage relation], honoring the woman as [physically] the weaker" (1 Peter 3:7). Your husband should protect you from such hard tasks as moving furniture, building fences, repairing automobiles, doing carpentry. Today you also need protection from physical or sexual attack just as your female ancestors did in the wilds of the frontier. When you try to develop the ability to protect yourself, you endanger your femininity.

Sometimes, too, your husband must protect your health by curtailing your many activities. If your husband has complained about your busy schedule, he may be worried about you. He may be expressing his love by saying your health is important to him. Thank him for his concern and let his advice be a reminder that you are doing more than God planned for you to do.

Your husband also protects you physically by providing you with food, clothing, and shelter. This is a sacred obligation given to him by God. "Whoever fails to provide for his own relatives, and especially for those of his immediate family, has disowned the faith and is worse than an unbeliever" (1 Timothy 5:8, WMS). This warning was not given to the woman but to the man.

Man's work is a blessing. It provides him with the opportunity to develop his God-given abilities as he faces struggles, burdens, and difficulties for his family. Be careful not to deny your husband the respect, the honor, and the deep satisfaction of fulfilling this role God assigned him: "Make it your ambition and definitely endeavor to live quietly and peacefully, to mind your own affairs, and to work with your hands, as we charged you; so that you may bear yourselves becomingly, be correct and honorable and command the respect of the outside world, being (self-supporting), dependent on nobody and having need of nothing" (1 Thessalonians 4:11-12).

Since God assigned man the responsibility of providing for his family, He rebukes the man who fails to do so, calling him "worse than an unbeliever [who performs his obligation in these matters]" (1 Timothy 5:8).

Even as it is your husband's job to provide the money, so it is your responsibility to support his financial plans. You should willingly make any effort necessary to make the dollar stretch, as described in Proverbs 31:13-14. "She seeks out the wool and flax and works with willing hands to develop it. She is like the merchant ships loaded with foodstuffs, she brings her household's food from a far [country]." You may learn to make the dollars stretch by finding bargains, cooking economical dishes, learning to sew, and by developing many other ideas God will give you.

As you limit your life-style to your husband's salary scale, God will direct your family finances. He will provide for you in a way that will not cause your husband to feel inferior. God may lead a neighbor to give you the very piece of furniture you need or an aunt to mail you the special dress you had prayed for. Too often, by using credit cards, you can limit God and place your family under unnecessary financial strain.

You must be careful never to belittle your husband's producing power. Such comments as "*We* can't afford this," or "I have to skimp and save to make ends meet" will discourage your husband. Try not to comment on the ways in which you have economized in order to help out, even though your economizing pleases you. Your thriftiness is good and will give you a feeling of satisfaction, but telling your husband about it only reminds him that it is necessary because of his limited income. You will help your husband in his role of financial protector by your quiet economy, open support, and gratitude for his provision for you and the family.

Many women have said, "My husband has hinted that I should work outside our home. I am trained in a certain area and we could use the extra money. Should I go to work?" No, it is your husband's job to meet the family's financial obligations. Do not feel guilty for not helping him. As a matter of fact, instead of helping him, you would be damaging his ego.

However, ask yourself why he suggested that you go to work. Is it because you have given him the impression that you are not satisfied with his provision for you? If so, set about to correct the impression you have made. Assure him that you are willing to move to a smaller house or make any other adjustments necessary to ease the financial burden. Any sacrifice on your part will be worth the satisfaction your husband will have, knowing that he can successfully meet his responsibilities.

If he insists that you go to work, take steps to obey him. Meanwhile, pray that God will change his mind or give you an alternate solution. God knows what you and your husband need to mature, so His answer to your prayer will fulfill your current needs.

Of course an emergency may arise. Your husband may become ill or lose his job. You may be forced to look for work to help out financially. The working woman is described in Proverbs 31:24: "She makes fine linen garments and leads others to buy them; she delivers to the merchants girdles [or sashes that free one for service]." Your helping out financially can be done without harm to your husband if you don't give the impression that you are a martyr or a rescuing hero. However, except in emergencies, I do not believe it is God's plan for a wife's work to supplement the family income.

In quite a different set of circumstances, you may find that outside work would be advisable for you. If you have no children, or if they are now grown, a job that does not interfere in any way with your role as a wife may be just the thing for you. Working under these circumstances, or as I do in writing and lecturing, should be an avocation rather than to supplement the family income. Any income from your activity should be incidental, like a bonus.

A good checklist to determine if your activity is within God's plan for you would be:

1. Does your activity conflict or compete with your husband's schedule or your duties as wife or mother?

2. Does your husband feel your activity is more important to you than he is?

3. Does your activity cause you to no longer be financially dependent on your husband?

4. Does your husband still feel the total responsibility of providing for his family?

Threats to you do not stop at the physical level. You also need psychological protection. Your emotions are a wonderful part of your femininity when they express themselves in loving response, appreciation, warmth, or kindness. But when you assume responsibilities that belong to your husband, you often encounter situations that subject you to undue emotional pressure. Your emotional response is then likely to be one of anger, frustration, and hurt. You may mishandle situations because you are so upset, and you may end up behaving like a shrew. This is often the case when you must deal with offensive salesmen, belligerent creditors, irritable neighbors, or even your own inconsiderate teenagers. Your husband is to serve as a protective agent between you and such pressures.

The next time your neighbor complains about your crabgrass getting into his lawn of fescue, simply say, "I'll speak to my husband about it." It's his problem, not yours. Isn't that comforting?

As you fulfill your role, you can even expect your husband to protect you from emotional conflicts with the children. He will demand that they respect you because he is learning to respect and appreciate your real womanhood. You will become like the woman described in Proverbs 31:25: "Strength and dignity are her clothing and her position is strong and secure."

When you do not understand that finances are your husband's responsibility, you may become emotionally upset about how the bills will be paid. However, if there is to be any worry involved, it is your husband's worry, not yours. Men are given the capacity to cope with this pressure. Of course you should be understanding and cooperative.

If you handle the family finances and write the checks, stop and ask yourself, "Why am I doing this?" Your husband has the right to delegate jobs, and it could be that he has requested your help. If he has given you the job of paying the bills, do keep him up to date on the family finances—so he'll know how to plan and spend. But if you are handling the finances in order to control the "purse strings," you are trying to lead. You're usurping your husband's role and will not have God's umbrella of protection.

You are usually least aware of your need for protection in the spiritual realm. Yet this is one of your more vulnerable areas. Being a more emotional creature, you may be deceived into making decisions on the basis of what appeals to you or what appears to be right instead of making decisions based on the principles set forth in God's Word.

Eve's decision to eat the forbidden fruit, for instance, was made on the basis of emotional appeal, and you know the consequences! "It was not Adam who was deceived but [the] woman who was deceived and deluded and fell into transgression" (1 Timothy 2:14). If you do not regulate your life by God's Word, you will be as easily led astray as Eve. "For among them [men who hold a form of godliness but deny its power] are those who worm their way into homes and captivate silly and weak-natured and spiritually dwarfed women, loaded down with [the burden of their] sins, [and easily] swayed and led away by various evil desires and seductive impulses. [These weak women will listen to anybody who will teach them]; they are forever inquiring and getting information, but are never able to arrive at a recognition and knowledge of the Truth" (2 Timothy 3:6-7).

It should be comforting to know that God will, literally, show you His will for your life through your husband. If you have prayed about a certain matter and feel you know God's will concerning it, use God's final check. Ask your husband what you should do. He may say "no" to what you feel God wants you to do, but God can change your husband's mind. The Bible says, "The king's heart is in the hand of the Lord, as the rivers of water; He turneth it whithersoever He will" (Proverbs 21:1, KJV). If God can change a king's mind at will, can't He also cause your husband to go along with the thing that is His plan for you?

You can trust God to lead you and your family spiritually without your defying your husband. When you get out from under God's umbrella of protection and become the spiritual leader in your home at the expense of your husband's headship, everyone suffers. Rebekah, for instance, conspired with her favorite son Jacob to deceive her aged, blind husband Isaac (Genesis 27). Through her deception, Jacob received his twin brother Esau's patriarchal blessing, but much heartache resulted. Esau's murderous hatred banished Jacob from his home for 21 toil-filled years, and Rebekah died without seeing her son again. It seems logical to conclude that her deceit also put a wedge between her and Isaac. God told Rebekah that Jacob would be the master (Genesis 25:23). How unfortunate that she did not trust God to work it out His way.

Your attitude toward your husband reveals your spiritual condition. You are rebellious to Christ's leadership to the same degree that you rebel against your husband's leadership. Sue had trouble accepting this principle until Christ made it very obvious one day. She was working in her flower garden when Bill asked her to empty the garbage can. *Why should I stop what I'm doing to do that?* she thought rebelliously. *I'll do it later, but not now.*

A day or two afterwards, the Holy Spirit prompted Sue to share with her neighbor how she might know Christ personally. Sue's immediate response was, "Lord, I'll do it later, but not now." Yes, her response to Christ was identical to her response to her husband—the one God had put over her.

God planned for your husband to stand between you and the world to protect you from the physical, emotional, and spiritual pressures that are harmful to you. As you allow your husband this privilege, you will begin to experience the pleasure of being a truly feminine woman.

How to Help Your Husband Become the Leader

At first you may say, "Sure, I'm convinced that my husband should be the head of our home, but he simply is not a leader." Remember, God would not command the man to be the leader ("For the husband is the head of the wife as Christ is the Head of the Church," Ephesians 5:23) without giving him the ability. With God's help and yours, your husband can be the leader God meant him to be.

If you have willingly or unwillingly assumed the role of leadership in your home, you can begin to ease out of it by *gradually* transferring to your husband the responsibilities he will most easily accept. When you begin to tell the children, "Go ask Daddy. He is the head of our home," they may be as shocked as their father, but this is a good way to start.

When your display of confidence in his leadership convinces him that his leadership is a permanent arrangement, not a temporary "kick" of yours, he should begin to respond positively. He very likely will enjoy the ego-boosting experience of taking charge and having you and the children follow his advice or decisions. He'll gradually gain confidence in himself and enjoy his new role.

Of course, you may have some reservations about your husband's leadership. "What happens when he makes the wrong decisions?" you may ask. Well, just remember that in trusting your husband, you are actually trusting Jesus Christ. He has promised to direct you through your husband. He can even use your husband's mistakes to teach him—and you—valuable lessons if you will stay under the "umbrella of God's protection." Remember Romans 8:28 says, "*All things* work together for good to them that love God" (KJV).

Suppose your husband has an important business decision to make and asks your advice. You warn against the venture, but he overrules your recommendation and goes ahead. As you predicted, the decision is a mistake. You now have the choice of ruining God's teaching opportunity by saying, "I told you so" or of maintaining a sweet, understanding attitude. If you have the proper attitude in this situation, you both can benefit from his mistake. You may learn, for instance, that you have been putting your trust in money rather than turning to Christ for your security.

As you maintain a sweet attitude and trust God, He will be able to deal with your husband directly and will not have to work against the interference of a nagging wife.

The promise in Romans 8:28 applies to both you and your husband. As you make mistakes (and you will), pray that God will work them out to glorify Him. I keep a button on my dressing table that is a comfort to me. It has these letters on it, "PBPGINFWMY" (Please be patient, God is not finished with me yet). Only God can take our mistakes and turn them into blessings as He makes us like Jesus.

Let go! Relax. You can enjoy the freedom of knowing that, along with the right to make the final decisions, your husband carries the responsibility for the consequences of his decisions. Resist temptations to interfere with his leadership because you feel his decisions or actions are too forceful, harsh, or wrong. Don't argue your point or try to manipulate him. Respond to his leadership in a relaxed manner, and you will find that your husband usually wants to please you.

Each year when they traded in their car, Peggy and Ken debated about whether they would buy the small car Ken wanted or the station wagon Peg wanted. Peggy's persistence usually won. After learning the principle of how to give advice, she simply shared with Ken her desire for a station wagon and left the final decision with him. She was sure he would come home with the small car because, after all, she had not argued or manipulated. Yet she decided to trust God regardless of the outcome, and Ken bought the station wagon.

I don't mean to imply that you will always get your way. Marjorie wanted very much to go to a Sunday School party, but Joe decided they would stay home and watch a football game on TV. Marjorie discovered a greater joy in committing her disappointment to Christ and watching the football game with Joe than she would have if she had gone to the party. Before learning to accept her husband's decisions, Marjorie would have pouted and made the evening miserable for both of them.

You will encourage your husband to take the lead by being a good follower and telling him how much you enjoy his taking charge. As you display trust in his ability, he will be more eager to continue as head of the house. Interestingly, as you follow, your husband will lead; but if you become aggressive, he may regress. You nag, and he will rebel. If you desire to please him, he will want to please you.

Be efficient in fulfilling your responsibilities to your husband, children, and home. Then your roles will be more clearly defined, and your husband will want to apply the same efficiency in his role. One lady commented, "As I have become a better wife, my husband has wanted to be a better husband. He can never be outdone."

Your husband can be head of the house even when he is absent if you faithfully follow his wishes for you and the family. For instance, you may not always agree with him that your teenagers should be home early on weekend nights. Yet you still make sure that they get in at their usual time, even though your husband is away on a business trip. You may tell them, "Dad wants you to be in by 10:30, so be sure to be home by then." Even if your husband is away for an extended time, you and the children can live under his protective leadership. God's provision is marvelous.

Ask God to show you any areas in which you have assumed your husband's role. Then go to him and tell him you have been wrong in assuming the role God has given him. Be specific; name the areas in which you've taken over: disciplining the children, refusing to move when he was offered a promotion, or not following the budget.

Tell him you know that since God gave him this role, God has equipped him to carry it out. Be sure to ask his forgiveness for challenging his abilities by interfering. Ask him to forgive you for your failure. Tell him that you are excited and comforted by the knowledge that God will lead you through him.

8
God's Best for You

Do you want God's best? This is an important question for you to settle. If you receive His best, you will experience *peace* of mind and heart: "Great peace have they who love Your law; nothing shall offend them or make them stumble" (Psalm 119:165). God's *joy*, too, will be yours if you choose His best: "But His joy is in those who reverence Him, those who expect Him to be loving and kind" (Psalm 147:11, LB).

Sarah chose God's best by responding to her husband as her authority. "It was thus that Sarah obeyed Abraham (following his guidance and acknowledging his headship over her by) calling him lord—master, leader, authority" (1 Peter 3:6).

God's best is revealed through His Word: "You are my hiding place and my shield; I hope in Your Word" (Psalm 119: 114). As the Word reveals Jesus Christ and His will for you, it will be like a flashlight to illumine the path ahead: "Your Word is a lamp to my feet and a light to my path" (Psalm 119:105).

His Word is permanently established and He will always

honor and fulfill its principles. "Forever, O Lord, Your Word [stands firm as the heavens] is settled in heaven" (Psalm 119: 89). "For You have exalted above all else Your name and Your Word, and You have magnified Your Word above all Your name!" (Psalm 138:2) The final authority in your life must be God's Word. His protection of you is based on your doing His will, not your will. "If you want Me to protect you, you must learn to believe what I say" (Isaiah 7:9, LB).

God's Authority for Wives

In His kindness and grace, God makes it clear in His Word that He wants you to obey your husband. "Wives, be subject —be submissive and adapt yourselves—to your own husbands as [a service] to the Lord" (Ephesians 5:22). Many other verses say the same thing. You might like to read them in your Bible: 1 Peter 3:1, 5-6; Genesis 3:16; 1 Corinthians 11: 3, 8-9; 1 Timothy 2:11-12; Titus 2:2-4.

The words "be submissive" in Ephesians 5:22 suggest or imply continuous action. Submission is to be a way of life. The wife never stops submitting. Submission is also used in the military sense—a position to which a wife is assigned.

Though God has assigned you that position, you still fulfill it voluntarily. He does not force you to take it any more than he forces you to receive His Son as your Saviour. The phrase "as unto the Lord" keeps this act of submission from being slavery and makes it a voluntary act of love. You willingly submit to your husband because you love the Lord and want to obey and please Him, not because you fear Him.

When you willingly, lovingly submit to your husband, your spirit of gentleness and love inspires your husband to treat you gently and to cherish and protect you.

Notice, however, that none of the verses listed say, "Be submissive if your husband is right, if he is a Christian, or if you can understand the outcome." No, God applies no such exceptions to your obedience to your husband.

Have you ever heard of a woman having a problem agreeing with the commandment, "You shall not steal"? (See Exodus 20:15.) Perhaps some do, but I myself have never heard one say, "It is all right to steal *if* you are hungry, *if* no one sees you, or *if* you strongly desire an object." God undoubtedly did not intend for us to steal. We accept this because He has made it clear. Yet, frequently women who would never consider stealing reject God's commandment to submit to their husbands. If you are such a woman and are unwilling to give God your total obedience, do not allow the Lord to be discredited by the blunders your disobedience produces. Admit you are living according to your plan, not His.

Most women I talk with do want to be God's women and be in His will. However, you can be in the center of His will only if you obey the one God has put in authority over you—your husband. You display your obedience to God through being subject to your husband. To refuse to recognize your husband's authority makes your life incomplete and unsatisfying—a direct result of breaking God's commandment relating to this issue. Remember, you do not degrade yourself or place yourself in an inferior position when you recognize and respect his authority. Instead, you gain dignity, fulfillment, femininity, and freedom to be the woman God wants you to be. God's plan is designed for your benefit.

Does complete obedience to Jesus Christ through your husband frighten you? "The Lord is fair in everything He does, and full of kindness" (Psalm 145:17, LB). Jesus Christ's love for you is so great and complete, it is hard to understand. "But God shows and clearly proves His [own] love for us by the fact that while we were still sinners, Christ, the Messiah, the Anointed One, died for us" (Romans 5:8). After dying for you, Jesus would not play a dirty trick by putting you in a position to make you miserable.

Do not put His love on the level of or below man's love (which you do when you feel that He would repay obedience with punishment). "Or what man is there of you, if his son asks him for a loaf of bread, will hand him a stone? Or if he asks for a fish, will hand him a serpent? If you then, evil as you are, know how to give good and advantageous gifts to your children, how much more will your Father who is in heaven [perfect as He is] give good and advantageous things to those who keep on asking Him!" (Matthew 7:9-11)

Suppose, to use a common illustration, that when I return home after a trip, my sons greet me with these words, "Mother, we've missed you and have decided that we'll do anything you want us to do, starting now."

Would I respond with, "Oh, good. I'm going to make your life miserable. You'll have brussels sprouts three times a day, and you'll never get to do anything you like to again. You'll be sorry you made such a commitment to me."

Of course I wouldn't say that. Once I finished hugging my sons, I'd probably go out and buy them the things they'd wanted. If we, in our incomplete human love, respond this way, surely we should not expect less from God. His love is perfect. He reaches out, wanting to minister to us in our deepest needs. If we can trust each other, surely we can trust the God of love and salvation. "We need have no fear of Someone who loves us perfectly; His perfect love for us eliminates all dread of what He might do to us. If we are afraid, it is for fear of what He might do to us, and shows that we are not fully convinced that He really loves us. So you see, our love for Him comes as a result of His loving us first" (1 John 4:18-19, LB).

It should comfort you to know that God's will for you is obedience to your husband.

The Wife's Protection

Since God states in Ephesians 5:24 (NASB) that "as the

Church is subject to Christ, so also the wives ought to be to their husbands in everything," do not think you are an exception. You may immediately say, "You don't know my husband! He's unsaved. He's unreasonable. That may work for some husbands and wives but not for us."

God deals with this specific problem in Scripture: "In the same way, you wives, be submissive to your own husbands so that even if any of them are disobedient to the Word they may be won without a word by the behavior of their wives, as they observe your chaste and respectful behavior" (1 Peter 3:1-2, NASB). Obviously, the Lord is talking here to the woman whose husband is unsaved.

Your submission to your husband is part of God's plan for order in our world (see 1 Peter 2:13-18). The words "in the same way" in 1 Peter 3:1 refer back to verses 13-14 and 18 in the previous chapter. "Submit yourselves for the Lord's sake to every human institution: whether to a king as the one in authority; or to governors, as sent by Him" (vv. 13-14), and "Servants, be submissive to your masters with all respect, not only to those who are good and gentle, but also to those who are unreasonable" (v. 18).

God is saying that His plan for you is submission to the one in authority over you—daily joyful submission to your husband even as you would submit to governments or a master. So if you allow the Lord to cleanse you, fill you, and control you, and if you take a position of wholehearted submission to your husband because God has said you should, you can depend on God to fulfill His Word in caring for you and helping you carry out His command.

Remember 1 Corinthians 10:13? "You haven't been tempted more than you could expect. And you can trust God; He will not let you be tested more than you can stand. But when you are tested, He will also make a way out so that you can bear it" (BECK). Now you don't know *how* God will fulfill His Word. You simply trust that He *will.* If your husband has asked you to do something unreasonable, God may change your husband's mind. As we noted earlier, "The king's heart [and your husband's!] is in the hand of the Lord, as the rivers of water, He turneth it whithersoever He will" (Proverbs 21:1, KJV).

Perhaps examples from life will help you understand God's gracious way of working things out for you when you obey Him and honor your husband.

Barbara had become a Christian, but her husband, Don, had not. She began to attend church faithfully and even took the children. Don seemed bewildered at first by her new faith and her interest in church. Then he became jealous and hurt because she was spending her Sundays away from him. He did not feel as if he was number one in her life anymore.

Some weeks had gone by when Barbara heard these principles of the wife's submission to her husband whether he was a Christian or not. She wanted to please the Lord, so she decided to concentrate on honoring her husband. Easter Sunday morning came, and she and the children were all ready to go to church when Don woke up.

Right away, Barbara sensed that Don was unhappy. "Honey, would you like me to stay home with you today?" she asked. "You know I want you to be happy. If you'd prefer to have me and the children home with you, we'll stay here." He didn't answer, but she could tell that he wanted her to stay home.

She and the children changed into more casual clothes, and she planned some relaxed games for the children. As the morning progressed, her husband's mood got better and better. Later in the day, Don called the children to him. He picked up the Bible and said, "Children, I want us to read some of the Bible together." He read from Proverbs and talked to them about what God said.

Naturally, Barbara's heart was warmed. She had given her husband his rightful place, and he was no longer jealous of her relationship with the church and Jesus Christ. Here he was taking the spiritual leadership, and he wasn't a Christian! Actually, the day ended up being far better than an Easter service because the family was united in reading and discussing God's Word together. Now, a year later, Don is a Christian too. True, there were times when Barbara had to stay home from church simply to give her husband his place in her life. But he might not have received Christ if she had not considered him.

Allison had an experience much like Barbara's. Only Allison had been raised to believe that churchgoing was the absolute right thing. When the church doors were open, you went. She was quite self-righteous about attending. But Allison had married a man who did not love Christ and did not care to attend church.

Allison's Sunday School teacher began to teach these biblical principles about the wife's role of submission. One Sunday she got Allison aside and told her, "Your husband simply doesn't understand what's going on in your life. He's jealous. He cannot understand spiritual truths, and if he wants you to stay home with him, then you should, until he is assured of his rightful place in your heart."

Allison was shocked. She had never heard anything like that before. But when she saw that the principles of submission came right from God's Word, she agreed to try them.

The next Sunday, Allison got herself and the children ready for church as usual. Her husband Andy, a traveling salesman, was sleeping late. He awoke, and seeing her getting ready for church, began to rave and curse and tell her he didn't see any difference in church people's lives or any good reason for her attending. Allison very quietly changed into a casual dress.

"What are you doing?" Andy asked in amazement.

"Well, it's obvious you don't want me to go to church," she said. "And I do love you. And I want you to be happy. After all, I haven't spent much time with you since you've been going out of town. So it would be the right thing for me to stay home with you. I'd like to hear what you've been doing this week, anyway."

Andy got out of bed and put his arms around her with tears in his eyes.

Allison said that for the first time that morning she saw something in him she had never seen before—just because she put herself in the position God intended. God was able to bring out qualities in Andy she didn't even know existed. They had a happy day together.

As the weeks went by, Andy began attending church with her and the children. The last I heard, he still hadn't received Christ as Saviour, but he was still attending church with his family and encouraging them to do so—all because Allison's relationship with Christ and her church were no longer a threat to him.

Men don't really want to be brutal or tyrannical. They act that way because they feel insecure in their relationships with their wives and are fighting desperately to gain the position God meant them to have. Once a man sees he doesn't have to fight for his wife's love, that he has her obedience, and her full attention, he in turn will allow her to have her own activities and interests—so long as she doesn't take advantage.

Now, as I said before, you don't know how God is going to work in your particular situation. Perhaps your husband won't change in the way Don and Andy did.

Laura's Jake gave her a bad time when she told him she was going to obey him and put him first in a way she hadn't before. He was not a Christian and decided to test her.

"OK, Laura, let's go to the Royal Three tonight." (It was a nightclub that featured lewd entertainment.)

Laura was shaken but didn't show Jake how she felt. "I said I'd do what you want me to, so I will," she told him.

He couldn't believe her and kept saying, "Well, what will you do when such and such happens?"

"I'll do what you say," she told him and proceeded to get ready. They were all dressed and ready to leave when he suddenly got a blinding headache. "Honey, I can't go," he told her. And they didn't. God had intervened.

Marilyn's husband also asked her to go to a nightclub with him and she went. However, she graciously refrained from taking part in some of the activities in such a way that she did not make her husband feel uncomfortable. Another woman, also sitting by and watching, noticed that Marilyn wasn't taking part and came over to talk to her. Marilyn explained that she was refraining from the activities because of her faith in Jesus Christ. So Marilyn was able to glorify her Saviour even at a nightclub.

Sally's problem wasn't so overwhelming. The family was visiting her mother one day. Her mother had some nice rich dirt and offered Sally some for her plants at home. Sally got a big bucket and filled it full. But as she started to put it in the car, her husband George said, "You're not going to take that home in our clean car!"

"Why, George, I can put paper on the floor and hold the bucket so it won't spill," Sally answered.

"No, I don't want a dirty pail in the car," he told her. And that was that. Sally didn't argue because she knew these principles of submitting to her husband. She figured she'd come back later in the truck and get the dirt, and just forgot about the incident. But as they were getting ready to leave, her husband surprised her. "Oh, go ahead and get the bucket of dirt," he said. "If you hold it like you promised, it should be OK."

This little incident made Sally think back to other times in their relationship. She realized that George felt at times as if he were no longer the head of the house. She could see that when he felt sure of himself and not threatened, he was as sweet as pie.

So many marriage problems result from a misunderstanding of the husband-wife relationship or from the wife's deliberate refusal to submit to her husband. It is significant that six verses in 1 Peter 3:1-7 speak to the wife about her role and only one verse instructs the husband. The woman's role is crucial, strategic, and it is a hard role to fill. God takes extra time, giving instructions to the woman on how she is to fulfill that role so she won't go to an extreme and become a slave but will still retain her individuality and her husband's love.

Basically, the woman's protection is God's Word. God has outlined in His Word the fact that he wants her to obey her husband without exception. If she does, she can depend on God to keep His Word and to deal with her husband in whatever way He sees necessary to enable the woman to do what He wants her to do.

The Wife's Responsibility

Your attitude toward God and your husband is the key to your success with God and man. If you do not want to submit to your husband, confess this to the Lord. Trust Him to control your life and change your desires. You will be thrilled to see God's Word become a living reality in your mind.

God holds you responsible for your attitude and motives. You must be transparent before Him. He cannot be fooled. "For the Lord sees not as man sees; for man looks on the outward appearance, but the Lord looks on the heart" (1 Samuel 16:7). Do not attempt to rationalize or justify your actions. "We can justify our every deed, but God looks at our motives" (Proverbs 21:2, LB). It is relaxing and comforting to be open and honest before God. He loves you!

You cannot play games with your husband either. He can

sense if you obey willingly or grudgingly. Do not be like the little boy whose daddy told him to sit down in the seat while riding in the car. The little boy refused. Finally, the father threatened to stop the car and spank him if he would not obey. The boy sat down but mumbled under his breath, "I'll sit down, but I'm still standing up on the inside." You cannot afford to "stand up on the inside." Such rebellion will destroy your joy and your husband's.

Remember, your husband's unreasonable demands or actions, whether he is saved or not, can be stimulated or minimized by your attitude. That is why it is so important for you to voluntarily obey him with pure motives. (Of course, the prerequisite to a right relationship with your husband is a right relationship with God, free from unconfessed sin.)

God's Word reminds us that husbands may be won to the Lord "when they observe the pure and modest way in which you conduct yourselves, together with your reverence [for your husband. That is, you are to feel for him all that reverence includes]—to respect, defer to, revere him; [revere means] to honor, esteem (appreciate, prize), and [in the human sense] adore him; [and adore means] to admire, praise, be devoted to, deeply love and enjoy [your husband]" (1 Peter 3:2).

In other words, your husband will see that you don't fall apart over the things that used to upset you. He observes that when he stays out all night and gives you no reason, you don't go into a tailspin or tantrum or nag him for days. You give him his freedom and accept him the way he is. He sees that you do not give "way to hysterical fears" (1 Peter 3:6), and you have more patience with the children. You're more thoughtful. You're considerate of him; you listen to him; you think about him; you respect him. You reverence him, adore him, admire him, praise him, and enjoy his company.

When your husband sees and lives with this kind of woman, he cannot help but be influenced! He cannot help but be softened and stimulated to be the man that God meant him to be. So it is your responsibility as a wife to fulfill the role God designed for you, keeping your relationship with your husband right and leaving everything else to God. Trust God to deal with your husband and work out difficulties in the way He sees best. God longs for you to trust Him.

What About My Reputation?

The wise woman will fix her mind on obeying God as we have discussed. Her first consideration is to build a successful marriage, not to look around and see what others think about what she's doing or to regulate her life to please others. In other words, if in obeying your husband and putting him first, you must attend a nightclub with him, do not worry about what others will say. Nor should you worry if you can't be in church every Sunday as you would like to be. In other words, do not be concerned about gossips or listen to well-meaning advice, even when it comes from Christian friends.

Some Christians will be very upset if you do not attend church faithfully. They will quote Hebrews 10:25 to you, where it says you should not neglect assembling together for worship. If they are critical, simply tell them you are only refraining for a time so you can later return to church with your husband's blessing, and, hopefully, with him.

Of course, you should study your Bible faithfully, so God can speak to you and guide you when you cannot get to church. You might even ask a friend to tape the Sunday services so you can enjoy them during the week. You may also attend a daytime women's Bible study or find other opportunities to assemble for Christian fellowship. Thus you will not be breaking God's command in Hebrews by submitting to your husband, so don't let anyone tell you that you are.

Your responsibility is to do the will of God, not to seek approval from others. Jesus Christ said, "I can of Mine own self do nothing: as I hear, I judge: and My judgment is just; because I seek not Mine own will, but the will of the Father which hath sent Me" (John 5:30, KJV). If Jesus could say that He had come to do God's will, not His own, certainly you should put God's will first in your life, too.

Jesus' reputation was not very good in some religious circles. Some religious people accused Him of being a drunk (see Luke 7:34, NASB). Others said, "What kind of Man is this that keeps company with tax collectors, prostitutes, and sinners?" (See Matt. 11:19.) Jesus "made Himself of no reputation, and took upon Him the form of a servant, and was made in the likeness of men" (Philippians 2:7, KJV).

Mary, the mother of Jesus, had a bad reputation among those who did not believe in the virgin birth. It has been said that one of the reasons Joseph took Mary with him to Bethlehem the year of Jesus' birth was to protect Mary from gossip at home. Even today some call Jesus the illegitimate son of Mary.

We belong to Jesus Christ. We can trust Him to care for us—His property. "He restoreth my soul; He leadeth me in the paths of righteousness for *His name's sake*" (Psalm 23:3, KJV). It is His reputation that is at stake when you obey Him and your husband, not yours.

Shadows in the Dark

Many questions and fears are the product of your imagination and worries. Do not become upset about someone else's situation or some unknown possibility. Jesus promises to be sufficient for all those who trust in Him for their *present* problems. "God is faithful—reliable, trustworthy, and [therefore] ever true to His promise, and He can be depended on; by Him you were called into companionship and participation with His Son, Jesus Christ our Lord" (1 Corinthians 1:9). Worry about "what ifs" is a sin. "Casting the whole of your care—all your anxieties, all your worries, all your concerns, once and for all—on Him; for He cares for you affectionately, and cares about you watchfully" (1 Peter 5:7). Let the light of Jesus Christ dissolve all your fears or "shadows in the dark"!

Guidelines in Accomplishing God's Will

Your role of submission to your husband will become an exciting adventure when you realize that one of the reasons for this role is to develop a mature attitude in you. God's desire for His children is that they become like Jesus Christ. "For from the very beginning God decided that those who came to Him—and all along He knew who would—should become like His Son, so that His Son would be the First, with many brothers" (Romans 8:29, LB). God wants to use any situation in which you find yourself to make you like Jesus.

Is there any area in which you are having problems with your husband? Has it occurred to you that those problems may be the result of some immaturity in you? Every person has a strong will (OSN). When the OSN is in control of your life, your marriage will be unhappy. God may use either a forceful husband or a husband who withdraws, leaving you with his responsibilities, to break your will.

"Even so consider yourselves also dead to sin and your relation to it broken" (Romans 6:11). When we exchange our desires for Christ's, the initial pain of dying to self is a healing pain which is followed by peace and fulfillment. When we are unwilling to exchange our desires for Christ's, we experience a kind of pain which produces heartaches.

Jesus Christ never promised a problem-free life. "The good man does not escape all troubles—he has them too. But the Lord helps him in each and every one" (Psalm 34:19, LB). These problems are for our benefit. "The punishment You gave me was the best thing that could have happened to me, for it taught me to pay attention to Your laws. They are more valuable to me than millions in silver and gold! Your faithfulness extends to every generation, like the earth You created; it endures by Your decree, for everything serves Your plans" (Psalm 119:71-72, 90-91, LB).

Another guideline to consider is your husband's position. He is a tool in the Father's hand. You are to honor and respect his position, not necessarily his personality. Your husband may not understand you and may have personality deficiencies that bother you, but God promises that He is able to work through these deficiencies if your attitude pleases Him. "When a man's ways please the Lord, He makes even his enemies to be at peace with him" (Proverbs 16:7). If God can enable you to live with an enemy peacefully, He certainly can help you live at peace with an ornery husband.

When a problem comes up, ask yourself, "What is God saying to me through this situation?" We miss many valuable lessons by not responding in this way to difficulties.

Jesus Christ had to take me through a particular lesson many times before I saw what He wanted to teach me. DeWitt had often expressed his disapproval of my talking on the phone frequently while he was home. I thought he was being unfair. Finally, the Lord got through to me and showed me that my behavior expressed more concern for the feelings of others than for my husband. Realizing what my actions implied, I saw how wrong I was. My stubbornness in not seeing earlier what God wanted to teach me, had caused much unnecessary friction. God sees weak areas in our lives—areas we are often unaware of—and wants to help us. The psalmist said, "For all my ways are (fully known) before You" (Psalm 119: 168).

Something else that will help you submit to your husband is to find out what his real motive is. This will help you be a helpmate to him. For instance, why doesn't he want you to buy the dress you are so crazy about? Does he want to hurt you or is he considering the family budget?

Some men are addicted to such things as drugs, alcohol, or gambling. The urge to gamble, the need for a fix, or drunkenness may make him unreasonable. Should you obey him under such circumstances?

If your husband drinks or has some other habit that affects his reason, find out what his basic goals are or his wishes in specific instances and obey these, not his unreasonable demands when drunk or obsessed. You are not disobeying him in this instance but are carrying out instructions he has given you when thinking clearly.

Bill was a gambler and seemed to have no control over his desire to gamble. At times he would win tremendous sums of money, but other times, he lost everything he had. Finally, he realized that his gambling could hurt his wife and children and himself. One day, right after winning a large sum of money, he went to his lawyer and had him put the winnings in savings. "I want you to draw up some kind of contract that says I can never touch this money. It's for my children's future and any immediate needs my wife might have," he told the lawyer. "If I come to you on my knees, begging you to break the contract and get the money, don't listen to me."

Later he did go to his wife and beg her to get some of the money out of savings, but she refused, knowing that in his "right frame of mind" he did not want her to touch that money except in real need.

God the Holy Spirit will enable you to be creative in responding to situations. You'll be surprised at the alternatives He will give you in following your husband's directions while maintaining personal convictions.

Coming home tired from work, your husband may say, "Tell anyone who calls that I'm not home."

What is his motive for asking you to say this? Obviously, he does not want to be disturbed; it isn't that he means to force you to lie. Therefore, you can tell him that you'll be glad to handle the calls so that he won't be disturbed. You can respond to those who call with, "May I have your name and number? My husband will call when it's convenient."

Choose your wording carefully when responding creatively to your husband's requests. Your response must not project any disapproval of him or make him feel guilty. Obedience to God's Word will help develop your common sense and good judgment. "Now teach me good judgment as well as knowledge. For Your laws are my guide" (Psalm 119:66, LB).

When your husband has made a wrong decision, remember that God is bigger than he or your circumstances, so give God time to change your husband's mind. Remember, "Just as water is turned into irrigation ditches, so the Lord directs the king's thoughts. He turns them wherever He wants to" (Proverbs 21:1, LB). "He changes the times and the seasons, He removes kings and sets up kings, He gives wisdom to the wise and knowledge to those who have understanding!" (Daniel 2:21)

Do not be surprised at what God may use to change your husband's mind! After DeWitt decided to purchase a motorcycle, several months elapsed before God changed his mind about it. God used this period of time to teach me about His faithfulness. Without too much difficulty, I had been able to trust Christ for DeWitt's buying and riding a motorcycle himself, but when he talked of buying a minibike for the boys, I felt he was going too far!

I exercised my privilege of sharing my feelings about the many dangers of cycling. He seemed to agree, and I thought the matter was settled. Later, however, he exercised his right to overrule my decision and bought the boys a minibike. I knew my part was to accept his decision and trust God for the results. I placed the boys' safety in God's hands and, by faith, entered into their joy.

Weeks later, DeWitt had a freak accident as he rode into our driveway one evening. He hurt his knee just enough to convince him of the dangers of cycling. It was his decision to sell the motorcycle three days later. It was also his decision not to repair an unexpected hole that appeared soon afterward in the minibike motor. When God changes one's mind, He does it completely.

Expect pressure while God is working to change your husband's mind. Your husband may give you a bad time just to see if you really intend to support a decision of his that you disagree with. Trust Christ's sufficiency through such pressures. "Bless the Lord who is my immovable rock. He gives me strength and skill in battle. He is always kind and loving to me; He is my fortress, my tower of strength and safety, my deliverer. He stands before me as a shield. He subdues my people under me" (Psalm 144:1-2, LB). God will use these very pressures to develop strong character in you. "We can rejoice, too, when we run into problems and trials for we know that they are good for us—they help us learn to be patient. And patience develops strength of character in us and helps us trust God more each time we use it until finally our hope and faith are strong and steady" (Romans 5:3-4, LB).

Each member of your family can develop strong character through problems and trials just as you do. Many times you do more harm than good by overly protecting your loved ones. They can learn valuable lessons through mistakes, suffering or trouble that they cannot learn any other way. Don't rob them of such opportunities.

When you "delight yourself also in the Lord . . . He will give you the desires and sacred petitions of your heart. Commit your way to the Lord—roll and repose [each care of] your road on Him; trust (lean on, rely on, and be confident) also in Him, and He will bring it to pass" (Psalm 37:4-5). The key is to delight yourself in the *Lord,* not in *your* desires. We must operate according to God's plan and timetable, not ours.

Be prepared! God may change your desires. Recently we bought new bedroom furniture. I wanted a nightstand, too, but DeWitt said we did not need one. My immediate response was one of rebellion. Then I committed my desire to the Lord. When I did, God changed my desire to correspond with DeWitt's. One cannot lose in God's plan.

As you apply these insights and are totally obedient to your husband "as unto the Lord," you can share David's response to the Lord. "How great He is! His power is absolute! His understanding is unlimited" (Psalm 147:5, LB).

9
Fadeless Beauty

Most women would give anything to have a beauty that grows instead of fading as they mature. Yet that kind of beauty is the inheritance of every woman who belongs to Christ. God describes this beauty in 1 Peter 3:4: "But let it be the inward adorning and beauty of the hidden person of the heart, with the incorruptible and unfading charm of a gentle and peaceful spirit, which (is not anxious or wrought up, but) is very precious in the sight of God." Incorruptible or fadeless beauty begins on the inside, and its radiance actually transforms your outward appearance.

You can get hung up on unchangeable features you consider ugly, such as a large nose or ears, a long face, or extreme height. When tempted to worry over such characteristics, remember that you had them when your husband chose you. Those features are unimportant to him because they are part of the whole you he loves. Thank God for them, knowing that they have a purpose in God's plan for your life. As you trust Him, he will use those very features to your benefit.

The sparkle in your eyes, a warm smile, a radiant, fresh,

feminine manner, and a gentle, peaceful spirit mean more to your man than your external features. Fadeless beauty is what a mature man looks for in a wife. Men do have different tastes, of course. One may choose a quiet, shy woman, another a dashing, outgoing woman, and still another the dramatic or glamorous type. But the basic characteristics of beauty are the same. Fadeless beauty satisfies the woman who possesses it as well as those around her.

Your inner beauty will be evident only when you realize that you are worthwhile and valuable. You are not "second-rate." You are royalty—a daughter of the King! "You were freed from the worthless life you inherited from your fathers not by a payment of silver or gold which perish, but by the precious blood of Christ, the Lamb without a fault or a spot" (1 Peter 1:18-19, BECK). Being aware of your true value because of what Christ has done for you, will enable you to gain self-respect and self-esteem. Those around you will, in turn, have the same respect for you.

The source of your incorruptible beauty is the spiritual condition of your heart: "For as he thinks in his heart, so is he" (Proverbs 23:7). A gentle nature and peaceful outlook will be mirrored in your eyes and registered on your features just as if your face were a sensitive cardiograph. Lovely attitudes dominating your heart will show up as pleasant expressions on your face. Sparkling eyes, a warm smile, and relaxed facial muscles are symptoms of a good "heart" condition. In contrast, dull eyes, harsh lines of the lips, and a scowl are symptoms of a bad "heart" condition. And the condition of the heart can be altered by only One—Jesus Christ, the Master Physician.

You were meant to be beautiful! Your Heavenly Father wants you, as a daughter of the King, to be especially appealing. As the psalmist says: "So will the King desire your beauty for He is your Lord; be submissive, and reverence and honor

Him. The King's daughter in the inner part of the palace is all glorious!" (Psalm 45:11, 13)

God's Beauty Salon

Your beauty will develop as you maintain a daily appointment with God in His "beauty salon." His beauty treatment is available without cost to all who want fadeless beauty and come to Him for treatment. Treatment involves regular Bible study, obedience to the principles He reveals through study, and talking with Him in prayer.

As God begins your treatment, realize that your natural thoughts and ways of doing things are opposed to His thoughts and ways. Your thoughts are influenced by the world system and your OSN which is opposed to God. "For My thoughts are not your thoughts, neither are your ways My ways, saith the Lord. For as the heavens are higher than the earth, so are My ways higher than your ways, and My thoughts than your thoughts" (Isaiah 55:8-9, KJV).

God works to develop your beauty as you surrender to Him much as you would surrender to the hands of a local beauty operator. "Let the beauty and delightfulness and favor of the Lord our God be upon us" (Psalm 90:17). His beauty treatment involves sitting under His beauty lamp and letting it clear up the defects in your life—transforming the darkness in your soul to the light of beauty.

In Ephesians 4:17-18 (KJV), our natural, sinful state is called darkness: "Walk not as other Gentiles walk, in the vanity of their mind, having the understanding darkened, being alienated from the life of God through the ignorance that is in them." The only solution to this darkness (wrong thoughts, attitudes, and actions) is the transforming light of Jesus Christ which produces true beauty. Jesus said, "I am the Light of the world. He who follows Me will not be walking in the dark, but will have the Light which is Life" (John 8:12).

You may think, "Jesus Christ is no longer present on earth in bodily form to be my light." You are right. He is now "seated at the right hand of the throne of God" (Hebrews 12:2). Yet though Jesus Christ is presently at the right hand of the Father, He has left total provision for you through His Word. He is the Living Word: "In the beginning [before all time] was the Word [Christ], and the Word was with God, and the Word was God Himself" (John 1:1).

Christ has left the Word, His thoughts in writing, to take His place in His absense. "We have the mind of Christ, the Messiah, and do hold the thoughts (feelings and purposes) of His heart" (1 Corinthians 2:16). In His Word He has given you everything He wants you to know while you are here on earth. You are not to look for any kind of special revelation. You need only to study the personal letter He has written to each of His children—the Bible—in order to know His will for your life.

His Word (wisdom) as described in Proverbs 4:9 "shall give to your head a wreath of gracefulness; a crown of beauty and glory." As you read it, you must decide whether or not you will believe it. If your response is positive, God the Holy Spirit, who lives in believers, will use this knowledge to illuminate your soul or inner self. The light of God's Word will chase away the gloom of sin, cleansing you and making you like Jesus Christ. "You are cleansed and pruned already, because of the Word which I have given you—the teachings I have discussed with you" (John 15:3).

If you say no to God's Word, the principle may remain in your mind as intellectual knowledge, but it will not transform you. But if you allow Christ's mind to be formed in your own, and you operate on the basis of God's principles, you will experience stability, inner peace, fulfillment, and beauty. Furthermore, Christ said, "If you live in Me—abide vitally united to Me—and My words remain in you and continue to live in your hearts, ask whatever you will and it shall be done for you" (John 15:7).

You can know whether you are saying yes or no to God's Word by your application or lack of application of God's Word to your daily situations. For instance, God says in 1 Peter 5:7 that you are not to worry but are to let Him take care of your problems. If you refuse to give Him your problems, saying, "Anyone would be upset in my situation," or "It's my nature to worry," you are living according to man's principles for life, not God's (see accompanying diagram on the next page).

God's Word can keep you panic proof as you realize that He has provided for every circumstance in your life. "He knows about everyone, everywhere. Everything about us is bare and wide open to the all-seeing eyes of our living God; nothing can be hidden from Him to whom we must explain all that we have done" (Hebrews 4:13, LB).

He not only knows all things but has already provided victory for you over every situation you will ever face (1 Corinthians 10:13; 15:57). And His light is sufficient for all of life's paths: "Thy Word is a lamp unto my feet and a light unto my path" (Psalm 119:105, KJV).

God's Word is also like a mirror, in that it reveals the defects in your beauty (James 1:23-26). Those defects or sins grieve the Holy Spirit (Ephesians 4:30) and dim your transforming light of beauty. Confession (see 1 John 1:9) returns the Holy Spirit to full control so that the light (Word) can shine into all areas of your life and transform you into the image of Jesus Christ. "I beseech you therefore, brethren, by the mercies of God, that ye present your bodies a living sacrifice, holy, acceptable unto God, which is your reasonable service. And be not conformed to this world; but be ye transformed by the renewing of your mind, that ye may prove what is that good, . . . and perfect will of God" (Romans 12:1-2, KJV).

Romans 12 : 1-2

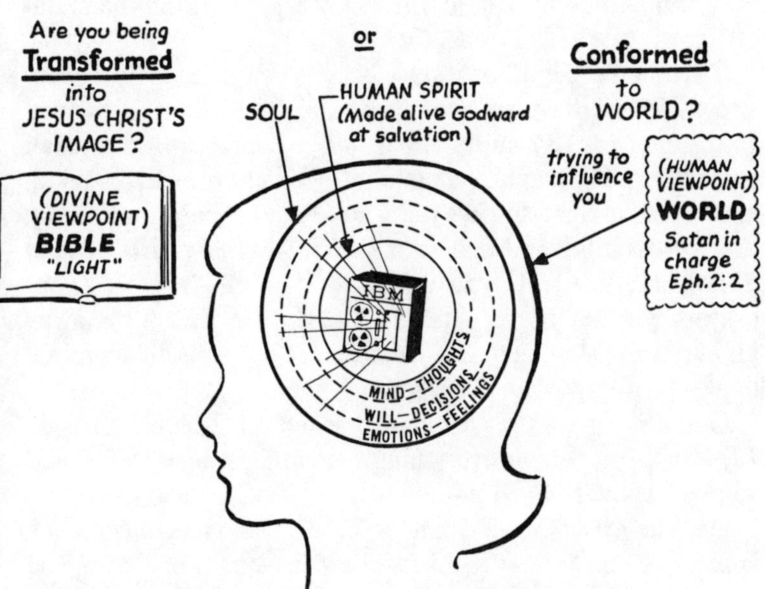

DIVINE VIEWPOINT: living according to God's principles (as taught in the Bible)

HUMAN VIEWPOINT: living according to man's principles (as taught in mass media and by other individuals)

= Storage area for principles by which our life is lived

Prayer is also an important part of God's beauty treatment. Jesus said, "If ye abide in Me, and My words abide in you, ye shall ask what ye will, and it shall be done unto you" (John 15:7, KJV). He also said, "Hitherto have ye asked nothing in My name; ask, and ye shall receive, that your joy may be full" (John 16:24, KJV).

As you share your praise, your requests, and your needs with God in prayer in Jesus' name, God promises to hear and answer and fill you with joy. And joy can transform the plainest face into a radiant one.

True, some conditions must be met if prayer is to be answered. If you harbor unconfessed sin, God will not hear you (see Psalm 66:18) and your joy will disappear. But you can pray with King David, "Create in me a clean heart, O God, and renew a right spirit within me. Restore unto me the joy of Thy salvation, and uphold me with Thy free spirit" (Psalm 51:10, 12, KJV). If you refuse to hear God's Word, your prayers will not be acceptable to God. "He who turns away his ear from listening to the law, even his prayer is an abomination" (Proverbs 28:9, NASB).

God also says, "Pray without ceasing" (1 Thessalonians 5:17, KJV). Pray about everything (see Philippians 4:6-7), and you will know His peace—another wonderful beauty aid.

Certainly if you spend time in God's beauty salon, reading His Word and letting it do its work in your life, and if you take time to pray, God's radiance will shine in your face and personality. There is no beauty like that.

Deadly Traps that Mar Beauty

The beauty that God is creating in you and revealing through you, can be marred when anger, fear, or depression control your life. Carnal emotions cannot control you without damaging your beauty and your physical and spiritual health. Medical doctors have estimated that these emotions produce 60-90% of all illness. Since you do not want your beauty to be marred, see what God's Word has to say about these deadly emotional traps.

1. Anger

Anger takes many forms: envy, intolerance, criticism, revenge, hatred, rebellion, jealousy, and unforgiveness. Many of these plus other forms of anger are mentioned in Ephesians 4:31: "Let all bitterness and indignation and wrath (passion, rage, bad temper) and resentment (anger, animosity) and quarreling (brawling, clamor, contention) and slander (evil speaking, abusive or blasphemous language) be banished from you, with all malice (spite, ill will, or baseness of any kind)." God commands you not to be controlled by these carnal emotions which flow from your OSN because He wants you to be happy and beautiful. Look at yourself in the mirror when you are angry and see how your beauty is blemished.

A wife controlled by Jesus Christ is a crowning joy to her husband, but when she is controlled by anger, her presence can be torture: "It is better to dwell in a corner of the housetop [on the flat oriental roof, exposed to all kinds of weather] than in a house shared with a nagging, quarrelsome, and faultfinding woman. It is better to dwell in a desert land than with a contentious woman and vexation" (Proverbs 21:9, 19).

Are you aware that one form of torture is the continual dropping of water on one's head? The Bible suggests that an angry woman is like this hellish torment. "The contentions of a wife are as a continual dropping [of water through a chink in the roof]. A continual dripping on a day of violent showers and a contentious woman are alike" (Proverbs 19:13; 27:15).

God needs to give a command only once for it to be important. The fact that He refers frequently to the repugnance of an angry woman should warn you of the seriousness of anger. God does not want you to miss the point.

Anger has a way of multiplying and reproducing itself in the lives of your husband and children. "The north wind brings forth rain; so does a backbiting tongue bring forth an angry countenance. It is better to dwell in the corner of the housetop than to share a house with a disagreeing, quarrelsome, and scolding woman" (Proverbs 25:23-24). Could outbursts of anger from your family be caused by your own, perhaps unconscious, bad humor? Your family can reflect your moods, attitudes, and aspirations.

The usual cause of anger is identified by the ugly word "selfishness." When you are angry, it is usually because you feel that your rights have been violated. Or you want something done for you that has not been done, or you do not want something done that has been done. You can excuse and justify your weaknesses and even indulge in vengeful, bitter feelings, but the motivation is still selfishness.

Recognize the symptoms listed above as evidences that you are controlled by the OSN, confess them as sin and trust Christ to change you.

2. Fear

Fear is a trap that is as damaging to your beauty and health as anger. No kind of cosmetic will cover the self-consciousness, doubts, and fears reflected on your face. Fear may be displayed through anxiety, doubt, timidity, indecision, superstition, withdrawal, loneliness, overaggression, worry, feelings of inferiority, cowardice, hesitance, depression, haughtiness, or shyness.

What causes fear? It may be caused by a conscience that is guilty because of sin. Adam and Eve's first sin—partaking of the forbidden fruit—brought fear. "They heard the sound of the Lord God walking in the garden in the cool of the day, and Adam and his wife hid themselves from the presence of the Lord God among the trees of the garden. But the Lord God called to Adam, and said to him, 'Where are you?' He said, 'I heard the sound of You [walking] in the garden, and I was afraid, because I was naked; and I hid myself' " (Genesis 3:8-10). Sin caused them to hide, fearing the presence of the Lord, whereas before their sin they had enjoyed God's presence and fellowship.

Sin produces fear from which you try to escape either physically or mentally. "The wicked flee when no man pursues them, but the [uncompromisingly] righteous are bold as a lion" (Proverbs 28:1). You do not have to prove or justify yourself if you are not guilty. You need not be afraid if you are innocent. "There is no fear in love—dread does not exist; but full-grown (complete, perfect) love turns fear out of doors and expels every trace of terror! For fear brings with it the thought of punishment, and [so] he who is afraid has not reached the full maturity of love—is not yet grown into love's complete perfection. And, beloved, if our consciences (our hearts) do not accuse us—if they do not make us feel guilty and condemn us—we have confidence (complete assurance and boldness) before God" (1 John 4:18; 3:21).

If you have feelings of guilt, perhaps you *are* guilty. Compare your actions with God's Word in order to determine your true condition. If God's Word reveals your guilt, confess your sin and thank Jesus Christ for paying the penalty for it when He died for you on the cross. The Father forgives and forgets your sin because of Christ's work for you. "As far as the east is from the west, so far has He removed our transgressions from us" (Psalm 103:12). Do not look back or remember the sin again. Let it be a closed case.

Because of Christ's work on the cross for you, you may be free from the burden of a guilt complex. If you are guilty, confess your sin and accept Christ's forgiveness. Should the thought of your confessed sin enter your mind again, simply thank God that He has forgiven you and move on.

Fear may also come from not knowing or not believing God's Word. Peter's lack of faith in Christ caused him terror: "In the fourth watch [between three and six o'clock] of the night, Jesus came to them, walking on the sea. And when the disciples saw Him walking on the sea, they were terrified, and said, 'It is a ghost!' And they screamed out with fright. But instantly He spoke to them, saying, 'Take courage! I AM; stop being afraid!' And Peter answered Him, 'Lord, if it is You, command me to come to You on the water.' He said, 'Come!' So Peter got out of the boat and walked on the water, and he came to Jesus; but when he perceived and felt the strong wind, he was frightened, and as he began to sink, he cried out, 'Lord, save me [from death]!' Instantly Jesus reached out His hand and caught and held him, saying to him, 'O you of little faith, why did you doubt?' " (Matthew 14:25-31)

At first, Peter did not recognize Jesus and was terrified. When you do not recognize His power to work out solutions to problems in the world, you can become terrified too. Then Peter's trust in Christ enabled him to begin walking to meet Christ on the water. But the strong wind whipped up the sea and frightened Peter into doubting Christ's sufficiency for him.

Is this not what happens to you? When the problems or anticipated problems of life threaten, you begin to fear for yourself and your loved ones. You fear that you'll have to face demands you aren't strong enough to meet. And it is true that apart from Christ you can do nothing (John 15:5). Yet you can say with Paul, "I have strength for all things in Christ who empowers me—I am ready for anything and equal to anything through Him who infuses inner strength into me [that is, I am self-sufficient in Christ's sufficiency]" (Philippians 4:13).

Jesus Christ commands us not to fear and promises to give us victory regardless of the situation. "Fear not [there is nothing to fear] for I am with you; do not look around you in terror and be dismayed, for I am your God. I will strengthen and harden you [to difficulties]; yes, I will help you; yes, I will hold you up and retain you with My victorious right hand of rightness and justice" (Isaiah 41:10).

Christ lovingly reminds us of our heavenly Father's watchful care. "Are not two little sparrows sold for a penny? And yet not one of them will fall to the ground without your Father's leave and notice. But even the very hairs of your head are all numbered. Fear not, then; you are of more value than many sparrows" (Matthew 10:29-31).

Recognize the deadly trap of fear set for you by Satan. Claim Psalm 27:1: "The Lord is my light and my salvation; whom shall I fear or dread? The Lord is the refuge and stronghold of my life; of whom shall I be afraid?"

3. Depression

The final deadly trap that can ruin your beauty is mental depression. The increased sale of tranquilizers and antidepressants indicates that depression is a major problem in today's society.

Depression can be caused by an abnormal physical or spiritual condition. You can be depressed because of improper balance in your body chemistry or because of other physical malfunctions. If depressed, first consult a doctor to determine if the source of your depression is physical. If so, you can still be controlled by the Holy Spirit.

A violation of God's principles can also cause depression. Living by God's principles produces an abundant life but violating these principles results in a defeated existence. "Your ways and your doings have brought these things down upon you; this is your calamity and doom; surely it is bitter, for surely it reaches your very heart" (Jeremiah 4:18). The Lord reminded Cain of this principle just before he murdered his brother Abel. "The Lord said to Cain, 'Why are you angry? And why do you look sad and dejected? If you do well, will you not be accepted? And if you do not do well, sin crouches at your door; its desire is for you, and you must master it' " (Genesis 4:6-7).

Depression can be an advanced stage of anger or fear that you've allowed to go unchecked in your life. We have already established that anger and fear are basically selfishness. Selfishness, when indulged, may take the form of self-pity. Self-pity is very subtle. Often we try to justify it by thinking, "I didn't deserve such treatment," or "How unappreciative my husband is after all I've done for him." Depression, the price you pay for self-pity, is not worth the sick satisfaction it gives.

You can avoid depression by focusing your thoughts on your position in Christ rather than on conditions around you. "If then you have been raised with Christ [to a new life, thus sharing His resurrection from the dead], aim at and seek the [rich, eternal treasures] that are above, where Christ is seated at the right hand of God. And set your minds and keep them set on what is above—the higher things—not on the things that are on the earth. For [as far as this world is concerned] you have died, and your [new, real] life is hid with Christ in God" (Colossians 3:1-3).

Your position in union with Christ is the basis of all your spiritual life and growth. This position was established for eternity when you received Jesus Christ as your personal Saviour. "Therefore if any person is (ingrafted) in Christ, the Messiah, he is (a new creature altogether,) a new creation" (2 Corinthians 5:17).

At the moment of your salvation, you obtained a permanent relationship with God which guarantees, among other things, that you will live with God forever. All your sins were paid for by Christ; you have the life of Christ (eternal life), and you share the righteousness and destiny of Christ. In other words, you are the beneficiary of an inheritance as an heir of God and joint heir with Christ. Concentrating on your privileged status in Christ is like drawing on a million dollars that a benefactor has deposited in your bank account. Concentrating on unpleasant conditions is like living in poverty, unaware of those available riches.

The principle of focusing on your position in Christ can

also be illustrated in the following way. A roomful of women will have their minds on various details of life. One will be thinking about her neighbor's hair-style or dress. Another will be thinking about a point of conversation. But when a celebrity walks in, all the women will focus their attention on the celebrity. Our lives and attention are to be focused on the Celebrity Jesus Christ and our position in Him. Then, the details of life will fall into place, and we will begin to enjoy the inheritance that is already ours.

One beautiful thing about being God's child is that if you fall, you do not have to remain under the control of the OSN which disfigures you. You can escape Satan's traps with their marring effects. "They may come to their senses [and] escape out of the snare of the devil, having been held captive by him [henceforth] to do His [God's] will" (2 Timothy 2:26). You will escape if you follow these steps: (1) face your anger, fear, or self-pity as sin; (2) confess your attitude or action as sin (1 John 1:9); (3) accept Christ's forgiveness based on His work on the cross for you; and (4) trust Him to make the necessary changes in your life.

10 How to Handle Problems and Trials

Certain problems are common to each of us and it will be helpful to know what God's Word has to say about our response to them. As you apply God's solutions to the various situations, your spiritual beauty will blossom.

What principles do I apply when I make mistakes? "A man who refuses to admit his mistakes can never be successful. But if he confesses and forsakes them, he gets another chance" (Proverbs 28:13, LB). Admit your mistakes; do not try to excuse yourself.

Millie reaped great dividends when she applied this principle. In the midst of a hurried afternoon of juggling children's schedules and activities, she accidently locked her keys in the car. Since her husband Ralph, busy at work, had the only other key, she had to call him late in the day. He had not been sympathetic to her blunders before and didn't sound very happy this time when she phoned him.

"I'm sorry for the inconvenience this will cause you after such a hard day's work," Millie told him. "We'll wait here for you until you can come get us."

When Ralph arrived, he seemed to be pleased with his wife's sweet dependency on him. Instead of fussing at her, he rewarded her by taking the family out to dinner.

Don't be disappointed if your husband does not respond positively to your mistakes as quickly as Ralph did. You may have to patiently and lovingly win back your man's approval over a period of time. If so, you can be comforted by the fact that God forgives you immediately even if your loved one has not yet learned to. Your peace will come from knowing you are living according to God's will through His Word.

What about the mistakes your husband makes? "Love forgets mistakes; nagging about them parts the best of friends" (Proverbs 17:9, LB).

His mistakes will not be corrected by mistaken behavior on your part. "Don't repay evil for evil. Wait for the Lord to handle the matter" (Proverbs 20:22, LB).

How should you respond to criticism from your husband? "Don't refuse to accept criticism; get all the help you can" (Proverbs 23:12, LB). "The man who is often reproved but refuses to accept criticism will suddenly be broken and never have another chance" (Proverbs 29:1, LB). Take your husband's criticism as a reminder from the Lord to investigate your actions and make the proper adjustments. Remember God holds him responsible for his household, and may be using him to correct mistakes in your home.

Proverbs 25:12 (LB) tells us, "It is a badge of honor to accept valid criticism." Sometimes you may receive criticism that you feel is not valid. However, if you maintain a sweet, gentle spirit by drawing upon Christ's power within you, God will use even invalid criticism to develop your inner spiritual qualities.

How should you deal with contention and strife? Be sure to come to terms quickly with your husband when there is any discord between you. "Come to terms quickly with your accuser while you are on the way traveling with him" (Matthew 5:25). Don't let hurt feelings stand in the way of your making the first move to correct an unpleasant situation.

I had the opportunity to apply this principle shortly after learning it. My busy schedule was keeping me from my household responsibilities. DeWitt pointed this out to me one morning at breakfast after asking me when I was going to mend the pants he had given me weeks earlier.

I realized I was not as good a wife as I wanted to be and felt hurt. I let the Holy Spirit act as the anesthetist for my pain and managed to respond correctly with, "I'm sorry I didn't mend them earlier, DeWitt. Thanks for helping me get my priorities straight."

Since this was a new response on my part, he was as shocked as I was to hear it. After a moment of silence, he said, "Oh, that's all right. I was just feeling grouchy this morning and took it out on you."

You see, he reacted kindly because I had responded properly and promptly rather than attempting to justify or excuse my actions.

Contention or strife is easiest dealt with before it gets out of control. "The beginning of strife is as when water first trickles [from a crack in a dam]; therefore stop contention before it becomes worse and quarreling breaks out" (Proverbs 17:14). When fighting is allowed to continue, strong walls are built up that are difficult to remove. "It is harder to win back the friendship of an offended brother than to capture a fortified city. His anger shuts you out like iron bars" (Proverbs 18:19, LB).

What about unkind remarks your husband makes to you or about you? First, realize that he may be teasing you, not knowing how he is hurting you by what he considers an innocent comment. You owe it to him and yourself to tell him how you feel about what he says. He is not a mind reader; you cannot understand each other without communication.

Choose a time when your relationship is good and your husband seems to be in an understanding mood. Be sure your words and attitude are loving and in no way violate other principles (trying to get him to change or making him feel guilty). "Rather, let our lives lovingly express truth in all things—speaking truly, dealing truly, living truly. Enfolded in love, let us grow up in every way and in all things into Him, who is the Head [even] Christ, the Messiah, the Anointed One" (Ephesians 4:15).

Remember, acting in love does not mean you are to be a doormat or have an apathetic or passive attitude. You may express love in many ways. You may express it forcefully but never with a condemning or martyr-like attitude. You should also be realistic. If you adopt an absurd, overly sweet reaction to your husband's indiscretions, you'll place yourself on a pedestal where your husband can't reach you and love you and have a normal and real relationship with you.

It might not fit your personality, but one woman I know communicates her feelings to her husband through exaggerated words and actions. When her husband says something she doesn't like, she playfully sticks out her tongue or lower lip at him. When he ignores her, she says in mock self-pity something like, "I'm going out to eat green worms till I die. Then you'll be sorry!" Through such antics, she lets her husband know how she feels without getting angry. Her husband knows she has spunk and is fascinated by her.

If your husband does not refrain from unkind comments after you have expressed your feelings, you can apply the principle in Proverbs 10:12 (LB): "Hatred stirs old quarrels, but love overlooks insults." If you trust Christ to give you a forgiving attitude, He will build strong character in you.

What should your response be to sinful mental attitudes (pride, jealousy, bitterness, vindictiveness, implacability, guilt complex, hatred, worry, anger, and fear) in the lives of others, especially your husband? As always, God has an answer. "Answer not a [self-confident] fool according to his folly, lest you also be like him" (Proverbs 26:4). Folly here is referring to sins of mental attitude.

If your husband is controlled by a sinful attitude such as bitterness and you become involved emotionally with his problem, you too can be overcome by carnal emotions. Your involvement should be limited and nonemotional. If you are not caught up in the emotion, God will be able to deal directly with your husband, convicting or disciplining him as necessary. Any animosity your husband expresses will be between him and God. "Beloved, never avenge yourselves, but leave the way open for [God's] wrath; for it is written, 'Vengeance is Mine, I will repay (requite), says the Lord' " (Romans 12:19).

If a response is necessary, it should be quiet and filled with love. "A soft answer turns away wrath; but grievous words stir up anger" (Proverbs 15:1). This is the only response that will be effective and reap the desired results. "By long forbearing and calmness of spirit a judge or ruler is persuaded, and soft speech breaks down the most bonelike resistance" (Proverbs 25:15).

Perhaps you say, "My husband is so gross in his attitudes and actions that I cannot respect and reverence him as Ephesians 5:33 commands. What do I do about obeying this command?" The Christian life is a life of faith (trusting Christ to be who and what He claims). (See Hebrews 11:1, 6.) You can be sure that what God tells you to do, He is willing to perform through you. If you follow the principle of reverencing and responding to your husband by faith, your actions will demonstrate love, respect, and reverence even though you do not feel those emotions. God is faithful and will, according to your need, reward your obedience to His commands.

Many times we women get hurt unnecessarily because we don't understand our men. Do not consider your husband's unpleasant actions or attitudes a personal attack on you. Realize that business, physical, or emotional pressures may be causing his reactions. Remember, it is God's job to deal with him concerning his problem, not yours. Help him by sympathizing rather than adding to his problems by pouting, fussing, or whatever you do destructively when you are hurt or offended.

Many women have said, "My husband does not admire and praise me as he does others. How can I get him to?" "It is not good to eat much honey, so for men to seek glory, their own glory, causes suffering and is not glory" (Proverbs 25:27). If you seek or demand your husband's praise, you'll cause trouble and hurt feelings.

You will attain praise and glory by focusing on Jesus Christ, His Word, and His will for your life. As you are occupied with Christ, He will provide you with praise and honor. "Prize wisdom highly and exalt her, and she will exalt and promote you; she will bring you to honor when you embrace her" (Proverbs 4:8). "Let not mercy and kindness [shutting out all hatred and selfishness], and truth [shutting out all deliberate hypocrisy or falsehood] forsake you. Bind them about your neck; write them upon the tablet of your heart; so shall you find favor, good understanding and high esteem in the sight [or judgment] of God and man" (Proverbs 3:3-4). As God's Word fills and controls your heart, you will gain the praise of your man. Wait for it; do not demand it.

How should you respond to praise from your husband or others? "The purity of silver and gold can be tested in a crucible, but a man is tested by his reaction to men's praise" (Proverbs 27:21, LB). You will not have a problem of pride if you are aware that you are simply a vessel God uses to do His good work. The most gracious way to respond to a compliment or praise is with a simple "thank you," reflecting a grateful heart.

Comparing yourself with others or fearing that others will not accept you as you are will always create problems. Do not spoil your beauty by getting your eyes on other people—allowing them to govern your attitudes, actions, and responses. "When they measure themselves with themselves and compare themselves with one another, they are without understanding and behave unwisely" (2 Corinthians 10:12). It is easy to think, "If I were like Sue, my husband would like me better." It never helps to try to copy another's dress, mannerisms, or personality. Your husband chose you because you were the one he preferred. You can pick up beauty hints or learn rules of etiquette from others, but do not try to be a carbon copy of another woman.

The fear of not being accepted is described in Proverbs 29:25: "The fear of man brings a snare, but whoever leans on, trusts, and puts his confidence in the Lord is safe and set on high." This fear is not from the Lord, "For God did not give us a spirit of timidity—of cowardice, of craven and cringing and fawning fear—but [He has given us a spirit] of power and of love and of calm and well-balanced mind and discipline and self-control" (2 Timothy 1:7).

Being overly concerned about others' reactions to your husband's behavior can create problems between the two of you. You can know if you are overly concerned if you find yourself correcting your husband, seeking to clarify his actions or comments by further explanation, or apologizing for his behavior. He will take your comments as an indication that you do not trust his ability to handle a situation or make a favorable impression on others. He'll feel that you are not accepting him as he is and are attempting to be a "go-between" in his relationships with others. And he will be *right*.

If your husband has not made himself clear or has been

misunderstood, let him work out the problem. Only then will he gain self-confidence and improve his ability to communicate clearly and interact with others. It is your responsibility to encourage and comfort him, not to mother him, correct him, or improve him. You can avoid needless frustration and tension if you ask yourself, "Am I assuming responsibility that is not mine as his wife?" Many frustrations and tensions come when you assume responsibility which is not yours.

No matter what may be causing you unrest, disharmony, or confusion, God has set forth a principle in His Word through which you can gain harmony and peace. Ask yourself, "Can the problem that is causing distress be corrected or removed?" Even as you oil a squeaky door, so you can set a disorderly house in order. Correct the problem if possible. Otherwise trust God to use it to mold you into His image. He promises, "When a man's ways please the Lord, He makes even his enemies to be at peace with him" (Proverbs 16:7).

Your inner beauty will be apparent if you learn to take even small irritations in stride and allow Christ to use them to make you a lovelier person. One day, June was in a big hurry and spilled milk in the back seat of the car. Instead of panicking or getting angry, she asked God what He wanted to teach her through this irritation. He immediately reminded her that she needed to slow down. When she shared this thought with her husband, he said, "You're beautiful on the inside and the outside!"

Accepting God's Complete Provision Through Faith

Faith is another word for believing what God says in His Word even though you have no visible proof. The Christian life is a life of faith (1 Corinthians 5:7). You take many steps by faith: you receive Christ by faith; you are forgiven of your sins by faith; and you are controlled by the Holy Spirit by faith. Yet the results are not based on the amount of faith you have but on the object of your faith—Jesus Christ.

God wants you to enjoy, through faith, His complete provision for your daily needs. And it is wonderful to know that at the moment you received Christ, you received, potentially, all He could give you to meet those needs: "Blessed be the God and Father of our Lord Jesus Christ, who has blessed us with every spiritual blessing in the heavenly places in Christ" (Ephesians 1:3, NASB).

You are not to seek some ecstatic new experience. All you have to do is discover what is already yours in Christ through the Word and apply it by faith (see Colossians 2:3).

Any decision you make must *always* be based on the solid, unchangeable facts of God's Word rather than on how you feel. Moods and emotions come and go, but God's Word never changes. Sometimes your feelings motivate and encourage you, but other times they pull you down. So you see, your feelings should never be the basis for your actions. Your decisions must be based on facts about God and what He has done for you. A life of faith in Christ will not always be easy, but it is the only life that offers incorruptible beauty.

God taught Moses that by faith he could obey anything God said (see Exodus 4:2-4). The Lord asked Moses, "What do you have there in your hand?"

Moses replied, "A shepherd's rod."

"Throw it down on the ground," the Lord told him.

Moses' rod was familiar and useful to him as a shepherd. He had no reason to cast it before God except in obedience to God. Moses trusted and obeyed God on the basis of God's word alone, not because the request seemed sensible to Moses. Once Moses obeyed and dropped his rod, it became a serpent and Moses ran from it.

Then the Lord said to Moses, "Grab it by the tail!"

Moses could have responded with, "But what about the head, Lord? I'm frightened!" Instead, Moses again trusted God and when he did, the serpent became a rod in his hand. When we fulfill our responsibility by obeying and trusting the Lord, we can be confident that He will work out each detail of a situation for our benefit. Moses' rod was returned to him, but the serpent (representing any harmful ingredient) was removed.

Do you hesitate to surrender some facet of your life to the Lord as Moses hesitated to obey the Lord and drop his rod? Could it be that you are unwilling to totally trust the Lord with your husband, children, career, possessions? You, too, can accept and experience God's complete provision for you, through faith, by surrendering each area of your life to Christ, knowing that if He returns it to you, it will be purified and safe for your enjoyment. When you surrender areas of your life to Him, you do not lose anything; you gain fulfillment. You *can* trust Him!

Another way you can accept God's complete provision for you through faith is by thanking God for *everything* in your life. "Thank [God] in everything—no matter what the circumstances may be, be thankful and give thanks; for this is the will of God for you [who are] in Christ Jesus [the Revealer and Mediator of that will]" (1 Thessalonians 5:18). Thanking God for everything in your life shows that you believe God's Word. He says that even though everything in our lives is not good, He will work out all things for our good as we trust Him (see Romans 8:28).

Is this concept new to you? I had learned that I should give thanks in all things, but I had not applied this principle in my life. I was in the habit of thanking God for those things in my life that I knew were good and I could understand, but I had never thanked Him for the unpleasant situations. Finally, I decided to give thanks in all situations.

One morning my decision was tested severely. A heavy ice storm had covered the Atlanta area when DeWitt left for work. Later in the morning, his office called to see if he were coming in. I told them he had left about two hours before. The gentleman replied, "Since it only takes him about 30 minutes to drive to work, I guess he's had an accident on the icy expressway."

At that point, I had the choice of trusting and thanking God or giving way to hysterical fear. Knowing that God loved DeWitt more than I did, that He is sovereign, and that He promises not to allow anything to happen to His children without working it out to their benefit, I said, "Thank You, Lord, for whatever situation DeWitt is in."

God honored my obedience to His Word by giving me peace. "Peace I leave with you; My [own] peace I now give and bequeath to you. Not as the world gives do I give to you. Do not let your heart be troubled, neither let it be afraid—stop allowing yourselves to be agitated and disturbed; and do not permit yourselves to be fearful and intimidated and cowardly and unsettled" (John 14:27). The peace God gave me did not hinge on DeWitt's circumstances. As it turned out, DeWitt was delayed because of other accidents, not his own.

Apply this principle of giving thanks in all situations, especially to minor incidents in your daily life such as dropping an egg on your freshly waxed floor, an inconvenient telephone call, or an unappreciative husband. As you learn to be thankful in the small problems in your life, it will be natural to be thankful for larger trials and crises. Of course, you can rejoice only when you focus on Jesus Christ's sovereignty and His ability to work everything out to your good. Because of His sufficiency, you live above your circumstances instead of under them and life takes on a new, wonderful dimension. With a thankful heart, you will experience real joy, realizing that God will allow nothing to happen in your life that He can't work out for your benefit.

You see, joy does not depend on circumstances but on your

relationship and fellowship with God, as we've mentioned. If you choose to react to circumstances and people around you, you will be happy when your circumstances and other people are pleasant but sad when they are unpleasant. In other words, reacting to conditions around you produces an unstable existence.

As you reflect Jesus Christ, you can have peace and stability whether or not you get the dress you want or have to live with a grouchy husband. Accept the victory Christ promises you in John 16:33: "I have told you these things so that in Me you may have perfect peace and confidence. In the world you have tribulation and trials and distress and frustration; but be of good cheer—take courage, be confident, certain, undaunted—for I have overcome the world—I have deprived it of power to harm, have conquered it [for you]."

Do realize, however, that as Christ controls your life, He will not assume responsibilities He has assigned to you. For example, He will not do such things as make decisions for you or open your mouth in order for you to witness. But He will be your power once you make a decision and, in faith, act on it. When I first understood that Christ desired to live in and through me (see Galatians 2:20), I excitedly shared His desire with my three-year-old son. "Isn't it good news, Ken, that we can trust Christ to live through us rather than trying to do it ourselves?"

"Yes," he answered. "That's good."

Later, when I told him to pick up his toys he said, "Let Jesus do it. I don't have to."

I reminded him that Jesus would live His life through him by using his arms and legs to pick up toys.

Ken said, "Oh, is that how it works?"

Christ will not make your decisions for you but expects you to make them on the basis of His Word. Then He is your Power for carrying them out.

11 Completing the Picture

Real, fadeless inner beauty is created by Jesus Christ, the divine artist at work in you. Your inner self (the living canvas) becomes radiantly beautiful under His workmanship. Your body (the picture frame) complements or enhances the picture. Both the canvas and frame must be attractive if people are to enjoy the painting. An unattractive or inappropriate frame can detract from a good picture. A wisely chosen frame will add that extra touch that can make even an ordinary picture look beautiful.

It should encourage you to know that both your body or picture frame and your inner self or canvas are precious to God. "And the very God of peace sanctify you wholly; and I pray God your whole *spirit* and *soul* and *body* be preserved blameless unto the coming of our Lord Jesus Christ" (1 Thessalonians 5:23, KJV). If God considers your body to be important, you should too.

Try to make your body as attractive a part of the whole picture as possible. People form ideas about the "real you" by the outward clues you furnish. They accept you on the basis of your own self-appraisal—often expressed in your grooming.

Since everything you do and are and even the way you look reflects on your Saviour as well as yourself, it is doubly important that you be well-groomed. "So then . . . whatever you may do, do all for the honor and glory of God" (1 Corinthians 10:31).

Your grooming should reflect self-respect and self-esteem. When you are not well-groomed, it is as if you are saying, "I consider myself unworthy of care. I don't think I'm valuable enough to spend time on." Yet when you remember that God considers your body important, that your looks reflect on your Saviour, and that you are a child of God, purchased by the blood of Jesus Christ, you can't help but rejoice and realize that you are a person of worth.

In fact you are a temple: "Do you not know that your body is the temple—the very sanctuary—of the Holy Spirit who lives within you, whom you have received [as a Gift] from God? You are not your own. You were bought for a price—purchased with a preciousness and paid for, made His own. So then honor God and bring glory to Him in your body" (1 Corinthians 6:19-20). Your body is a palace where Royalty lives! You will want it to be glorious and beautiful, shining and polished, to honor the King of kings. The psalmist expressed the desire "that our daughters may be as cornerstones, polished after the similitude of a palace" (Psalm 144:12, KJV).

There are those who say good grooming is worldly, that you are not spiritual when you are well groomed. These people often take the verse in 1 Peter 3:3 (KJV) as their basis and say you should not care for your hair, wear jewelry, or dress attractively. "Whose adorning let it not be that outward adorning of plaiting the hair, and of wearing of gold, or of putting on of apparel." Such people always stop in their reasoning before they finish the verse or they would have to conclude that we are not to put on clothing!

Man (OSN) is always trying to *do* something to make himself spiritual, whereas his spirituality is determined by whether or not Christ is controlling his life. A dowdy or "odd ball" appearance limits your effectiveness for Christ, but a pleasing, socially acceptable appearance gives you a wider witness for Christ. Good grooming is looking your best for Him, not drawing attention to yourself. Your overall appearance should be the best you can accomplish within your budget and should be in keeping with your role and position.

Your *role as a wife* involves developing a relationship with your husband that will bring joy to both of you. A *career* would involve spending time updating your skills so you could be successful in your field. In the same way, your *identity as a woman* requires you to spend time making and keeping yourself attractive. Of course you should not spend all your time, thought, and money on your appearance, but you will need to take some time to make yourself as lovely as possible: "sugar and spice and everything nice," as the old rhyme goes.

Sugar and Spice through Good Grooming

1. Cleanliness

One of the most important ways to be lovely is to be sure your body is as clean as possible. It has been said that "cleanliness is next to godliness." Reverence for God should produce reverence for your body. Bathing daily will help you stay clean and sweet-smelling all day and will help you feel dainty and feminine. Of course, your freshness will last only if you use a good deodorant to control unpleasant body odors.

Choose your favorite fragrance as a delightful finishing touch to your daily bath routine. When Ruth was preparing to win her husband-to-be, Naomi told her to "wash and anoint yourself therefore, and put on your best clothes and go" (Ruth 3:3).

2. Diet

Are you aware that what goes inside shows up on the outside? It is important to provide a healthy body for Jesus Christ to live in. And it requires self-discipline. If you want to maintain a healthy weight, you must prepare wholesome, nourishing, well-balanced meals for yourself and your family. If you have gained a few extra pounds, it is important to your health, your self-image, and your husband to lose them. But do consult a doctor before trying any severe reducing diet.

You can take sensible precautions against an over intake of calories by cutting down on between-meal snacks, heavy pastries, and rich desserts. You do not have to stop eating. Just train your taste buds to enjoy nonfattening, nourishing foods. Generally speaking, when you eat moderate portions of nourishing food, your weight will not fluctuate much. Find out how many calories you need to maintain your correct weight and eat accordingly.

3. Exercise

If you don't get enough exercise, you will feel sluggish, gain weight, and/or get flabby. Be sure you get exercise each day, outdoors if possible. If it is necessary for you to do some calisthenics, you might enjoy them more if you do them with a TV exercise program. However you do them, you will find that they move your blood, limber you up, and give you a firm, trim figure and more enthusiasm for life.

4. Rest

An active wife and mother also needs time to rest and relax. If you have small children, you may be able to rest only while they are taking naps. Regardless of when you do it, take time to relax and do not feel guilty about it. Jesus told His disciples to "come away by yourselves . . . and rest awhile" (Mark 6:31, NASB). If the Son of God saw the need for relaxing, you should. It will help you stay fresh and alert through the evening when your husband and older children are home. Their day may be coming to a close but yours may last until late at night.

5. Makeup

Proper complexion care and makeup aids are important in achieving and maintaining a lovely complexion. Most cosmetic studios or large department stores have skin-care and makeup analysts to serve you without charge. Make use of their free service. They will give you tips on how to apply makeup for the most natural look. Remember that when makeup is skillfully applied, others will be aware of your loveliness, not your cosmetics.

Watch yourself in a mirror to see if you have any distracting facial mannerisms when you talk. Or ask a friend if she has noticed any. Do you chew or lick your lips? Do you grit your teeth or move your jaws from side to side? Make a conscious effort to correct such mannerisms.

6. Hair

A lovely face should be framed with a halo of beauty—your hair. A woman's hair is a symbol of her femininity. One of the ways your femininity contrasts with your husband's masculinity is through the care, style, and length of your hair. "Does not (experience, common sense, reason and) the native sense of propriety itself teach that for a man to wear long hair is a dishonor (humiliating and degrading) to him, but if a woman has long hair, it is her ornament and glory? For her hair is given to her for a covering" (1 Corinthians 11:14-15). Tousled, unkempt, and unattractive hair does not glorify God or add to your femininity.

For your hair to look as attractive as possible, it is necessary to brush, shampoo, and set it regularly. First, however, empty your piggy bank and get a professional haircut or, if you prefer long hair, a trim to get rid of split, dry ends.

The style of your hair should enhance the shape of your face. Consider current styles but do not choose one just because it is fashionable. After experimenting with your hair or trying on wigs or getting the help of a professional, pick a style that is best for you.

7. Hands

Nothing expresses the inner you more completely than your hands. Dry, shiny hands suggest that you are getting old. Red, chapped hands prove you wash dishes and floors but don't care about the aftereffects. Ragged nails and cuticles reveal that you are a nervous chewer. Dirty nails suggest that you are not completely clean.

Since neglected hands and nails definitely spoil the overall sugar and spice effect you want to project, keep your hands clean and soft and your nails shaped and clean. This will not take too much time if you keep hand lotion, an emery board, and a pair of rubber gloves (for dirty work or washing) ready.

Then be sure you do not spoil the effect of lovely hands by restless, nervous, fidgety actions. Nervous practices such as twisting your handkerchief or ring, gesturing, rubbing or stroking your chin, chewing your nails, or cracking your knuckles will mar your charm. Practice holding your hands in a graceful, relaxed position while sitting, standing, or talking.

8. Clothes

Carefully chosen clothes add the final touches to your feminine appearance. Clothing can create an illusion of a well-proportioned figure. You can accentuate your good points and camouflage your bad points through the use of line, color, fabric, and pattern to make yourself look taller, shorter, fuller, or thinner. You can get specific instructions on how to complement your individual figure at the larger department stores' modeling and fashion shows or through books or magazine articles.

The wise woman, as described in Proverbs 31, dresses well: "Her clothing is of linen, pure white and fine, and of purple [such as that of which the clothing of the priests and the hallowed cloths of the temple are made]" (Proverbs 31:22). It is better to choose a few well-made, fashionable dresses than many poorly-made garments. Trust Christ to guide you in choosing your wardrobe, and you will be amazed at the bargains you can find. Remember, though, that a bargain is not a bargain unless you need it. You can make your wardrobe appear larger than it is if you buy a few basic garments that you can vary through the use of scarves, belts, jewelry, vests, or mixing and matching.

And you can add to your wardrobe inexpensively by sewing. "She seeks out the wool and flax and works with willing hands to develop it" (Proverbs 31:13). If you do not know how to sew, you may be able to get instructions reasonably at a sewing center or in an adult education class at a local high school, college, or YMCA. You can get ideas for sewing by browsing in the more fashionable dress shops and noticing the trim, material, color combinations, and styles in use. Even looking through Sears', Ward's, or other catalogs will help you make your sewing look both professional and fashionable. The Lord tells you to ask Him for wisdom. He'll help you express your own personality through your dress.

Your clothing, like your hair, expresses your femininity in contrast to your husband's masculinity. God gives strict orders about a woman not wearing men's clothes and vice versa. "The woman shall not wear that which pertains to a man, neither shall a man put on a woman's garment; for all that do so are an abomination to the Lord your God" (Deuteronomy 22:5). This does not mean a woman cannot wear slacks, but slacks or pants outfits should be feminine. Unisex clothing does not glorify God. God wants a man's dress to be masculine and the woman's dress to be feminine, according to the culture's standards.

Yes, you will want to choose styles that flatter your figure and pick colors that enhance your skin tone. But be sure your husband approves of your clothing. You will please God when you dress in a way that pleases your husband.

9. Posture

No matter how well-groomed and daintily dressed you are, you will ruin the whole effect if you slump, hunch, or swagger. Practice standing, walking, and sitting gracefully. Stand tall, chest high. Keep your feet together when you sit or walk by keeping your feet parallel and your knees together.

These points about hair, hands, figure, dress, and posture may seem troublesome and time-consuming but as they become part of your outlook and routine, you'll find they are not a burden. Increasing your feminine charm will be worth all the time and effort you must take.

Everything Nice through Domestic Tranquility

Your sugar and spice appearance should be matched by "everything nice" around you. In other words, you want a setting of a tranquil, orderly household. That will mean planning, organization, and self-discipline on your part. If you feel you can't handle a home and family in an orderly manner, ask God's help. Since you are His child, you can go directly to Him in Jesus' name. "Let us then fearlessly and confidently and boldly draw near to the throne of grace—the throne of God's unmerited favor [to us sinners]; that we may receive mercy [for our failures] and find grace to help in good time for every need—appropriate help and well-timed help, coming just when we need it" (Hebrews 4:16).

God is orderly and wants you to have a peaceful life. "For He . . . is not a God of confusion and disorder but of peace and order. . . . But all things should be done with regard to decency and propriety and in an orderly fashion" (1 Corinthians 14:33, 40).

Jesus Christ promises to help us use our time wisely when we trust Him. "Reverence for God adds hours to each day; so how can the wicked expect a long, good life? I, Wisdom, will make the hours of your day more profitable and the years of your life more fruitful" (Proverbs 10:27; 9:11, LB).

When we are not organized and purposeful in our living, Christ is dishonored. "Look carefully then how you walk! Live purposefully and worthily and accurately, not as the unwise and witless, but as wise—sensible, intelligent people; making the very most of the time—buying up each opportunity—because the days are evil. Therefore do not be vague and thoughtless and foolish, but understanding and firmly grasping what the will of the Lord is" (Ephesians 5:15-17).

Design a plan by which you can accomplish your responsibilities. Then look to God for help. "We should make plans—counting on God to direct us" (Proverbs 16:9, LB). Keep in mind your priorities: (1) personal relationship with Jesus Christ, (2) husband, (3) children, (4) personal grooming and rest, (5) household responsibilities, (6) outside ministry. Before you schedule your daily activities, the following outline might be helpful in keeping your priorities in order:

1. Time with the Lord (studying His Word and prayer)
2. Meals, dishes, housework
3. Washing, ironing, grooming
4. Time with the family
5. Time to rest and relax
6. Individual hobbies, interests, and activities.

Start by making a list of the jobs you have to do. Then work out a reasonable schedule for getting them done. You may have to cut out some TV, unnecessary shopping, or long phone conversations. You may have to learn to say no to some good activities that are not essential. But if you know what your priorities are, you will not sacrifice the best for something that is merely good. You owe your husband your best, whether it's your attention, appearance, or providing a tranquil household.

Learn to make wise use of your time by carrying a book, or handwork such as sewing or writing, with you when you must wait in the car, at the doctor's office, or when you watch TV with the family. Save steps by placing items that go to the basement near the basement door. Make one trip at the end of the day rather than several during the day unless you need the exercise. Make good use of your time by having a long telephone cord on your kitchen phone so you can cook, clean your kitchen, sew, or iron while visiting with friends or making necessary calls. You can do some housework while listening to Bible study tapes that help you to grow spiritually.

Take the necessary time to train your children to care for their rooms, clothing, toys, and personal appearance. It may be easier to do their work yourself at first, but once your children are properly trained, their help will save you time. Besides, part of your job is to train your children to be self-reliant. You should not be doing things that the children can do for themselves.

Plan ahead and your life will not be regulated by the unexpected. Again, the wise woman of Proverbs 31 is a good example: "She fears not the snow for her family, for all her household are doubly clothed in scarlet" (v. 21). Her life was not regulated by disaster (snow). Sunday morning did not find her scurrying around ironing her son's pants. She foresaw his need and planned ahead.

Yes, you should plan and be organized but not inflexible. "We can make our plans, but the final outcome is in God's hands. Commit your work to the Lord, then it will succeed" (Proverbs 16:1, 3, LB).

Among your many responsibilities is that of buying and preparing food that pleases your husband. "She is like the merchant ships loaded with foodstuffs, she brings her household's food from a far [country]. She rises while yet it is night and gets spiritual food for her household and assigns her maids their tasks" (Proverbs 31:14-15).

It is well to rise early in the morning to fix your husband a good breakfast. Christ will help you enjoy cooking—even early in the morning—if you ask His help.

Discovering new and different ways to serve food can be fun. "Variety is the spice of cooking." Avoid preparing the same thing each week by adding new dishes that friends recommend or that look good in your cookbook. If your husband's likes are limited, try to fix the foods he likes as tastily as possible. But do serve a new dish occasionally for your children's sake.

When you prepare a favorite dish of the family, try doubling the recipe and freezing half for unexpected company or a quick family meal.

God has given you the exciting, fulfilling, rewarding ministry of being a wife and mother. You have inexhaustible opportunities for supporting and complementing your husband's ministry as well as for training your children. Their lives will, in turn, affect hundreds of other lives. No other person can have the influence on your family that you have as wife and mother.

Your role includes a wide range of skills. As God enables you to develop these, you will find that in your own home you are teacher, nurse, interior decorator, manager, dietitian, seamstress, purchasing agent, counselor, consultant, photographer, you name it. What greater challenge could any woman want?

Your ministry in your home can be an exciting creative adventure. And most important, if Christ is controlling your life, you are serving Him as you care for your family. You are serving Christ just as certainly as the evangelist who is seeing hundreds saved each day. God's plan for you as a woman will completely satisfy you if you allow Him to direct every area of your life.

Everything Nice Via Emotional Stability

"Everything nice" includes your emotional stability. One way to maintain balance is to develop a sense of humor. Do not take yourself too seriously. "A happy heart is a good medicine and a cheerful mind works healing. . . . He who has a glad heart has a continual feast [regardless of circumstances]" (Proverbs 17:22; 15:15). You are to your family atmosphere what a thermostat is to the temperature of your home. If you are relaxed about life, your home will have a relaxed atmosphere. If you can laugh with your children and husband (especially at his jokes) and laugh at yourself, your home will be a happier place for your family.

Avoid crying to get attention or your own way. Your husband may give in to you in frustration, not knowing any other way to handle you, but you will have damaged your relationship. Crying to get your way is like demanding love but getting sympathy; you get results but not the ones you really want.

There will be times when household tasks, mistakes in household management, routine child care problems, and decisions regarding meals may cause you to become discouraged. Do not bother your husband with these routine problems. Instead, go to Jesus Christ for your strength and guidance. "Work hard and cheerfully at all you do, just as though you were working for the Lord and not merely for your masters, remembering that it is the Lord Christ who is going to pay you, giving you your full portion of all He owns. He is the One you are really working for" (Colossians 3:23-24, LB). These words, addressed to servants, apply to anyone who has tasks to perform.

One of the qualities of an emotionally stable person is a grateful attitude. This attitude is developed through Christ's controlling your life as you regularly study God's Word. "And let the peace (soul harmony which comes) from Christ rule (act as umpire continually) in your hearts—deciding and settling with finality all questions that arise in your minds—[in that peaceful state] to which [as members of Christ's] one body you were also called [to live]. And be thankful—appreciative, giving praise to God always" (Colossians 3:15). You can be grateful for every person in your life as you realize that Christ promises to work out all things (or use any persons) for your benefit as you trust Him. If you have a grateful spirit, your husband will enjoy your company and be more likely to become the husband you need.

Let gratitude be your response when your husband gives you a gift. Remember that your husband and his thoughtfulness are more important than what he gives you. Therefore accept anything he gives you with a joyful spirit and sincere appreciation.

Never reject a gift he buys for you. If he should buy you a size 16 dress when you wear a size 10, let him go with you to exchange it for something he likes. If you cannot stand the perfume he gave you, use a little more than necessary when he is around, and he may suggest that you stop wearing it. Let it be his decision, not yours.

What if he does not give you gifts? Examine your past actions to see if you have violated any of the principles we have established. If not, you simply may be married to a man who does not enjoy shopping (by the way, few men do). Accept him as he is!

You foster an "everything nice" atmosphere when you understand how to ask your husband for what you want or need. Do not hint. Men are usually so preoccupied with their activities that they do not catch subtle hints. Then their wives feel hurt, thinking their men do not love them. Avoid trying to convince him of your need in order to get your way. He may feel trapped and rebel. Demanding your way does not work either because in demanding you are usurping his authority, and he feels offended by your actions. Instead, ask for things with a simple "May I, please?" or "Will you, please?" When you use this simple straightforward method, you will find him more willing to grant your requests. Of course you should be careful not to ask for things he cannot afford.

Try not to be shaken if your husband should have a reaction known as "Pandora's Box" when you start applying God's principles to your marriage. He may have suppressed hateful feelings toward you through the years, fearing that if he vented his real feelings his marriage would break up. Now that he knows you accept him as he is, all these suppressed feelings may suddenly come rolling out. If this happens, ask Jesus Christ to relieve any hurt feelings you may have. Do not argue with your husband, but encourage him to share his feelings with you. When he is through expressing his hostilities, he will, hopefully, be free of bitterness toward you and be free to begin loving and cherishing you.

Everything Nice through Your Individuality

Many women are afraid that they will lose their individuality if they subject themselves to their husbands. Yet the wise woman of Proverbs 31:10-31 is definitely an individual though she obviously seeks to please her husband: "She will do him good and not evil all the days of her life" (v. 12, KJV). Paradoxically, only when you submit to God—in any area—do you know the fullest freedom and power: "If the Son therefore shall make you free, ye shall be free indeed" (John 8:36, KJV). See also John 14:21, 23; Galatians 3:28, and Galatians 5:1.

Having cared for your responsibilities as wife and mother, you can find ways to express your individuality: thinking up new menus or recipes, decorating your home, planting a vegetable garden, planning a surprise party for some family member, inventing some new activity to keep your youngsters occupied or some new means of settling their quarrels, following the stock market, writing letters or stories, painting pictures. Whatever your interests are, develop and enjoy them, even put them to work in your home. Because your husband knows he is first in your life, he will be glad for you to express your individuality in your home and even have outside interests and hobbies—so long as they don't take too much of your time and attention.

Your husband will actually be comforted and fascinated by the fact that you are an individual in your own right. "Strength and dignity are her clothing and her position is strong and secure" (Proverbs 31:25). Your husband can be relaxed if his business detains him, knowing that you have plenty of interests to keep you busy in his absence. He may enjoy your dependency but not the yoke of your helplessness.

As you work at making yourself and your home attractive, your husband should be able to say, "There are many fine women in the world, but you are the best of them all!" (Proverbs 31:29, LB)

12
Physical Fulfillment

God has provided a way in which you and your husband can experience and express the deep, intimate relationship He intends for you. That way is through your sexual union. God's plans are so perfect that there is no area in which He has not made total provision for your needs whether they be spiritual, psychological, sociological, or physical. He is interested in your complete personal fulfillment.

Sex—God's Idea

We see that sex is God's idea because it was part of His plan in making the man and woman. "And the Lord God said, 'It is not good that the man should be alone; I will make him an help meet for him.' So God created man in His own image, in the image of God created He him; male and female created He them. And God said unto them, 'Be fruitful, and multiply, and replenish the earth, and subdue it' " (Genesis 2:18; 1:27-28, KJV).

After God made Eve from Adam's rib, He gave Eve to Adam and said, "Man shall . . . become united and cleave to his wife and they shall become one flesh" (Genesis 2:24). Thus, God instituted the marriage relationship. The marriage of Adam and Eve set a pattern for mankind so that the human race could be perpetuated in maximum freedom, protection, and happiness.

God designed the sexual union of husband and wife to be an expression of love for each other. This union is described by the word "cleave" meaning "to be joined"—a sexual relationship. God meant this relationship to be a fulfilling, enjoyable part of the lives of husband and wife. The Song of Solomon, as well as many other Scriptures, describes in vivid language the physical delight experienced in the union of the bodies of married lovers (Song of Solomon 6:1-10 and 7:1-9).

Since Scripture teaches that, for married people, an effective Christian life and good sexual adjustment go together, you should strive for the latter as well as the former, remembering that "marriage is honorable in all and the bed undefiled" (Hebrews 13:4, KJV).

The physical union of you and your husband should be good and satisfying because it is an expression of your inner oneness. Being one in the soul means that your mind is filled with thoughts of your husband, you commit your will to doing his will, and no one will ever take his place in your affections. The sexual union, then, becomes more than just a physical act since it portrays a much deeper soul relationship between you two. Without unity of soul, the sex act is an improper union of bodies and is not fulfilling.

Distortions or Abuses of God's Plan for Sex

Distortions or abuses of sex come from the OSN or from Satan himself. Satan is a master distorter and counterfeiter of God's wonderful provision for mankind. Distortions will emphasize the body or sex without the soul relationship or vice versa. Since God has designed a complete, satisfying relationship for you, He has set certain boundaries or prohibitions. This is because He loves you and desires you to be happy.

God has prohibited adultery (sex with someone other than your mate), for example, because it destroys your soul oneness with your husband. The fact that adultery can destroy you as a person is revealed in Proverbs 6:32 (KJV): "But whoso committeth adultery with a woman lacketh understanding; he that doeth it destroyeth his own soul."

God also says that adultery affects the body: "Any other sin which a man commits is one outside the body, but he who commits sexual immorality, sins against his own body" (1 Corinthians 6:18). Adultery can affect your body by causing you not to be able to function properly, sexually, and by taking away full enjoyment with your mate. In a woman, promiscuous sex can lead to nymphomania (insatiable sexual desire)or frigidity (lack of or decreased sexual desire). The corresponding effects in a man would be satyriasis and impotence.

Furthermore, both man and woman can become laden with guilt as a result of adultery. God warns us not to distort or misuse sex but to enjoy it within the boundaries He has set.

Another abuse of sex is the practice of autoeroticism or masturbation. God says in 1 Corinthians 7:4 that married people are not to arouse their own bodies sexually. This is the right of your husband only. "The wife does not have the right to do as she pleases with her own body; the husband has his right to it. In the same way the husband does not have the right to do as he pleases with his own body; the wife has her right to it" (1 Corinthians 7:4, WMS). Since masturbation is a means of self-gratification only, it is an abuse of God's plan for sex to be an expression of love between husband and wife. Also, the sexual drive should never control you, but it may if you become engrossed in self-gratification.

When you enjoy sex according to God's plan, distortions

and abuses of sex such as masturbation, homosexuality, lesbianism, bestiality, wife-swapping, pornographic activity, sensitivity concepts, and polygamy will not be part of your life.

Sex itself is not wrong; but the misuse or distortion of it is. "Marriage is honorable in all and the bed undefiled, but whoremongers and adulterers God will judge" (Hebrews 13:4, KJV).

Sex can be compared to another of God's good gifts—food. "For everything God has created is good, and nothing is to be thrown away or refused if it is received with thanksgiving. For it is hallowed and consecrated by the Word of God and by prayer" (1 Timothy 4:4-5). Food, when eaten in the proper proportions and balance, provides health and pleasure. When you violate these boundaries, you can become a glutton. The sun, also God's gift, provides warmth and light but can cause pain when you overexpose tender skin to its rays. The Bible gives a balanced, healthy view of sex. God does not hide the details; neither does He glamorize or glorify the wrong use of sex. God's information is complete and perfect!

If you have been involved in immoral sex practices, remember that Jesus Christ paid for that sin also. Confess your immorality as sin, accept Christ's forgiveness, and move on to a life of fulfillment in His will. As Jesus said to the adulterous woman, "Go and sin no more" (John 8:11, LB).

Marital Delights

God gives beautiful, positive instruction in Proverbs 5:15, 18-19 (LB) on how a couple's sexual needs are to be fulfilled through union in marriage. "Drink from your own well, my son—be faithful and true to your wife. Let your manhood be a blessing; rejoice in the wife of your youth. Let her charms and tender embrace satisfy you. Let her love alone fill you with delight." The wife is referred to symbolically in these passages as a well and in some translations as a "cistern," as "fresh running water," and as a "fountain." The beautiful parallel is between a person's thirst being satisfied by drinking cool, fresh water and a couple's sexual thirst being satisfied by regular sexual union in marriage.

Notice that God says, "Rejoice in the wife of your youth." The sexual relationship is to provide you with great pleasure. The wife is described as tender, charming, loving, and *satisfying*. You are to concentrate on making your sex life a satisfying, fulfilling experience for your husband. Otherwise, how can he "let her love alone fill [him] with delight"? There are no sexual perversions when a wife is satisfying her husband's sexual desires and needs.

You must realize that your husband needs the freedom to initiate whatever sexual actions he desires, knowing you will respond lovingly. You can be relaxed in the knowledge that it is God's will for you to meet his needs enthusiastically. As you do, your mutual fulfillment and enjoyment will grow.

Mutual sexual fulfillment has not always been a reality in Karen and Fred's life, but it is now. While growing up, Karen had not been taught God's plan for sex. As a result, she had many hang-ups. The sordid stories she had heard about marital sex caused her to think of her role in physical relations as an obligation or duty she dreaded. The books Karen read on sex did not release her from her warped ideas. Almost any techniques of love-play and sexual arousal left Karen burdened with a deep sense of guilt. She felt that to enjoy such activities would be perversion.

After hearing the lectures on which this book is based, Karen got a different perspective. Her eyes sparkled as she said, "I had no idea God had so much to say in His Word about sex. The Scriptures you mentioned showed me that sex is God's idea, not man's. It's designed to give pleasure to both my husband and me. I've learned to relax totally and enjoy the genuine desire we now have for each other."

Solving Sex Problems

You must look for the source of sex problems if you want to find permanent solutions. Since sex in marriage is an expression of the inner oneness of two people, it follows that problems can relate to any facet of either mate's life. Problems can be spiritual or personality maladjustments, or they may simply stem from not understanding each other.

Realizing how you and your husband differ sexually may help correct some sexual problems. Generally, the man has a more aggressive, stronger sex drive than the woman. This is understandable since God created the man to be the leader. Knowing this, you can simply respond to his sexual leadership and expect complete satisfaction for both of you rather than being "turned off" by his aggressiveness and need. Furthermore, a man is usually stimulated sexually by sight but a woman normally is not. Should your husband watch you undress for bed, he may become sufficiently aroused to be ready for intercourse while you are simply ready for bed.

Also, a man and woman may differ in sexual response after an argument. Your husband's way of saying, "Please forgive me and let me show you how much I love you" may be to have sexual union. But you may prefer to be reassured of his love with tender words and caresses before you are ready for sex. Furthermore, sex can serve as a tranquilizer for your husband, enabling him to relax and go to sleep. When you are tired, the last thing you may want is sex.

It may help you, too, to realize that your husband may feel his masculinity is tied in with his ability to satisfy your sexual needs. If your husband is unsure of his masculinity, he may attempt to cover up or compensate for real or imagined deficiencies. He may display his insecurity by refusing sexual relations or accelerating sexual behavior. He may be afraid that you will reject his sexual advances, or he may fear that he won't be able to adequately meet your needs.

You can help your husband avoid these fears if you realize that he has a greater physical-emotional challenge in the sexual union than you do. The success of the act depends on his ability to obtain and maintain a strong erection. Support him by displaying your confidence in his sexual ability through word and deed. You may convey this by embracing him eagerly, kissing him warmly, or by sighing in appreciation at the right time. Your actions should give the unmistakable impression that you can hardly wait to enjoy union with him.

You may be thinking, "Am I to pretend?" Since you know God planned this relationship for your enjoyment, pretending should never be necessary. Therefore, look at it as if you are simply anticipating your own sexual excitement and communicate this eagerness to your husband. The most effective way to give your husband pleasure is to let him know you care about him and desire to have intercourse with him.

What if your husband is not interested in you sexually? Remember, a beautiful sex relationship does not start when you go to bed. The relationship is an expression of lives lived in an atmosphere of love. Ask Christ to show you if you have unintentionally been critical, cutting, sarcastic, or jealous, or if you have implied that your husband's sexual abilities are inferior or inadequate for you.

Joan tried to get her husband to go for a medical checkup, feeling his inability to have union with her was a physical problem. Finally, her husband handed her an article he had clipped from the paper. It said in essence that a man does not find a woman appealing, sexually, if she is constantly bickering or has attacked his masculinity by not allowing him to be the leader, provider, and protector in his home. As you trust Jesus Christ for your attitudes and actions and fulfill your role as wife, your inner "oneness" will be right and sexual problems will begin to disappear.

Never be guilty of using sex as a weapon, whether to punish your husband or to get something from him. When you withhold your body for such reasons, you are making a prostitute of yourself because you are selling your body to your husband in exchange for something you want. Paul tells us: "For the wife does not have [exclusive] authority and control over her own body, but the husband [has his rights]. . . . Do not refuse and deprive and defraud each other" (1 Corinthians 7:4-5). If you place a price tag on your sexual relationship, your husband may feel the price is too high and go shopping for a better bargain.

Sexual problems can also result if either you or your husband has a warped idea of love, sex, or marriage because of childhood experiences. For instance, as a child you might have asked your mother the very normal question, "Where do babies come from?"

Your mother may have said, "Nice little girls don't ask such questions. When you get bigger you will learn about such things."

Because of her attitude, you may have concluded that there is something wrong about "where babies come from" and you did not question her any more about such things. You may have gotten the rest of your sexual education in an atmosphere of secrecy, causing you to feel sex was "dirty" rather than a beautiful, God-given expression of love. If your mother's attitude or an unfortunate childhood experience has been the root of your resentments and frigidity, renounce your wrong feelings about sex. Accept God's forgiveness and allow Him to give you a positive, healthy reaction to sex.

Sometimes a wife is not satisfied, sexually, because her husband doesn't understand her. Even though the greater percentage of sexual success is a result of your attitude, at least 20% depends on his education. Your husband may not be aware that a woman is not usually sexually aroused as quickly as a man and needs tender words and longer love play before she is ready to enjoy orgasm. If this is true in your marriage, guide your husband gently, showing him actions and expressions that please you. Then respond with enthusiasm.

When you respond to his efforts positively and with enthusiasm, he will be encouraged to make other efforts to please you. Let him know how much you enjoyed his efforts by telling him, "You were just wonderful tonight." If you did not reach a climax, you can still respond positively. A climax or orgasm is not always necessary for your sexual union to be a pleasing experience. You will discover, however, that as you wholeheartedly desire to satisfy your husband and respond positively to his actions, you will also have sexual satisfaction.

Should you ever take the initiative sexually? Yes. It is good for you to take the initiative at times. When you do, any fears your husband has that you may reject him sexually will be dispelled immediately. Also, he will likely be stimulated by the idea that you find him sexually desirable. Many times a man's impotence is overcome by being near his "turned-on" wife. He is made aware of his sexual ability and is encouraged to enjoy the sex act. However, do be careful not to become too aggressive in your sexual initiative.

As a result of your aggressiveness and sexual demands, your husband could be repulsed, feeling that he is not "the man in charge." Your sex life, as well as all other areas, must be balanced. When your husband's leadership in your home is not threatened, he will enjoy and be encouraged by your taking sexual initiative at times.

The wise woman plans ahead in order to meet her husband's sexual needs. Get the rest necessary in order to be alert, responsive, and available to your man. When you are tired or are not particularly interested in sexual union, trust

Jesus Christ to give you a new excitement and enthusiasm since it is His will for you both to receive pleasure and fulfillment through this union.

Let your schedule be flexible so that you will be available to meet your husband's needs at night, in the morning, or in the middle of the day.

Sense when your husband is interested in love-making. Don't be like the wife who finds all sorts of things to do before going to bed or reads *Good Housekeeping* in bed until her husband turns over and forgets the whole thing. True, you can't be a mind reader, but do be sensitive. Know your husband.

Prepare yourself to make love by thinking positive thoughts that would arouse you rather than cause you to be irritated. If you fulfill your role as a wife by accepting your husband as he is, admiring him, making him the center of your life, and responding to his leadership, provision, and protection of you, you will not need to be afraid of losing him to another woman. The basic reason for most unfaithfulness in marriage is emotional rather than sexual. Your husband's infidelity may be revenge for real or imaginary mistreatment. You should know more about his needs and wants than any other woman. By acting on this knowledge, you will tip the scales significantly in your favor.

Regardless of your sexual needs or problems, you can trust Jesus Christ to provide solutions. He promises to give wisdom to all who ask. "If you want to know what God wants you to do, ask Him, and He will gladly tell you, for He is always ready to give a bountiful supply of wisdom to all who ask Him; He will not resent it" (James 1:5, LB). He may provide this wisdom through His Word, the counsel of your pastor, a mature Christian, or through information received from a book. The heavenly Father is interested in your sexual life being totally fulfilling for both you and your husband. As you begin to understand your husband, you will become the wife he needs.

"Newness" in Marriage

Do not ever let it be said of your marriage that the "newness" has worn off or that life has become dull and routine. You can give new life to your marriage by saying or doing the unexpected. For instance, after you greet your husband with a kiss when he comes home from work, whisper in his ear, "I'm in the mood for love; how about now?" Of course you don't literally expect him to take you up on your suggestion since there may be children around and dinner to prepare. The thought, however, will stimulate him and remind him that he is desirable. This is just another way of saying, "I love you."

Some men want their wives to read dirty books or go to X-rated movies to see how they can add variety to their sex life. Show your husband you can provide variety and excitement without such "aids."

You can add freshness and variety to your marriage by making yourself beautiful, your bedroom irresistible, and your bed beautiful and comfortable. "She makes for herself coverlets, cushions, and rugs of tapestry" (Proverbs 31:22). Here are some suggestions you might use to gradually add "newness" to your marriage. Notice, I said gradually since your husband could be overwhelmed or even suspicious if you used all suggestions at once.

1. Keep your bed clean and sweet smelling. If your husband likes perfume, spray a little of his favorite on the pillows or sheets. Satin sheets and fur throws and pillows add a nice variety.
2. Use candlelight, soft light, or black light to produce a romantic atmosphere. Millie said her husband had never been the "candlelight type." However, when she introduced candle-

light to their bedroom, they both were thrilled with the effect.

3. The use of soft music can add a touch of newness to your sex life.

4. When circumstances permit, variety may be obtained by having sexual union in different rooms, perhaps in front of a glowing fireplace. Be responsive and be willing to have sexual union in a variety of positions.

5. When children are around, be sure you have privacy and a relaxed atmosphere. Lock your bedroom door if necessary.

6. Do not spoil the inviting scene you have created by appearing in curlers or face cream, and do use breath mints, spray, or mouthwash. A thing as simple as bad breath may keep your husband at a distance.

7. If possible, splurge on a new gown, and dress attractively for him, drawing his attention to your best features. Every woman has at least one good feature on which she can capitalize. It may be beautiful ankles, thighs, shoulders, neck, or breasts. *Make the most of what you have and don't fret about what you do not have.* Your most appealing outfit may be your "birthday suit." Never be embarrassed at being naked in front of your husband. Remember, your body belongs to him (1 Corinthians 7:4).

8. Keep your husband aware of your womanliness—the fact that you are an exciting woman and his lover, not just his children's mother. You can exhibit your stimulating, challenging womanhood through your creativity as you add spice and variety to your life. For instance, arrange for the children to spend a night or weekend with friends and have your husband's favorite meal by candlelight. Wear his favorite perfume, relax, and enjoy him.

Your bedroom should be the most beautiful room in your home since this is the room where you and your husband regularly display your love for each other. Always reserve this room for love—not for quarrels, though a Christian couple may well come to God on their knees in the bedroom to ask His forgiveness for sharp words and wrong attitudes.

You are glorifying Jesus Christ when you think and plan toward being a good sexual partner for your husband. You are reminded in 1 Corinthians 7:34, "The married woman has her cares [centered] in earthly affairs, how she may please her husband." When you make your sex life an exciting and satisfying part of your life, you will please your husband and, at the same time, you will be obedient to Christ's instructions to you.

If you do not fulfill your husband's sexual needs, you may be a stumbling block in his life and cause him to be led away from spiritual truths instead of toward God. "Do not refuse and deprive and defraud each other . . . lest Satan tempt you [to sin] through your lack of restraint of sexual desire" (1 Corinthians 7:5).

As you make sex an exciting and meaningful part of your lives, your husband will not be tempted to feel that he is "missing out" or that the "newness" of marriage has worn off. He will look forward to the sexual and emotional gratification he has with you.

In Conclusion

Your husband will be the happy man you want him to be when he feels that you accept him as he is, admire him for his masculinity, and put him first and foremost (after God) in your life. He will feel needed at home because he knows he is respected as the family leader, provider, and protector.

As you respond to your husband and fit into his plans according to God's order, you will see God perform the impossible in your marriage. When your husband is with you, he will feel complete and fulfilled, because you are his counterpart—giving him what he does not have alone.

This beautiful relationship between you is focused in a

sexual union where your love and affection are expressed, increased, and fortified. The sexual union makes possible a tender understanding, communion, and communication that cannot be expressed in language. As "one flesh" you are able to do together what neither of you can do alone.

When the principles set forth in this book become a part of your life, you will find fulfillment in your personal life and marriage. You will have a closer relationship to God, who ordained marriage. And you will discover that you are a real woman—the wife of a happy husband.

We Became Wives of Happy Husbands

Introduction

Daylight had hardly broken one morning in early March when the phone rang. As I reached for it, I wondered who would possibly be calling at such an early hour.

When I answered, Anne Carroll's voice greeted me. She said that during the night she had been quite ill and unable to sleep. While lying in bed wondering whether to call her doctor, a thought began to take shape that she decided to share with me.

"Darien," she explained, "I have been thinking more and more about many of the women who attend the seminars or women who began to read your first book but were just not ready to trust God completely for their marriages. I believe that if women could read some of the marital transformations that we hear and see, they would not hesitate to accept God's way and His principles.

"What do you think about putting a variety of true testimonies in a book so that any woman picking it up could in some way identify with at least one of them? When they see that these women, in the same situations or with even more serious problems, were able through Christ's power to turn their lives around, they too would be encouraged to apply God's principles in their lives. I feel deeply that all some women need is hope, and such a book would offer that hope to many."

I agreed with Anne that there was a need in this area, but I expressed my reservations. I was convinced that another person's experiences could not alter a woman's life unless that woman could understand the principles through which these marital innovations took place. Changes might occur as the result of reading someone else's story, through trying to mimic her actions, but these would be short-lived. Lasting changes would not come to pass unless women could understand how to apply God's principles through His power.

We prayed about Anne's idea. In a short time, God impressed my heart as He had Anne's that this book would be in God's will if the principles could be provided at the end of each story. Then women could see that the failures and heartbreaks in these marriages were not a matter of "bad luck" or fate but were a result of violating principles in God's Word. Just as bad luck hadn't caused the marital problems discussed, neither did a sudden turn of fate mend them. Women must see that the turning point in each of the situations came when each woman realized that she alone was totally insufficient to correct the existing problems in her marriage. When she understood how and when to apply the truths set forth in God's Word through His power, then and only then did her life become fulfilling, happy, and complete.

We both felt that it couldn't be stressed enough that changes seldom occur without some pain, and that deep and lasting transformations do not happen overnight. We both know that Christ wants an abundant life for us, but only through consistent reliance on Him and application of His principles can this become a reality.

A few weeks passed as we prayed and talked about the book. Finally we said, "If it is Your will, Lord, that we write this book, You will have to provide us with the women who will be willing to share their testimonies." With little effort on our part, we obtained the stories you are about to read.

We now want to thank all the women who have shared with us the intimate details of their lives. We realize that for many of them it has been extremely painful to go back into the past and relive these heartbreaks and failures. All of the women whose stories are presented here felt as we do, that if their experiences might help even one woman find the peace and happiness they have, then the pain of recounting their lives would be worth it.

For obvious reasons, most names and locales have been

changed to protect identities, but all of the situations, lives, pain, heartbreak, and happiness are real.

We express our appreciation to each of the contributors and also to: Dot Baker and Vivian Price for their excellent and untiring job in editing, and to Anita Spaugh, Annelle Swilling, Lattie Garrett, Jan Kerr, and Peggy Sosebee for typing the manuscript.

Both Anne and I were blessed by the cooperation of our families.

I, Darien, wish to thank my husband and three sons for patiently supporting and loving me, even when I overextend myself and violate the principles I hold so dear.

I, Anne, want to express my deepest love and appreciation to my husband, Jim, for allowing me to write this book. His faith in me and encouragement have meant much during the past months. My sincere thanks to my two sons for all the duties they performed for me so that more of my time could be free.

1
My Journey Back to Love

Anne Kristin Carroll

While men and women drifted from group to group, mingling, talking, and looking, I sat watching. I was 21, the mother of an infant son, newly divorced, uncertain, searching. The rodeo was in town this chilly midwinter evening, and everyone was sporting his best western attire, from jaunty jeans, shirts and boots to the ultimate in garish, "boudy" Texas style.

I was sitting at a table in Mid Lane Gardens, a bar in the southwest area of Houston. The name doesn't sound illustrious now, but in the early '60s it was one of the "in" spots for singles. Being a nondrinker, I was in very unfamiliar surroundings. Grant, the guy I was currently dating, had brought me here more than once, but I never felt comfortable. I didn't know what was expected of me in this crowd, and whatever was expected I felt I couldn't handle it.

Strains of "Moon River" drifted on the smoky air as people wandered about. Bored and scared, but curious, I left our table and strolled into the other room. There a friendly male voice startled me.

"Hi, there."

"Hi," I replied uncertainly.

My mind whirled as I tried to place where I'd met him. He must have sensed my confusion.

"I'm Jim. We met here last Friday."

Vaguely I remembered him.

"Oh, yes, yes."

The scene flashed back through my mind. I had been sitting at a table with a friend, trying to fit in, and Jim was one of the strangers at the table.

He interrupted my reflections. "Hey, would you like to go to a party?"

He certainly gets to the point, I thought.

"Well," I explained, "my date is in the other room."

Jim dismissed my reasoning. "So what? Mine is, too. Why don't we just split?"

I responded to his positive lead. "Sounds great! Let's go." I really wasn't interested in another Saturday night of fending Grant off.

The party we went to was in one of the singles' complexes in the heart of what some Houstonians called "Sin Alley." The rocking beat of twist music met us as we joined the party. My new date was momentarily appalled to find I didn't know how to dance, but he offered to teach me. Amused at my attempts to learn the twist, he finally suggested: "It's like drying your bottom after a bath without moving your upper part."

But I couldn't seem to coordinate body and feet in anything that resembled dancing. I felt as though I must have been put together differently from the rest of the girls.

I had always felt different. I had no brothers or sisters. My father was 41 when I was born, my mother 31. My parents' friends had no youngsters or else their children were grown, so I spent most of my time with adults. I believed that my Daddy, a successful businessman, could solve any problem and fix anything for me. With him, I felt loved and wanted, and Mother anticipated my every need. Therefore I was never forced to cope with the demanding realities, responsibilities, and consequences of life.

As I remember myself at 13, I looked like a Roman elephant with my protruding ears and patrician nose. Wanting me to feel proud and to help me gain some much-needed confidence, Mother arranged for my protruding ears to be corrected through plastic surgery. I was pleased with my neatly pinned-back ears, but instead of being happy I refocused my inferior feelings on my nose.

At 14, insecurity so plagued me that I once took my mother along to a youth meeting at our new church. Before I was 15, I met Dan, a reserved high school senior. Our dating throughout my last three years in high school gave us both a sense of acceptance without competition.

To many parents I might have seemed like a model child. I didn't smoke or drink, or even go to parties, but spent most of my time in school and church. Mother knew, however, that it wasn't my "goodness" that kept me in line. Perhaps she did not realize that my lack of self-acceptance was my basic problem, but she took me to psychologists, hoping to help me. I made up fanciful stories about their ink-blot pictures, and the doctors asked me interminable questions, all with the same gist: "What do you think are the answers to your fears and insecurities?" I felt like screaming, "I don't want questions! What I need are answers!"

One of the places where I looked for answers was at church. I remember vividly my experience at 12. Our family regularly attended a church where the expressions "making a profession of faith" and "joining the church" were nearly synonymous. Either decision was signified by going to the front of the church sanctuary at the end of the service. Many of my contemporaries had already joined the church, and I decided before a service one evening that tonight was decision night for me.

As the "invitation" began, the front of the church seemed to move farther and farther away, and the aisle grew longer and longer. I kept saying to myself, "I'll go on the next verse of this hymn." Finally I admonished myself, "Self, you're moving out into that aisle."

I did. But it was as if my stomach and heart remained in the pew. Mechanically I walked the aisle and faced the minister at the end of it. He said something like, "Do you believe in Jesus Christ?"

With no real understanding, I answered weakly, "Yes." And I was accepted into the church.

But my problem of feeling worthless and insecure remained. By the time I was a junior in high school, the awareness of a void within drove me to spend more and more time in church. Dan and I still shored each other up, and we often went to meetings together.

At church "revival services" I'd get all charged up—but it wouldn't last. My life was a constant roller coaster: one day I felt beautiful, spiritual, so close to the Lord the way I believed a Christian should feel; the next day the harps stopped playing and the "spirituality" left me.

Troubled because I longed for the life I thought Christianity offered, I sometimes "went forward" in other services. Again I heard the same question, "Do you believe in Jesus Christ?" I always answered, "Yes."

No one ever followed up by asking me whether *I* had any questions. I had been around the religious circuit so long that I knew the pat answers anyway. In fact, I knew all the right Scripture verses and I carried a Bible faithfully. Like the rest of my facade, it was only an act. I didn't know a thing about the role I was playing. Jesus was neither my Saviour nor my Lord.

When I graduated from high school, I faced a new world that was asking me to play a different part. I felt the next thing expected of me was to enroll in college. I chose to attend the University of Houston so I would not have to leave home or Dan. But once there, I could not adjust to the competitive college life and I dropped out.

My sense of worth further damaged, I turned to the prospect that marriage might provide the magic to fulfill my life. Dan and I had dated for three years, and we had seen plenty of movies that showed romance plus marriage equals happiness ever after. Our parents preferred that we wait until Dan had finished college, but after much talking they finally consented, and we were married.

After the newness of marriage wore off, I realized acutely that this was not filling my inner void. We attended a church associated with a Bible college, and the students there radiated peace and happiness—everything that I was searching for. I decided to go to school there and find what they had. When my first attempts failed, I thought, "If I do everything they do and refrain from doing what they don't, I should have what they have." But imitation of their actions didn't give me what they had, and I left school, defeated again.

If that's not the answer, I thought, maybe I need a career. So I went to work for Pan American Airways and stayed on the job until I learned I was pregnant.

Dan's graduation from the university and our baby's birth occurred in the same month. We had never been responsible for anything but our daily schedules, as our parents had always supported us. Now we were faced with parenthood responsibilities and a job for Dan.

It was too much for me. I couldn't cope—perhaps I didn't want to. I had never even held a baby, and the whole idea of motherhood scared me to death. Little Kevin was sick and he cried almost constantly the first few months. The walls of our small apartment seemed to close in on me. Afraid I would do something wrong, I sat up all one night on our living room couch, holding my screaming child. All I could think of was that I would call Mother and go home if we both lasted until morning.

With the first light of day, I phoned. "Mother, I can't handle this. I don't know what to do. The baby is sick. Please come get me."

Dan went with us to Mother's. She and the maid cared for the baby, carefully feeding him with a special formula, holding and soothing him as he struggled with a serious digestive problem. Dan had already elected to go to school for his master's degree. Since the baby's constant crying disturbed his studying, it seemed natural for Dan to move back with his parents.

I wandered about in a daze, with no purpose. Motherhood does not come naturally to all women. I wish someone had explained that to me; I felt like a freak—a failure with my own baby!

By September, boredom and the search for my identity pushed me to take another job with a large international importer. There I compared my appearance with other girls and decided I needed some improvement, so I enrolled at John Robert Powers School of Modeling.

Suddenly I became fascinated with myself. School personnel told me I was very pretty, with real potential for modeling. My long, sandy-blonde hair in a knot made me look like an old-maid school teacher, they said, and changed it to short platinum-blonde. They highlighted my eyes with make-up and taught me how to sit and move gracefully. I emerged from the course a different girl—on the outside.

Following the transformation, I remember the first time I walked into a room full of people. Confident of my good looks, I felt approval from the group. That confirmed my belief that physical attractiveness means acceptance in this competitive world. I clutched this new self-confidence for dear life, feeling nothing else about me had any value. People scared me, I had blown the motherhood role, and I couldn't make it as a wife; but I could control my looks.

My marriage to Dan had deteriorated to weekend visits, and before winter began we were divorced. We used the excuse of "incompatibility." The truth was we didn't have any legitimate grounds for divorce. Looking back, I can't recall any of our conversations while we were married. I cannot think of a time when Dan said "no" to me, and "no" sometimes means, "I care about you."

It amazes me now that no one tried to stop our divorce. No one counseled with us. It was as if we were kids who'd gone steady for a long time and were breaking up. The attachment that we thought was love—that first love which we expected to last forever—bent and broke at the first prolonged strain. As I think back now, I look at Dan more as a brother that I never had. We are still friends, and I am pleased that he found a marvelous woman with whom he enjoys a happy marriage.

I knew no one else who was divorced, and the awful reality filled me with fright and loneliness. Then another blow hit: doctors diagnosed my dad's illness as cancer. It was unthinkable that my father, who I thought was invincible, could be mortally ill.

My world went into a tail spin and my search for stability and fulfillment became frenzied. That's when I met Jim in the singles' bar, ditched my date, and went off to another party.

Jim was the opposite of Dan in many ways. Dan was quiet and a loner; Jim was carefree, exciting, and gregarious. He was tall, with beautifully broad shoulders and wavy brown hair that dangled a marvelous curl over his forehead. To bring more sophistication into my life, he taught me to drink and to dance. I discovered that he had a self-supporting job, while most of my friends were still supported by their parents. Within six weeks Jim and I were married.

But Jim wasn't any more ready for a real marriage than I. He'd spent years in a military school and his home background was totally different from mine. We had a few good weeks before the newness of a live-in wife wore off and Jim gravitated back to his old group. He began staying out with them, partying until all hours.

Shocked, I tried to force him into the role of a "good husband." Then I discovered I was pregnant. Through that summer and fall I cried and nagged, driving Jim to spend more time away from home.

In late November, uncomfortable with my pregnancy, I drove to my parents' house every morning to see Daddy. One morning as I neared the house I saw an ambulance parked in front. Outside a neighbor sadly informed me: "Your dad just passed away."

I did not cry. I couldn't. My mind accepted only information that I could cope with, and I couldn't accept the void he would leave. Somehow I lived through the next few days in numb disbelief.

I remember some of the funeral. As a line of mourners came by to pay their last respects, I was screaming in my mind, "This isn't right . . . it can't be . . . get up, Daddy, get up!" But it was real. Daddy was gone.

I believed death wasn't final, but I was sure I couldn't face life without my dad. Who would reassure me now and say, "Sugar, everything will be all right"? I thought, "No one will ever feel I'm special again." Like a long nightmare, I had continual dreams of him. Soon I was sure I had seen Daddy and he was trying to reach me from the next life. So I launched into the dark world of the occult.

As I searched, I became enamored with the writings of Edgar Cayce. I prayed, meditated, and used the various methods to try to contact the spirit world. Because Cayce used Christian terminology, I thought he was giving biblical insights. It never occurred to me that the Bible might give specific directions about horoscopes, spiritist mediums, and the black arts. No one suggested I read such Scriptures as Isaiah 8:19-22 or Isaiah 47:13-15. Cayce and his followers even taught reincarnation of the soul, and my skimpy knowledge of the Bible gave me no clue that Cayce's teachings were diabolical perversions of God's Word. My search for identity continued through this tangle of intellectual Christianity and occult beliefs.

Jim's employer transferred us to Atlanta, Georgia, and we were happy while our two children remained with my mother and we searched for a house. When the children joined us in a rented home, problems flared again. Up to this time, my mother had provided a live-in maid to care for the family, and I had not changed more than ten diapers! Jim, as immature as I, could provide little help for my insecurities, and I spent the next year running back to Mamma. She would bandage my hurts, cheer me up, and off I'd go again until the next crisis. We finally bought a lovely home and things were more pleasant for a while.

But I couldn't leave well enough alone. I would have been ripe for women's lib, had it existed in the early '60s. Home bored me, the children frustrated me, and I wanted a maid again. It seemed logical that a woman as talented as myself should not waste her time in the dull routine of housework! As my interest turned from home, Jim's wandered also. The more independent I became, the more Jim seemed to look for someone who needed him. Obviously, I didn't!

The solution to the new problem seemed simple: I must become smarter, prettier, or sexier than my phantom competition. I say "phantom," because I accused Jim of more things than a romantic superman could have done. At the time I didn't recognize that my main competition was *me*. God says in Proverbs 14:1, "Every wise woman builds her house, but the foolish one tears it down with her own hands." Word by word, and brick by brick, I was tearing it down.

As I became more anxious, I developed into a super-detective. I checked for traces of make-up on his shirt, searched between car seats for hair pins of the wrong color, checked his address book for unfamiliar female names. Or I trailed Jim at a discreet distance to a club, waited a bit, then popped in and feigned surprise at encountering Jim. My sleuthing produced nothing productive.

Instead, my antics often humiliated me. When I chased him down by phone, I might hear Jim's voice in the background yelling, "Hey, I'm not here!" to a buddy who answered my call. Or worse, a bartender gave the guys a chortle with the version: "He says he ain't here."

Jim had good reason to stay away from home. No peace existed there for either of us.

One morning after I'd found traces of lipstick on the shirt he'd worn the evening before, I proceeded with a Spanish-style inquisition.

"Where were you last night?" I asked, knowing full well he hadn't been where he reported.

"Oh, after I finished work I got together with some of my buyers," he replied.

"Really?"

"Why?" he asked.

At a fever pitch, screaming, tears streaming down my face, I dragged out the shirt, pointing a finger at the lipstick stain.

"Look at this! I guess your buyers wear lipstick now!" I said, sarcasm etching each word. "Jim, I can't take any more; I can't stand it; you're driving me crazy!"

After the outburst, I collapsed with a stream of tears.

"I'm sorry," he said as he tried to embrace me and soothe my hurt. I was enraged again that he thought "I'm sorry" could eradicate the waves of pain and humiliation flooding over me. Although he was repentant, episodes like this did nothing to improve our relationship. Jim would leave, feeling guilty; and I would feel crushed.

Distractedly, I thought a new nose might make a difference. I contacted a plastic surgeon back home, left my children with Mother, and by the time Jim found out, I lay in the hospital looking as if a truck had run over my face. I would have done anything for Jim's approval and to bolster my frail self-image.

Being prettier did not entice him to stay home. I lay in bed at night, listening for his car, crying, dying a little as each hour passed. I wondered why I had failed, what I lacked, and I longed for Jim to hold me in his arms and love me.

I remember a scene that ran and reran for many years: I lay in bed yearning and dreading to hear the sound of his car in the driveway. When he did arrive, I found myself torn between painful bitterness because he'd been out and relief because he was home. It's as if two people lived in my body: the one wanting to reach out, forgive and love; the other wracked with icy hate, wanting to turn away. In utter frustration I'd cry, "Why? Why?" And Jim would say, "I don't know."

As this drama unfolded, I was convinced that Jim's "I

don't know" was a cop-out. Not until much later would I realize that he really didn't know. Although he would swear he'd never wander again, this scene was repeated with heart-breaking frequency.

On a visit to my neighborhood doctor, I told him some of my problems and he said, "What you need is a pill."

I said, "Yes, that's what I need."

That began four years of antidepressants, barbiturates, uppers, downers, anything I could legally get my hands on. I lived in a daze. If there were no current problems, I still took the pills because I knew I couldn't cope when a difficulty arose. It seemed logical to me, when I felt nervous, afraid, insecure, that the answer was to relieve the anxiety. Eliminating the source of the problem didn't dawn on me. I was putting medicine on the rash and ignoring the cause. As I became more addicted, there were days when I hardly got out of my bedroom.

During one visit to my mother, I read a newspaper article about the treatment of schizophrenics in a mental institution. I learned I was taking twice the dosage of medication prescribed for them! I said to myself, "Either you belong in the institution or off the pills." I started a do-it-yourself kick—and I did kick the pill habit.

Without the pills, however, problems piled on me again and I fell apart. After searching everywhere for answers to life, I considered one more answer: suicide. One lonely night, with no hope for a life that was any different, I sat down to plan my suicide.

Something deep inside wanted to reach out just once more for help, but where? Only my mother, who had borne the brunt of my childishness and failures, knew our real situation. I had played Miss Super Cool with everyone else, never discussing my deep feelings. Not only had we faked a happy marriage in front of our friends, but I had the feeling that even if I had the humility to call them, they didn't have any answers either.

That seemed to be the longest night of my life. I cried,

then phoned all the social-help numbers in the directory, one by one. I heard, "Pray." Another said, "Christ is the answer." But how? I'd tried all that.

Morning came, and a phone call from a neighbor whom I hardly knew, Xara Ward. The subject of religion came up. Xara said, "I'm going to a ladies' Bible class today. Why don't you go with me?"

I was glad Xara couldn't see my face. I had searched the whole world of religious answers, and the idea of a "ladies Bible class" was ludicrous to me. But I couldn't reveal my true feelings, and weak with the emotional turmoil of a sleepless night, I agreed to go.

When Xara and I arrived at the class, a young woman was teaching from the book of Ephesians. I thought: What can a housewife named Darien Cooper teach educated, liberated me?

My first impression of Darien was of a tall, slender, obviously intelligent young woman, with a distinct East Tennessee accent which didn't seem to fit the rest of her demeanor. She spoke with authority and yet with such heart-warming knowledge of the Lord. He was obviously her best friend, her strength!

As I settled into a chair, I looked around at the women with mixed feelings. Many of them looked happy, and it wasn't fair. What curse had been put on me? With disgust I thought: This Christ-is-the-answer stuff is okay if your problem is the neighbor's dogs upsetting your garbage, or your husband has forgotten your birthday. It wouldn't work if you had problems like mine!

I don't know what held me together emotionally for another week, but Xara persuaded me to return to that horrid class with her. This time it seemed different, as though the message was meant for me.

Mrs. Cooper said that God had a design for *my* life. He loved *me,* she said, but the reason I wasn't experiencing the abundant life He wanted me to have was because I was sinful, and sin separates us from God. Jesus, however, came to bridge the gap between humans and God. Alone, I could never be good enough for God, but God had given His perfect Son, who took the judgment for *my* sin when He died on the cross. It was a *personal* thing. I could accept Him as my Saviour, a transaction between Jesus Christ and Anne. I, Anne, could have a one-to-one, fulfilling relationship with the Son of God!

Excitement ran through me. I understood for the first time that my belief in Jesus had been only an intellectual acknowledgement of His existence. *I had not trusted Jesus Christ to make me acceptable to God,* as He offered to do.

I had always thought of the death of Christ as a mass project ("Christ died for the world"), but now I saw that if I had been the only person in the world, Jesus still would have come and died for *me* . . . Anne . . . to reconcile me to God!

It was instant identity, a beautiful self-image. God loves me!

Now I knew what I had spent all those years searching for. I was 28, and I had found the One who could be the solution to all my problems!

I must have hit Jim with all my new enthusiasm like a loaded freight train. With a taste of what Christ could mean to our lives, I proceeded to stuff salvation down Jim's throat. I preached day and night, too busy giving out my unseasoned truth to him to learn any more for myself, let alone apply it to my life.

God said, "My thoughts are not your thoughts, neither are your ways my ways (Isa. 55:8). I didn't realize that, nor did I understand what it meant to "wait on the Lord." I ran full-steam ahead, trying to drag Christ along, to make Him fit into my plans. I'm sure He tried to slow me down a few times, but I was running too fast to hear.

In the summer I spent a week at a Bible conference and came home brimming with spiritual energy—to find Jim gone! When he finally got in, it was obvious he hadn't been pining away for me. Still I didn't catch on that I was asking him to compete with Jesus Christ. I wasn't the girl Jim married, nor was I yet the woman Christ was trying to design. But on I rushed.

I had clear notions about how I should look, act, and dress. Single handedly, I hoped to convert the world. It would be nice to have Jim's approval, but it seemed more important that he please me and further my ministry. By Christmas time I was about to blossom into full sainthood and ascend Mt. Sinai to receive a second set of Commandments. At that point Jim decided he'd had it with his live-in "Billy Graham" —he asked for a divorce.

I couldn't believe it. To some people looking on, it seemed that Jim was all wrong and I was altogether right. For a while it seemed like that to me, too.

But Jesus Christ had something to teach me through the alienation. God waited patiently while I retraveled the singles route and discovered the pastures none too green. Meanwhile my deep love for Jim persisted. Tired and disgusted, feeling I'd done all I should and still failed, I cried, "My God, I've tried everything. I quit."

It was as if He said, "Great. Now, Anne, I can get to work."

By this time, Darien and I were close friends. I spent many hours seeking her counsel and her knowledge of the Bible. She was so patient through those difficult times. I'm sure she became weary at times when I'd talk out the same problem for the tenth time, or ask for an explanation of principles we'd gone over many times before. Sometimes I felt as if the Lord were using me to give Darien counseling practice for her course, "Will the Real Woman Please Stand Up?"

The first principle we worked on was my acceptance of Jim. I recognized that I had used many ways to let Jim know I wanted him to be different. But Jesus hadn't demanded that of me. Although Jim and I were now divorced, we saw one another frequently. I started to accept Jim just as he was, with no hope of his changing.

As the Bible principles took shape in my life, I learned that God is the Father who never lets me down. Repeatedly my experiences strengthened my sense of being worthwhile and very special to God.

As I obeyed Him, Jesus rekindled the fires of devotion between Jim and me. Better than that, we developed a deeper, more precious relationship. Two and a half years after our divorce, Jim asked me again to become his wife! I wrote the thoughts and words of our love into the wedding ceremony which reunited us.

Working out our new relationship was a gradual yet exciting process. With my acceptance of Jim, I learned to give my expectations to the Lord. The psalmist wrote: "Delight yourself also in the Lord, and He will give you the desires *and* secret petitions of your heart. Commit your way unto the Lord—roll and repose [each care of] your road on Him; trust . . . also in Him, and He will bring it to pass" (Ps. 37:4-5, AMP).

I tried to keep these verses constantly before me. I stopped asking him where he was going, unless I needed it as business information. Whenever he showed up, I let him know I was glad to see him. No more pouting fits or complaints marred his ties at home. He spent more and more time with me. Often now, Jim comes home sooner than he's planned. I guess home is a nicer place to come back to, today.

My goodie-goodie image had to go. Owing to my preconceived ideas of Christian behavior, I had been very careful about where I was seen. And I had changed from really swinging fashions to things that made me look like Granny Grunch. My self-righteous attitudes and actions made for a Madonna complex, and I learned that no man can relate to a Madonna. As part of making amends, I told Jim I would wear whatever he liked. He tested me for a short time, but when he saw that I really did it to please him, we agreed on fashions that we both enjoy.

Part of the principle of letting him lead the family helps me as much as it does Jim. He had been used to my handling things like any business*man,* but I learned to let him handle even some small things. For instance, when I was harassed by a collector for a newspaper bill we didn't owe, I told the man that he would have to come back when my husband was home. When I told Jim, he called the person responsible and told him not to send anyone again to his home and insult his wife. Now when I'm asked to make a decision when Jim is not around, I say, "I'm sorry. You'll have to talk to my husband about that." Of course, Jim knows I will take care of anything he delegates to me, but he tries to keep undue pressure off me.

Following the leader works in three specific changes that I made in my approach to problems: I now leave the preaching to preachers; I share my opinions with Jim, but leave the final decision to him; and I give him responsibility for the rules and discipline of our children. I have learned to relax and enjoy the protection of my husband's leadership.

I don't mean to imply we are without problems, for who is? When I think of Jim's and my relationship, I am reminded of Song of Solomon 8:7, "Many waters cannot quench love, neither can floods drown it," and 1 Corinthians 13:8, "Love never fails—never fades out or becomes obsolete or comes to an end" (AMP). These things speak to me of the permanence which God intended for love. I wouldn't take anything for our having struggled through the bad years. I love Jim more than words could ever express, and I thank the Lord for reuniting us because truly now, "My beloved is mine, and I am his" (Song 2:16).

Jim has done a lot of maturing. His devil-may-care air is mellowing with an underlying strength. A real warmth and concern for others are emerging elements of a beautiful new personality. His faith is still a private matter between him and God, kept close to his heart with the other profoundly personal subjects nourished in his individualism.

When I revert to seeing things from a human viewpoint, Christ gently corrects me; it's as if He says, "Anne, you've taken your eyes from Me and you're looking at the world and at yourself." I remember that He is painting the picture of my life, and He sees the full image. Then I affirm that when Jesus is in control of my life He is responsible for "working all things to our good."

When my faith wavers, I remember what a bomb I made out of my life, and how looking through His eyes changed a hopeless situation into a bright beginning.

Jesus is my constant companion and friend. I talk to Him continually. "Look at this," I say. "Isn't this fantastic!" Or, "What should I do now, Lord? I know You want the best for me; don't let me goof." I may need to confess: "Lord, I sinned, I've fallen short. But I know You can work it out for my good. Lord, it is so comforting to know You love me more than I love myself, and you love Jim even more than I do, and Lord, I just thank You for being with us, for loving us. Thank You, Lord."

Jesus loves me even when I'm unlovable. That's what I needed to know in order to live and to journey back to love.

Reminiscing With Darien:

The neighborhood Bible class seemed like any other on that wintry Wednesday morning except for the very stylish, sophisticated young woman sitting on the front row. Later I learned her name was Anne Carroll. I wondered about her, "Why did she come? What did she hope to find, and would she return?"

She continued to come each week and gradually began staying longer and longer after the classes to talk with me. At first, she seemed so knowledgeable on every subject that I wondered if I dared reveal how uninformed I was about the things of the world she was discussing. My newly learned truth of simply being myself—open and honest with no pretense—was challenged. I wanted her to respect and like me. Could I risk losing it? Yes, God was teaching me that as long as I had His approval, He would draw to me needed and dear friends (Prov. 3:1-16).

Only God could have brought together two people so opposite in background and personality to teach each so very much and to establish such a beautiful friendship.

Periodic phone conversations soon became a daily occurrence. I began to learn through our relationship what had only been a theory before: regardless of the mask we wear or the impression we give to others of ourselves, we are *all* alike on the inside. Anne had searched from early teens to find peace and fulfillment as a person. So had I. While I had not been able to hide my feelings of inferiority, she had covered hers deftly with a mask of "Miss Self-Sufficiency." But her disguise hadn't helped any more than my admitted inadequacy.

Blaise Pascal, physicist and philosopher, identified this universal need when he said, "There is a God-shaped vacuum in the heart of each man which cannot be satisfied by any created thing, but only by God, the Creator, made known through Jesus Christ."

It was exciting to watch the reversal in Anne's thinking as

she started seeing herself as God saw her, a person of tremendous worth. Since the value of anything may be judged by the price placed on it, she saw that she was infinitely precious since the life of Jesus Christ, infinite payment, had been given for her. Not only did accepting the death of the Son of God for herself give Anne the right to fellowship with God, but God also declared that He was *richer* by her receiving His Son as her Saviour (Eph. 1:8). Anne gained comfort from God's *unconditional acceptance* of her in Christ and at last she began to experience fellowship with God through the Saviour.

As Anne's relationship with God deepened, she learned to deal with others in proper perspective. God said she was His *ambassador* (2 Cor. 55:20); she had no need to worry, because God promised to *meet all of her needs*—personal and marital (Phil. 4:19). These needs were met through our searching the Scriptures together and applying the answers we found there.

As Anne began to see herself from God's perspective, her direct, almost abrupt manner began to soften, and her tender, caring nature began to be manifested. By becoming God-centered, the identity crisis was over and she was well on her way to becoming the "divine original" that God had created her to be.

Perhaps you have some of Anne's problems. Or maybe you'd profit by the self-evaluation and Bible study afforded in the following questions and Scripture passages.

Thinking Through With You:

Question: *What kind of life does God desire for us?*
Answer: "I have told you these things that My joy *and* delight may be in you, and that your joy *and* gladness may be full measure *and* complete *and* overflowing" (John 15:11, AMP.).

Q.: *What separates us from God's approval and blessings?*
A.: "Your iniquities have made a separation between you and your God, and your sins have hid His face from you, so that He will not hear" (Isaiah 59:2, AMP.).

Q.: *How can we get rid of these sins?*
A.: "God caused Christ, who Himself knew nothing of sin, actually to *be* sin for our sakes, so that in Christ we might be made good with the goodness of God" (2 Corinthians 5:21, PH). "Who [Christ] personally in His own body carried our sins onto the cross, so that we might abandon our sins and live for righteousness" (1 Peter 2:24, BERK).

What remains for us to do?

"Believe in the Lord Jesus and then you will be saved" (Acts 16:31, PH). "In view of God's mercies, that you present your bodies a living sacrifice . . . to God . . . And do not conform to the present world scheme, but be transformed by a complete renewal of mind, so as to sense for yourselves what is the good and acceptable and perfect will of God" (Rom. 12:1-2, BERK).

2
God Didn't Take Over Until I Let Go!

Bonnie West

With mixed feelings, I joined my friends in the waiting car. We were going to hear Darien Cooper teach "Will the Real Woman Please Stand Up?" I was excited because I loved to hear the Bible explained, but I was apprehensive because I didn't want to receive a set of rules to follow. And I hated to take study notes.

Worse yet, I had heard that the course would teach me submission to my husband. I had carefully circumvented that Bible concept. The Scripture phrase "as unto the Lord" seemed too deep for me. Recently, however, I had decided to let Christ have full control of my life, and I thought there *might* be something in the course to help me with my problems.

I had grown up not knowing my father, as he died when I was a baby. Out of necessity, my mother made a place for herself in the business world of our small, typically Southern town. She was independent and quite capable in her real estate field. I deeply admired her. There was one thing, however, I wished she had time to do. In my daydreams I envisioned her wearing an apron and humming while working over a warm stove baking a cake. But since she had to be the family breadwinner there seemed no time to bake cakes.

In spite of that, we lived a satisfying life. We went to a church where, at nine, I accepted Jesus Christ as my personal Saviour. Mother and I shared many friends in common. Our closest companions were our neighbors, who were mostly widows.

We had no close relatives living nearby and there was little chance for me to observe a husband-and-wife relationship. For a reason I didn't understand at the time, I found playing with my school friends to be an unsettling experience when their fathers came home. I would leave immediately—even when the mother was humming and lovingly baking a cake! Now I realize that, not having a father, I was insecure in this unfamiliar relationship. Since I had little idea what marriage was supposed to be like, I concluded that I was to be just like my mother: self-sufficient.

Mike and I had our first argument on our honeymoon trip. I wanted to purchase a dog and take him several hundred miles back home with us. Mike suggested we wait until we got home to buy a pet. I insisted we do it my way; he decided we would do it his way—and he drove past the pet shop. Consequently we rode 500 miles in frigid silence, while I wondered what I had got myself into!

We discovered that our interests went in opposite directions. I loved libraries and reading. I even tried to write for magazines. A romantic at heart, I was also definitely the indoor type. Mike's world seemed to revolve around football and basketball games, mostly on television.

I learned to loosen some tubes in the television set when a "big game" was coming up—there was a big one every week! But Mike soon figured out that I had been tampering with the TV, and he readily fixed it while I crept away to sulk.

Mike was meticulous, always checking on details. I ignored them and worked out my own way to do things. It seemed Mike never, *never* got in a hurry, and I was always ready for things ahead of time. Mike thrived on talking with strangers at a gathering, while I couldn't think of a thing to say. He stayed up late; I went to bed early. He relished traveling and I preferred staying home. The clincher was that Mike liked to eat—and I hated to cook!

Four children certainly gave us something in common, but we argued about discipline and my having to care for them. Some days I imagined myself running away and leaving Mike with the kids for a while—until he would welcome me back with due appreciation!

I finally admitted that there must be a better way to live than the one Mike and I were following. That's when I heard my friends talking about "Will the Real Woman Please Stand Up?" They said 500 or more women attended each seminar. I understood that the principles taught there helped a wife to become what her husband wanted her to be. If that were true, it seemed to be just what I needed, because I felt that I wasn't anything like what Mike wanted.

As I sat waiting for the class to begin, I looked around at the other women. I wondered if my problems were like theirs, or worse. Then Darien arrived, and as soon as she started talking everyone began taking notes. Even though I knew I'd lose mine, or couldn't understand them when I got home, I pulled out my pen and scribbled away.

Suddenly I felt as if Darien were talking about me—just me—and I looked around to see if anyone was staring at me. But, of course, no one was. Then I became so fascinated with what she was saying that I put down my pen and just listened.

God works through the husband for the benefit of the wife, she said. When the wife understands and believes this, she can trust God in any situation. She is released from the pressure of trying to change her husband, of manipulating him into doing what she wants. Favorable results are then produced by lovingly responding to her husband's leadership and leaving the results to God.

Realizing Christ accepts her just as she is, a wife can then thank God for her husband *just as he is.* If he asks her to do something she isn't interested in or hasn't the appitude for, she can do it lovingly, recalling the verse which says "Wives, be subject—be submissive and adapt yourselves—to your own husbands as [a service] to the Lord" (Eph 5:22, AMP). An "I'll-do-it-even-if-it-kills-me" attitude isn't the same thing!

Darien read Scripture verses to underscore the principles she was sharing. She stressed that she wasn't talking about the wife as a namby-pamby doormat. God gave us our own beautiful individuality; God created the wife to be a helpmate for her husband—a complement to him.

The idea that God would work His will for my life through my husband entranced me. I went away from the class with the idea boldly in front of me, like a giant billboard.

I began applying some of the practical principles Darien had suggested. I didn't complain when Mike went to play golf, or when he tracked mud into the house, or when he isolated himself behind the sports page. He began watching me with suspicion. One day he acknowledged my new attitude with, "What's happened to you? Why don't we fuss anymore?"

As the class continued to meet, I began to realize that I had been asuming a lot of responsiblilities that weren't mine. For instance, I thought it extravagant for Mike to buy new tires for the cars while the old ones were still rolling. Consequently, when he announced, "I bought two new tires for your car today," he knew what to expect: I would name all the things I could have bought with that tire money, and I'd tell him I didn't want to hear about treads. Now I realized that the care of the cars is Mike's responsibility. Like a wet puppy shaking itself, I shook myself free of his responsibility.

The next time he said, "I got you a new tire today," I replied, "Thank you." Then I went out to look at it on the car. I told him, "You picked out a lovely tire." He chuckled, and I grinned. There was appreciation for me beneath his laughter.

But there were times when I didn't manage so well. There was the day Mike told me about the rotten tomato in the refrigerator just after I had (1) waxed the kitchen floor,

(2) scrubbed the cabinets, and (3) cooked his favorite supper. Feeling very unappreciated, my human nature took over and I wouldn't have removed that moldy old tomato or apologized for anything!

Generally, though, I began reacting differently about the things I'd wanted my way for years. While listening to Darien during one of the class sessions, I began thinking, "Surely God doesn't want me to like football for Mike's sake—not that!" Just at that moment Darien said, "If your husband is a football nut and wants you to enjoy the games with him, ask Jesus to take over. He will."

On the way home that day, I asked God to help me "endure football." Then I changed it to "like football." And I added, "I'm trusting You to do this for me."

Sure enough, within a few days, Mike asked me to go with him later in the season to a football game. I heard myself answer "yes" in a small but animated voice.

I had never seen him so excited. For two months he talked about the game we were going to "together." As for me, I felt no bitterness or resentment, though I didn't share the same degree of anticipation.

The sun shone warmly as we walked into the stadium that December afternoon. Mike explained some of the more exciting plays and I actually began to understand some. Sitting with Mike in the midst of thousands of screaming fans, I looked up at the bright blue sky and thought, "You really take over when we let you, Lord. Thank You."

It didn't occur to me right away that Mike had acted differently by planning so far ahead. I am the one who loves to plan things months in advance and scrawl the upcoming events on my calendar. Mike likes to play things by ear and "hang loose." Consequently it was hard for me to let go of a problem and trust God to work through my husband when I had to wait so long for Mike's decisions.

Waiting is hard for me. I tend to work out solutions and pray, "God, this is ready for Your blessing. Isn't it a terrific idea!" Of course, I may disguise my prayer in pretty language, using "Your will" or "make me teachable," but often the attitude of my heart is "Let's get going, God."

Mike and I had been married nearly 17 years and the Lord was doing so many exciting things in my life and my marriage that I wanted to write about them. Writing was a dream come true for me. Within a few months' time my articles had been accepted by several magazines. Then, after praying about it, I began rewriting a book which I had started four years earlier.

Since Mike objected to my writing when he was home, I stopped whenever I heard his car in the driveway. I also tried to have supper ready in the evenings and to keep the house looking fairly neat.

But one morning with the writing going great, I didn't stop for eight hours straight. I paid no attention to the house, the children, the telephone, supper, nor to Mike when he drove up. I heedlessly kept on typing. Obviously, my priorities were out of order.

When Mike entered the house, he saw I was exhausted. He said I had no right to drive myself so hard and to ignore the children and our home. An argument ensued and Mike picked up the manuscript and threw it across the floor. His contempt seemed almost as horrible to me as if he had swung violently at one of our children!

I ran upstairs and slumped to my knees. Sobbing to my Father in heaven, I asked Him to help me give up the book if Mike didn't want me to write it.

When I went downstairs, Mike apologized. He didn't beat around the bush, either. He said the words, "I'm sorry." Then he told me to go ahead with the book. He was concerned, however, for my physical and mental well being. So I tried to work less frantically.

When the book was finished, I asked Mike to read what I had written, because it was about us. I wanted his approval before I sent it to a publisher.

Mike didn't get around to reading it for two weeks. In his spare time he watched television and read the papers. Inside

I was screaming, "Read it, read it, you stubborn man! Why don't you read it?" Then another thought whispered through my mind, "Trust God. Be patient."

I mourned in silent anguish as Mike enjoyed television. When I could stand it no longer, I tried asking him again to read it. He replied that he'd get around to it. I felt as if I were being torn apart inside. I kept telling myself I was trusting God to work through Mike, though I wasn't.

Finally Mike started reading. Ever so slowly, it seemed to me, he perused it. One day he said it would be all right to mail.

I was at the post office within the hour.

But serious damage had been done. A few days later I awoke with pains in my chest. The spasms grew to an unbearable intensity. I was hospitalized with one of the largest stomach ulcers my doctor had ever seen. I knew immediately that my impatience and lack of trust had caused it. My first reaction was, "Oh, I don't want God to know about this ulcer. I'm so ashamed."

I believe God had to teach me this lesson the hard way: the danger of trying to make a drastic change in behavior on my own. I realized that Christ can do things—change us and others—only when we totally let go. Trusting isn't saying, "It's Yours, Lord," and then thinking behind His back you can continue to apply your own solutions. You'll never find the quote, "God helps those who help themselves," in the Bible.

I bowed my head and prayed for forgiveness. Then I asked God to heal the ulcer. I wanted no reminder of my disobedient attitude. Within six weeks the ulcer vanished without a trace. The doctor even allowed me to resume following a normal diet.

When I truly give a problem to God—completely let go of it—it is amazing how He takes over. Our pastor approached me one day to ask if Mike and I could attend a "lay renewal weekend" coming up in a couple of months. My answer surprised me, and the pastor mirrored my astonishment. I said, "I'll tell Mike about it, and whatever *he* says, we'll do."

Normally I would have tried to push Mike into anything I wanted to do. Demand an answer from him. Make him commit himself. Put it on my calendar, So a part of me wanted to insist: *get an answer from Mike tonight.* But, against my nature, I gave the matter to the Lord. Even though I wanted terribly to go, I trusted God to work through my husband for our good.

When I told Mike, he replied right away. "We can't go." Then he paused as if waiting for my rebuttal.

"OK," I said with a smile. It wasn't a gushy response. Nor was it a martyred, goody-two-shoes attitude. The desire to attend left me completely and I was somehow glad we weren't going!

A couple of days later Mike asked me what time he'd need to get off work in order for us to attend the first session of the conference, if we went. We had not been away for a weekend, just the two of us, in years. Planning for the care of four children would be a problem, and it was a bad time for Mike to get away from the office. I realized that Mike was reasonably and responsibly weighing his decision.

Weeks slipped by and the pastor needed a definite yes or no. I put the question to Mike. "Is it all right to tell him we can't go?"

"No, we're going."

"Really!" I squealed. My desire to go returned and intensified in a split second.

Then it hit me! I hadn't suffered while waiting for Mike to make up his mind—I had been trusting Christ to do what was best for us. Those dates on my calendar remained blank all that time, and it didn't matter in the least!

I thank God that each day gives me new chances to be Mike's helpmate. I've relinquished many "'rights" from my grasp and since I opened my fist I've discovered that Mike wants to hold my hand!

Reminiscing with Darien:

Ring-ring-ring. The telephone interrupted my thoughts as I sat at the kitchen table writing.

"Hello."

"My name is Bonnie West. I attended your spring class entitled, 'Will the Real Woman Please Stand Up?' Since I did not get to meet you at that time, I wanted to share with you some of the things I am seeing God do in my life."

Bonnie's enthusiasm over the biblical truths God was teaching her was not minimized by the miles of telephone line. I could immediately identify with her excitement. God had begun teaching me those same truths a few years ago.

Such an interruption of my writing was truly welcome. Getting to know Bonnie as we talked about the reality of Jesus Christ in our everyday living was very rewarding to me.

Bonnie became a Christian as a child, but had not learned how to live the Christian life. She was discovering that the Christian life is not only difficult to live but is impossible—by oneself! Only Jesus Christ can live such a life. Not only had Christ died to pay for Bonnie's sins, but He rose again to relive His life in and through her, moment by moment.

Bonnie realized that such power had not been a reality in her life for two reasons. First, she was unaware of the provision God had made for her as His child. She was living in spiritual poverty when God had provided an abundance. Her condition could be compared to having a million dollars in her bank account while living in poverty, unaware of her wealth.

Second, God's power had been limited in her life because of unconfessed sin. Bonnie learned that worry, jealousy, a critical attitude, bitterness, revenge, self-pity (to name a few) were symptoms of self rather than Christ being in control. The Holy Spirit was grieved by these sins. The moment she confessed her sins, claiming the promise in 1 John 1:9, she was cleansed and again controlled by the Holy Spirit as she yielded to Him.

Even though confessing one's sins is imperative in the Christian life, confession is not enough to break the old habit patterns. For instance, if you found a beetle on his back kicking his feet in the air, you might conclude that his problem would be corrected by placing him on his feet. After doing so, you observe that he starts back up the same incline that caused his fall. Then you realize that he needs to be headed in another direction. Likewise, we must begin to respond to our husbands, children, in-laws, and others as God instructs, as well as ceasing harmful actions.

Bonnie began to realize that her relationship to Mike was to have the same ingredients as her relationship with Jesus Christ. At first she was frightened to accept Mike exactly as he was. Wouldn't he take advantage of her and start doing everything "wrong" if he knew she'd respond lovingly, regardless? Then she remembered that she didn't respond spitefully to Christ when she learned He loved her equally at all times. She had been drawn to Him, desiring to be all that He wanted her to be.

Bonnie realized that acceptance of Mike must not be conditional. She was to respect his God-given right to make his own decisions without coercion from her or being penalized by her if he didn't do what she had desired. Such acceptance provides the atmosphere necessary to bring out the best in a person. Mike immediately began to respond, showing appreciation and admiration for the sweet spirit she displayed. Other men may test their wives to see if their acceptance is genuine or just a new gimmick to get their own way. But Christian wives can have perfect peace, knowing that this is God's way for them to respond. After all, the wife is responsible only for herself, not for her husband.

Accepting your husband as he is provides a basis for his dignity as a person. A man's self-esteem can be undermined when you attempt to coerce, set limits, or put conditions on what he does. He may react by withdrawing into himself, becoming passive and suffer in an attempt to keep a peaceful attitude. Outwardly he turns into a "mouse." Or he may rebel against the restraints and resemble a roaring "lion" around the house. Either way, the traits are hard to respect in a man. But manly qualities require the self-esteem you can help build in your husband.

God never asks you to accept your husband or fulfill any other request in the Christian life without providing the means whereby His will can be accomplished. Philippians 4:6-9 gives the formula for responding properly to problems —marital or otherwise.

The first step is to give your problem to God: "Be anxious for nothing, but in everything, by prayer and supplication, with thanksgiving, let your requests be made known to God" (Phil. 4:6, NASB).

Bonnie faced the fact that even though God's way is not always easy, it is easier than doing things her way. She began to consistently place marital problems into God's hands. When the problems entered her thinking, she simply said, "Thank You, Lord, that You are handling that problem. It's going to be exciting to see how You work it out."

Once God has been given access to our problems, the next step is to cooperate with Him as He works out the solution. Verse eight describes this: "Whatever is true, whatever is honorable, whatever is right, whatever is pure, whatever is lovely, whatever is of good repute, if there is any excellence and if anything worthy of praise, let your mind dwell on these things" (Phil. 4:8, NASB).

God's way of working out problems varies. He enabled Bonnie to enjoy the football game rather than taking away Mike's yen for sports. But He led Mike to approve her desire to write. Bonnie learned from their argument that her priorities should be as follows: (1) maintaining her relationship with Jesus Christ through Bible study and prayer, (2) being her husband's help-mate, (3) caring for their children's needs, (4) caring for her personal needs—diet, exercise, rest, and appearance. (5) housekeeping responsibilities, and (6) personal hobbies and activities. With her priorities in order, Bonnie's writing enhanced rather than destroyed precious relationships.

Verse 9 of Philippians 4 is important to remember also. "Practice these things" (NASB). Some days the spiritually sensitive wife may feel that all she does is confess her sins, give problems to God, and focus on positive truths. But as we are obedient each time to these directions, we find ourselves experiencing God's peace more and more.

Thinking Through with You

Question: *How is the Christian life lived successfully?*
Answer: "I have been crucified with Christ and I no longer live, but Christ lives in me. The life I live in the body, I live by faith in the Son of God, who loved me and gave Himself for me" (Gal. 2:20, NIV).

Q.: *What kinds of qualities will be manifested in my life when I am under Christ's control?*
A.: "The fruit of the Spirit is love, joy, peace, patience, kindness, goodness, faithfulness, gentleness, self control" (Gal. 5:22-23, NASB).

Q.: *If insisting on my rights involves constantly checking on my husband, expecting him to share every thought and move, demanding meal attendance at my time and convenience, and criticizing his failures, what does love involve?*
A.: "Love is patient, love is kind. It does not envy, it does not boast, it is not proud. It is not rude, it is not self-seeking, it is not easily angered, it keeps no record of wrongs. Love does not delight in evil but rejoices in the truth. It always protects, always trusts, always hopes, always perseveres" (1 Cor 13:4-7, NIV).

Q.: *What relieves you of the responsibility and burden of changing your husband?*
A.: "Each of us will give an account of himself to God" (Rom. 14:12, NIV).

Q.: *What can you expect from God if you take your problems to Him in prayer and thank Him for taking over?*
A.: "The peace of God, which surpasses all comprehension, shall guard your hearts and your minds in Christ Jesus" (Phil. 4:7, NASB).

3 The Fans Are Silent But My Praises Ring

Chris Sorpenski

Cool breezes blew off the bay and the California sun cast giant shadows across the football field as the 49ers ran on for the last game of the season. Fans slowly filled Kezar Stadium. Taking my regular seat, I wondered if Dusty and I would miss the glamor and glory of the past years. Would anything else match the roar of the crowd, instant recognition at restaurants, and the advantages of being a professional football player?

Waiting for the game to start, I thought back to the first time I met Dusty. After my parents divorced, I had lived with my grandparents in Carmel. It was at a charity bazaar one summer afternoon that I had first seen Dusty. After graduating from Stanford University in the spring, my summer had been filled with parties and trips. Only at the last moment had I decided to go to the bazaar.

After greeting my hostess, I talked with many of the girls that I had grown up with. Much time was spent in "catch-up" conversation. Grandfather had brought me and he was insistent that I meet some of the young men.

Dusty was one of them. I was instantly taken with him, but his name, Duston Sorpenski, was a bit much. As we talked, I learned he had recently graduated from Ohio State and had come to San Francisco to play professional football.

A few weeks later, Dusty called and asked me to go to a party given by one of the rookies. After the party we drove back up the coast to Carmel. There we stopped the car and sat on a ridge overlooking the Pacific. A gnarled old tree stood on the edge of the cliff, twisted by the constant ocean winds. Looking at Dusty, I thought, "I could stand up through the storms of life just like that old tree if I had this man beside me."

When Dusty proposed marriage a few months later, I was thrilled. I felt that he was the greatest thing that could ever happen to me. He was so tall, dark, and handsome. He was sweet, patient, loving, kind, and a truly gentle man. Being a professional athlete, he had a marvelous physique. When I fell in love with Dusty, I fell so hard that I thought I loved him as much as it was humanly possible to love anyone.

After becoming a Christian at the age of 12, I had not made Jesus a prominent part of my life. But as I approached marriage I became aware of this lack. I spoke with our minister, and the morning of our wedding I reaffirmed my commitment to Christ. Dusty and I had briefly discussed Christianity. He told me that he, too, came to know Christ at an early age. I wanted a Christian marriage, with never any thought of divorce. I wanted our future children to have a happy home and the family togetherness that I never had.

After Dusty and I were married, we faithfully attended church each Sunday, but our spiritual training began and ended there. After two years of marriage, the Lord gave us a beautiful baby girl, and we were thrilled. Three years passed, and we were again blessed with a precious baby boy. Our family was now complete. We loved our children dearly and sincerely wanted to raise them in the ways of the Lord.

As soon as they were old enough, we started them in Sunday School. They were taught to ask the blessing before meals and to pray before going to bed. Bible stories were taught to them, but I now know that Jesus was not vital in any of our lives. We never mentioned Christ in ordinary conversation.

We realized the lack of Christian instruction one Christmas when our daughter Oma confused Jesus with Santa Claus. I wanted Christ's birthday to be meaningful to our children, so I went out and bought a manger scene. We shared with the children the real meaning of Christmas. I realized then that all of us needed more than a manger scene could give, but pride still dominated my personality.

Dusty's decision to retire from football was going to bring a great change in my life. I had spent all my years in California, and now for the first time I would be moving away.

I knew Dusty felt that time was catching up with him. Almost ten years as a professional football player was more than most players could expect. But giving up the "good life" in California was not going to be easy for either of us.

The throbbing notes of the National Anthem broke through my thoughts and returned me to the reality of the moment. I watched the players run out on the field and listened to their names being announced. "Number 63, center, Duston Sorpenski." Tears welled up in my eyes as I realized this was the last time I would hear that announcement. The game itself became something of a blur in my memory.

Dusty had bought a large motor-hotel in Gatlinburg, Tennessee. We were going into a new business, in a totally different part of the country. Since Gatlinburg is basically a resort town at the western entrance to the Smoky Mountains, we had decided to make our permanent home in Atlanta, Georgia.

The children glowed expectantly as they watched the movers place the last piece of furniture in the van. It was warm as we left Carmel in mid-February. Arriving in Atlanta, we found the ground, trees, and telephone wires weighted down with ice. Like a Disneyland fantasy, the whole city seemed to be frozen. I longingly thought of the warm California sun.

After a few weeks of eight- and nine-hour days with a patient real estate agent, we found a lovely home in the Indian

Hills section. The children adjusted quickly to their new schools and friends, and life went on as usual.

Dusty spent a lot of time in Gatlinburg, getting the motel ready for the tourist season. There was much work to be done. The rooms needed remodeling, new furniture was being delivered, and menus had to be planned for the motel restaurant.

I met wonderful new friends. Much time was spent decorating our new home. As spring came to Atlanta, I was astounded by the beauty of the dogwoods and azaleas. Memories of California quickly faded from my mind.

Spring turned into fall and again into spring. And the steady strains of business, life, and marriage began to bear down on us.

I had always considered myself a good woman. I thought I was a good Christian, a good friend, a good wife, and good mother. But if I had been entirely truthful as far as my marriage was concerned, I would have admitted I was a domineering, possessive, stubborn, demanding, and immature partner.

One of our periodic hangups arose when Dusty and I had a disagreement and I would insist that it be settled before we went to sleep. "It just isn't right to go to sleep with this strain between us," I would cry.

"Chris, don't you realize it's 3 o'clock in the morning?" His voice was taut, disgusted. "Let's talk about it tomorrow. I'm tired."

But I could never let it drop.

And I usually wanted my own way. One evening Dusty came home and said, "Hey, Chris, why don't you fix a quick dinner for the kids and let's us go out?"

"Fantastic!" I said, and began making sandwiches. "Where are we going?"

"Oh, I thought we'd go to Aunt Fanny's. I've had my mouth set all day for some of that country ham."

"Really, Dusty . . . not Aunt Fanny's. I'm in the mood for violins and the Midnight Sun."

"You have got to be kidding," he said. "I don't want to

get dressed up and I don't want to drive that far. I just want ham."

"Well, I don't, and if we can't go to the Midnight Sun I don't want to go out at all!"

The rest of the evening simmered in silence, with Dusty watching TV and me pouting in the bedroom.

Sometimes I was downright irrational. For Christmas one year, I got Dusty a beautiful Browning 300 magnum rifle. I had asked one of his friends to go with me to pick it out, since I didn't know much about guns, and I wanted it to be just what he wanted.

The problem arose when Dusty wanted to use the beautiful equipment I had given him—a hunting trip was planned or a fishing trip was in the offing. I would pout and cry because I didn't want Dusty to go! I wanted Dusty to have all that gear but I didn't want him to enjoy activities which excluded me.

Possessiveness wasn't all that plagued me. Resentment and a profound feeling of not being wanted filled my being at times. Once upset, I turned skirmishes into drawn-out battles. It took days and even weeks to get over my horrible feelings of the hurt and malice. Dusty could explode one moment and in the next be happy and loving. Not me! He would apologize repeatedly, whether he was right or wrong.

"Chris," he'd say, "I'm sorry; I didn't realize that I had upset you so."

"It just doesn't matter," I'd reply. "You wouldn't have acted like that if you loved me."

"Chris, I do love you. You're just impossible at times."

"See, you said it again. You don't love me!" Like a child denied candy, I'd pooch out my lip and stomp out of the room.

There were many happy times, of course, and for the most part people thought we were an ideal couple. And as long as things were going my way, peace prevailed.

Early one spring a horrible argument boiled up. Dusty told me he was going to Gatlinberg to prepare the motel for the coming season. He had never gone this early before, and I was dead-set against it.

He said, "Chris, don't you understand? The rooms need painting, the gutters need cleaning, and you know if I'm not there the work won't get done."

"We've got a manager to oversee things like that," I protested. "I can see no good reason for you to go right now. This is two weeks earlier than you've ever gone before."

"Well, if you can't understand, I'm not going to stand here all night trying to explain it to you," he said, and walked into the bedroom.

I wasn't going to let him get away with that. If it took all night, I was going to get things settled—my way.

Walking into the bedroom, I said, "Dusty, we're not going to drop it just like that."

"Yes, I am," he said. He walked out into the hall to pick up some business papers, and I followed him, fussing with every step.

He went back into the bedroom and shut and locked the door. Obviously, he had had enough for the evening. Knowing that I wasn't about to drop the subject, he tried to retreat and find some solitude.

Totally enraged, I screamed and hollered, beating on the bedroom door. Knowing I would wake everyone in the house, he furiously jerked open the door, grabbed my arm and pulled me in.

When he let go, I was off balance and stumbled and fell into an end table. A crystal vase fell as I upset the table and broke under my arm as it hit the floor. With blood dripping from the cut on my arm, I walked pathetically into the bathroom.

The accident ended our conversation that night. But the next morning I found Dusty had packed his bags and left. I wasn't sure whether he had left me or had just gone to Gatlinburg.

I realized that if he hadn't left me for good, it might not be long until he did. I prayed that the Lord would help me and help our marriage. I knew I was destroying it, but I didn't have the slightest idea how to begin to make changes.

My Sunday School teacher had often asked me to attend a Bible class which met every other week. Needing help so very much, I decided to go. One day at Bible study, someone was reading Ephesions 5. When she read verse 24, "Now as the church submits to Christ, so also wives should submit to their husbands in everything" (NIV). I immediately asked the group if they *really* obeyed their husbands. There was a moment of silence, and then one of them asked me if the word "obey" was in my marriage vows. I quickly said yes, but I sat there thinking that obeying my husband would be the last thing I would do.

It is ironical that the minister who married us referred us to Ephesians 5 as an important chapter for marriage, and yet I had never applied it to mine.

A few months later when I was discussing a current book on marriage with a friend, she asked me if I had read *You Can Be The Wife Of A Happy Husband*. She let me borrow her copy and I began reading the Christian principles and truths taught by Darien Cooper. I realized what kind of wife God expects a Christian woman to be and I saw how far short I fell.

The Lord began to counsel me about not being possessive, demanding, domineering, and holding resentments. As I was responsive, Christ began to change me. When I heard that Mrs. Cooper would be teaching a seminar on the book topic, a friend and I began to attend.

When we arrived at the first class, Anne Carroll was speaking. I was fascinated with her story and was encouraged to see the transformation the Lord had performed in her life. I knew then that no matter how strained my relationship with Dusty had become, Christ could make the necessary changes if I made myself totally available to Him and applied His principles for a Christian marriage.

After listening to Mrs. Cooper, I became aware of the necessity of obeying God's Word. I developed a hunger to read and study, to learn exactly what God wanted for my life instead of what I wanted. I learned that the Lord would guide my life through my husband.

Almost immediately I had an opportunity to follow my husband's leading. I prayed about a car that Dusty seemed set on buying. I believed the decision he made would be from the Lord. The very next day Dusty announced that we would not be buying the car. I quietly thanked God for His answer.

I learned to keep short accounts with God. When feelings of resentment reared their ugly heads, I immediately confessed them and other wrong mental attitudes as sins, claiming Christ's promise: "If we confess our sins, He is faithful and just and will forgive us our sins and purify us from all unrighteousness" John 1:9, NIV).

Darien's knowledge of the Scriptures is exceptional. Her insight into the male ego seems phenomenal to me. Her words really hit home when she talked about accepting your husband as he is, and helping him to like himself. She said that a man who is not happy with himself cannot possibly relate correctly and lovingly toward his wife.

Right after that particular lesson I read an article in the newspaper about husbands running around on their wives. The majority of people think the reason is sex, but the report said that most straying husbands were looking for someone who would admire them, praise them, and love them as they are.

Of course, that is exactly what God commanded a wife to do. I became aware that a man needed to feel love, security, importance; then he becomes liberated to love, protect, and honor his wife. As Darien was quoting these biblical truths, I understood the need in my marriage to make Dusty feel important, admired, liberated.

Dusty was out of town for a week when I started the course. The day that he was to return, I received a call saying he wouldn't be back for two more weeks. I knew how he must have hated to call and tell me that.

Normally I would have gotten mad. This time I said

nothing unpleasant. I told him I really appreciated his calling, to take care of himself, and to get home as soon as he could. Before he hung up, I said softly, "Dusty, I love you."

At the next lesson, Darien asked us if we had ever thanked our husbands for making us a living. I certainly never had. I thought that was simply his duty.

A few nights later, Dusty called again. He began telling me how hard he had been working. This presented an excellent opportunity for me to thank him. I said, "Honey, have I ever thanked you for making us such a good living, or told you how much we appreciate the hard work you do?"

There was stunned silence on the other end. I continued the conversation, talking about the children, and asking Dusty about himself.

When he got time I began rebuilding the ego I had bruised. I told him, "You have got to have the broadest, most beautiful shoulders in the world." That was the beginning—and I am still learning. Now when there is furniture to be moved or heavy jobs to be done, I ask Dusty to do them for me. Afterward I thank him, and compliment his ability to do them so easily.

One afternoon he asked me to go to a baseball game. "I'd love to," I said. My heart almost broke as I saw his face light up. He was thrilled. I thought of the many times I had denied him my company and bound him because of it. Bound him, because there were many places he would have gone but I refused, and he didn't want to go alone.

We had a marvelous time at the game. I don't mean to imply that I fell in love with baseball. I didn't. But the joy in my husband's heart and eyes were payment enough!

Many times Dusty used to ask me to walk in the rain with him. I thought that was the dumbest idea I ever heard. Since I learned the joy of giving happiness instead of being obsessed with my own desires, he hasn't yet asked me—but you'd better believe every time it rains I sit expectantly waiting. This time, I'll go.

All during our marriage I had tried to make Dusty fill the

void in my life that I now realize only Christ can fill. By allowing Christ to enter in, all those self-centered desires that caused us so much pain and frustration have completely gone.

I'm amazed how beautiful life can be when I follow God's plan for a wife. How serene life can be when a wife is under her husband's "umbrella of authority and protection," as Darien teaches.

We certainly haven't reached perfection. No one will until Christ takes us to heaven. But when we do have disagreements I have learned to say, "I'm sorry." Those two words had never been in my vocabulary where Dusty was concerned.

A few weeks ago Dusty told me he looked forward to coming home to be with me because it was so much fun. He shared how much he enjoyed our quiet times alone. *Praise the Lord*—I have waited eagerly to hear that!

I have learned the reality of appreciating my husband; I now know the magic of praise, the simple, binding beauty of the words, "thank you."

This summer we drove to Gatlinburg and took our friend Phyllis along. As we stopped for lunch, Dusty began talking. "Phyllis," he said, "you know since Chris learned God's plan for her as a woman, our marriage has completely changed. I wish next fall you would go with her to that seminar. I know you think things are over for you and Jerry, but with Christ nothing is impossible."

It is now Dusty who is recommending Darien's seminar. When we arrived in Gatlinburg, I shared with some of our friends the wonderful changes that had taken place in our relationship. I was so thrilled with what I had learned that I wanted to share these truths with other women.

I had ordered a complete set of Darien's tapes. With Dusty's encouragement I invited some friends over to begin a tape class. I was amazed at the number of women who were hungry to know God's will for their lives. We had 25 women in attendance, and this was our first attempt at a home study. Through the class, two women came to know Jesus Christ as their personal Saviour and others have written since we returned to Atlanta that they are beginning to see wonderful changes in their marriages.

I thank God for a Saviour who has completely filled the longing and void in my life. I know He can do the same for anyone who sincerely seeks Him. For those who are enmeshed in the web of self-centeredness, for those who never appreciated the man they married, for those who think that maybe they married the wrong man, I want to say . . . STOP . . . the Lord can change all that! Think for one minute what that man of yours might be if *you* became completely available to the Lord!

Well, the roar of the football crowd for my Dusty is long silent. But I thank You, Lord, that my praises will go on and on!

Reminiscing with Darien:

Chris had just returned to Atlanta after spending the summer in Gatlinburg, Tennessee, and my heart warmed as she shared how God had used her to help other women claim God's blessings for them as wives. She said, "The amazing part of it is that I didn't plan anything; it just 'happened.' That's unusual for me because I am normally a planner." I rejoiced with her over the thrills that come from being available to Christ's plan for our lives.

Chris' life parallels Eve's, the first woman, in many ways (Gen. 3). Chris never intentionally set out to hurt her husband and children. Like Eve, her downfall came from following her desires rather than God's plan. She discovered as Eve did that her actions had a far-reaching influence on her husband and children.

Our nature and desires apart from Christ's purifying power are selfish and demanding. Chris learned that Christian behavior involved more than going to church on Sunday and wanting to be a good wife and mother. She had to learn God's will through His Word, then to make His ways become a reality in her life by His power. She learned that happiness was achieved by being in right relationship with God and seeking to meet her husband's needs rather than trying to get her own needs met.

As Chris praised Dusty's admirable traits, she observed that he began to love, protect, and cherish her as never before. She helped him like himself by building his self-esteem or self-image. He, in turn, was loving her as he loved himself (Eph. 5:28–29).

Sharing Dusty's interests and hobbies made Chris a part of her husband in a deeper way. She learned the joy of sending her husband off on a weekend hunting trip because she wanted him to be happy. She now listens when he talks, not necessarily because she's enthralled with the subject but because she can discover in this way how Dusty feels and thinks.

Chris' experiences confirm that a wife regulates the home atmosphere as a thermostat controls the temperature of the house. As she seeks to comfort, encourage, and bring happiness to her family, she basks in the same benefits.

Thinking Through with You:

Question: *How does God say a good wife responds to her husband?*
Answer: "She will comfort, encourage, and do him good as long as there is life within her" (Prov. 30:12, AMP).

Q.: *What attitudes and actions of a wife build the husband's confidence?*
A.: "Let the wife see that she respects and reverences her husband—that she notices him, regards him, honors him, prefers him, venerates and esteems him; and that she defers to him, praises him, and loves and admires him exceedingly (Eph. 5:33, AMP.).

Q.: *In God's created order, what is woman's role in relation to the man?*
A.: "The woman is the glory of man" (1 Cor. 11:7, NIV).

Q.: *How will service and submission to your husband benefit both of you?*
A.: "Husbands ought to love their own wives as their own bodies. He who loves his wife loves himself. After all, no one ever hated his own body, but he feeds and cares for it" (Ephesians 5:28-29, NIV).

4
He Has the Same Heart Toward Me

Renate Dowler

Unless you've been through it, you can't realize the turmoil of being in the middle of the ocean, leaving your homeland and family, and heading toward a strange place where your beloved awaits you.

Even now, years later, I can remember the clashing pain and happiness in my heart as I left my family in Germany and traveled toward America to join my husband-to-be.

I would lie awake nights in my stateroom, my thoughts racing faster than the propellers of the S.S. *United States* as they churned through the mighty ocean. Early in the morning I would get up and climb to the empty deck to stand quietly as the wind blew away my tears.

"Ach," I would tell myself, "how foolish you are, to feel happy and sad at the same time."

One moment my mind would be filled with thoughts of Paul, our coming marriage, and his country that would be mine. It was a wonderful place, he said.

The next moment, as I looked over the rail at the deep and ageless sea, homesickness would sweep over me.

Munich. How I loved my home. It had been so beautiful—before the war.

Until I began this long journey, every day of my life had been spent in Munich. When the air was pure and silvery, I could see the Bavarian Alps from my window.

As a child I'd perch in a windowseat and watch the people pass below—merchants rushing to deliver their wares and women pushing their baby carriages to the park.

School, skiing in the nearby mountains, church, and Christmas were memorable parts of a normal childhood in Munich. Then came Adolf Hitler and the war. Bombs fell all around us and fires burned day after horrible day, night after endless night.

When it was over, Munich was a hollow shell of her former self. One-third of her homes had been destroyed and three-quarters of her buildings were in ruins. Then the foreign occupation began.

The townspeople began to rebuild—binding up the wounds of our beautiful city. Once again the tortured earth began to spring alive with grass and trees and crops.

Our soldiers began to return, some in wooden boxes, some broken in body, and others in spirit, but like a child struggling for its first breath, we all began to live again.

Khaki uniforms, leather boots, jazz, and American faces became a constant reminder of our defeat. The G.I.s built a replacement depot near our town. It was a stop-off where soldiers were sent for reassignment to other areas or cleared for return to the States.

I began working at the depot as a clerk in the snack bar. One afternoon as I sat in the snack bar talking to my friend Helga, a tall, broad-shouldered American soldier approached our table.

"May I have a cigaret?" he asked.

We replied in German that we didn't understand. Actually, we knew what he wanted.

He pointed to the cigarets and again asked for one. I laughed and stopped my masquerade to speak to him. In broken English, I introduced Helga and myself.

He said his name was Paul, Paul Dowler.

We exchanged the usual information—where do you work, what do you do, etc. The three of us talked for awhile, and then the conversation seemed to narrow down to Paul and me. He asked me many questions about Germany, the war, customs, and personal things. He asked me to write in German things like Munich, Renate, and the main streets and theaters. We had a pleasant afternoon and then said goodbye.

One afternoon a few weeks later I saw a jeep stop in front of our house. Momma said, "Renate, that looks like an American man coming here. I wonder who he is looking for."

My heart was fluttering inside. "Momma, I know him," I said. It was Paul. I couldn't believe it.

"Well, you go out there; tell him to come on in," she ordered. She acted like inviting Americans into one's home was a normal occurrence, which it certainly wasn't.

I was terribly embarrassed. What if the neighbors should see me? At this time in Germany, a girl could ruin her reputation by dating an American. This feeling was not directed against the soldier personally; most people just felt it wasn't right to date "the enemy."

There was an old saying which still expressed the feeling in my country: "Honor that you stay in your own country and that you stay with your own people."

Neighbors' opinions, old sayings, and the like were soon forgotten, however, as I began to date the genial American on a steady basis. Paul was in the Air Police, and instead of being a temporary soldier passing through he was permanently stationed in Munich.

After the confinement of war I found almost everything fascinating outside my home. Much of our time was spent in night clubs. I had discovered dancing and I couldn't get enough. The GI bands beat out the songs popularized during those years, and we "swung and swayed" to "Now Is the Hour" and "Tuxedo Junction." For the next four years the world was ours and we savored every moment we spent together.

Then one day a piece of paper dropped like a huge oak into the gears of my merry-go-round world: Paul's new orders. Somebody in the U.S. who seemed to be related to everyone—"Uncle Sam" the boys called him—wanted Paul back in America.

Months before, Paul and I had realized that our time together was not a passing interlude. We truly and deeply loved each other. When Paul's orders came through, he asked me to return with him as his wife.

"Wife"—what a beautiful word. "Mrs. Paul Dowler"—what a beautiful sound that had.

Excitement coursed through my body as a new world flashed into view. When I returned home that afternoon my feet hardly touched the floor. I burst through the front door yelling, "Momma, Momma! Paul wants to marry me and take me home with him."

Momma faced me silently.

"Momma," I cried, "do you hear what I'm saying? Paul wants to marry me. He loves me!"

Momma sat down and waited till I calmed down. Then she said, "Renate, I want to tell you something. I think the thing you do is—you let Paul go home first, alone. You know, Paul has been away for a long time."

Momma seemed to think that perhaps Paul was just passing time with me; maybe there was a girl back in the States. Possibly he'd feel differently about me when he was again in familiar surroundings.

"Renate, you just let him go," she said, "and then wait and see if he still has the same heart toward you."

I waited as Momma asked. Then one day a letter arrived from Roswell, Georgia, U.S.A. A letter from Paul! When I opened the envelope, a bank draft for my passage fare drifted to the floor. As I read his message of love, the letter blurred before my eyes as tears of joy rolled down my cheeks.

All I could say was, "Momma, oh, Momma, Paul, he has the same heart toward me."

Now that I am older, I can understand how my family must

have dreaded seeing me off on that ship carrying me so far away. But there was no other way for me.

The long days and nights on the ship came to an end finally. I will never forget the excitement as we neared New York Harbor. The deck was crowded with passengers on their first ocean voyage, and they were filled with the awe and expectation of a child at his first Christmas.

There she stood, the Statue of Liberty, the symbol of everything this land of promise held for us. There were tears and cries of joy, each person reacting in his own way. What a day!

"Oh, America," I thought, "you are truly beautiful."

In New York City I boarded a train to Atlanta, Georgia, where Paul awaited me. I met Paul's family—his mother Ruth, his brother Donald, and his sister Carol. They were all so warm and welcoming.

Ruth helped me so much with our wedding plans. She contacted the minister of her church, who arranged to perform our ceremony in his study.

The big day came. As I got ready, standing before the mirror, I wished that Momma and my sisters could be with me to share my wedding day. My dress was white linen with long, graceful sleeves. I'd put my long, dark hair up in a large bun and fluffed out curls all around my face.

During the service I looked every minute at Paul. He looked so handsome with his sparkling blue eyes and dark-blond hair. So neat and distinguished in his blue serge suit.

After the ceremony we said our good-byes to Paul's family and enjoyed a quiet dinner before driving to the Henry Grady Hotel where we spent our wedding night.

The splendor of that day was going to have to last a long time, for we rented a small, old apartment in the Buckhead area of Atlanta. Three dull-gray rooms with hardwood floors and bare walls became our first home.

Paul carried a complete course in law school and then worked a full-time job in the afternoons and evenings. There was just enough money to fill our basic needs. But it was thrilling as we began our life together—and such fun.

A friend of Ruth's donated an iron bed. And an old dresser was rescued from somebody's garage. At first there was no table to eat at nor chairs to sit on. We were the proud owners of two spoons and two knives; most of our meals were eaten from cans as we dined on our big iron bed!

One day I had the opportunity to do some sewing for a lady who lived near us. I took great pains to make every stitch perfect. When finished I received four dollars for my work!

What a grand time I had with that money! I bought a 75-cent aluminum coffee pot, a hammer, two dishes, and a cannister set.

I'm sure the emperors of Rome, lying on satin pillows and feasting on grapes, could not have known the pleasure that Paul and I shared during those days.

I suppose we could have used extra money, but I never went to work. Paul never wanted me to take a job, and I considered it a real privilege to stay home. My experience as a child contributed to my attitude about working wives. My mother worked in a mill during my childhood and I silently resented it. Daddy was a hard-working man who provided well for his family. Momma worked because of her desire for unnecessary extras.

I was jealous of my friends whose mothers stayed home. Their mothers were always there to pack their lunch and slip in that special piece of cake baked early in the morning, and at home to greet them when school was out.

There was always work for me with Momma gone so much —dishes, cooking, and cleaning. And those important talks—moments to share a special joy or disappointment—didn't fit well into Momma's schedule. I determined then that if I ever married, even if we had to eat beans out of a can, I'd never work outside my home.

Between Paul's work and his studies, we had very little time together. Aching loneliness took root in my soul. I felt, "Here I am in America in a three-room apartment with nothing to do." Some days I'd wax and rewax the floors just to keep busy. And the ache grew.

Some afternoons I'd stand by the window watching cars returning home from the day's work. I would think back to Germany and wish, "Oh, if I could just go home." It was a confused feeling I couldn't understand because I was happy with Paul; we had a beautiful marriage.

My desolate feeling was soon replaced by a wonderful one: I discovered I was expecting a baby.

Paul and I were blessed with a beautiful, blue-eyed, black-haired girl. We named her Anna. That baby was the biggest thrill of my life.

Paul was so busy that I immersed myself with the baby. I would read to her and we would play. My life revolved around Anna. For a time she quenched all my feelings of loneliness.

One evening after I'd put Anna to bed, I walked through the living room and was attracted by music coming from the TV. Like many other "poor" people, we had a big TV.

On the television screen I saw a stately looking man standing before a massive crowd and singing the most beautiful song I'd ever heard. The words, "Blessed assurance, Jesus is mine," floated through the room.

When the singer concluded, another tall, dignified man appeared and began speaking. It was Billy Graham.

I didn't know Billy Graham then. I'd never heard of him, and I didn't realize he was a minister. If I had known who he was, I wouldn't have listened because I had "my religion" and I wasn't looking for anything else.

The program was coming from a place called Madison Square Garden. Beyond the speaker's stand was a huge poster that read, "I Am the Way, the Truth, and the Life." Like the words Mr. Graham was speaking, I understood the meaning, but they had no relevance for me.

The only reason I watched was my hope of hearing more of that beautiful song. When the program ended, the announcer said they would be on again the following week.

I faithfully tuned in for the next couple of weeks, waiting for that song from George Beverly Shea. The song wasn't sung, but one evening as I watched, everything changed.

Mr. Graham was talking about the feeling of loneliness that I had experienced. He would say "lonely," and I completely identified with what he said. I still didn't know he was a minister. He could have said "The Bible says . . ." all evening long and it wouldn't have meant anything to me. We had many prayer books in our home, but no Bible. No one had ever taught us from the Bible, and I had never held one in my hand. I didn't even realize what it was—God's Word.

As he spoke I thought, "He's smart. I would really like to talk to him." There were feelings in me that I couldn't identify till he named them. The mysterious ache in my heart had proved that all the nice things in my life couldn't make me happy.

On previous telecasts I'd watched people go forward at the end of Mr. Graham's talk, and I wondered what they were doing. This time I thought, "If I were there, I would follow those people so I could talk to that man."

At that point Billy turned from the crowd and looked at me from the television screen. "You, there in the living room . . ." he said. That's where I was—and I felt he was talking to me personally. "You, too," he said, "if you have never accepted Jesus Christ as your Saviour you can do that right now!"

Paul was still at work and Anna was asleep. Slowly I slipped to my knees by the sofa and began to pray. I don't remember what I said; I wanted whatever that man had, whatever he was talking about.

I wept and I prayed. Sometime later I got up and turned the television off. I didn't want to be disturbed; I had such a beautiful, peaceful feeling. I just wanted to bathe myself in it.

The next week after watching Mr. Graham, I wrote down the address given by the announcer. I wanted to send this wonderful man a gift so I sent a whole dollar! I thought that was a lot.

His Minneapolis office began to send me little booklets called "Decision." I devoured each one as it came. At the back of each was a space to write your name and address if you'd made a decision for Christ. Each time I filled out all the blanks and then tucked the booklet away for safe keeping.

One evening a few weeks later I was sitting on the front porch when a car drove slowly by, stopped, and backed up. A young man got out and walked toward me. "There is a lady who looks like she needs a Bible," he announced. He said he had just finished work and was on his way home when he saw me.

I had never thought about a Bible, but I said, "Well, I need a Bible."

"What type of Bible do you want?" he asked. He said he had a King James Bible and a Catholic Bible.

I thought for a moment and said, "I think I'll take one of those King James kind." It was a huge, family-size Bible, but it felt light in my hands.

That evening I couldn't wait to read this book of God. I put Anna to bed and went to the kitchen with my big book. Opening it on our oilcloth-covered table, I began reading in "Revelation." I struggled through the whole book, noting seven-this and seven-that. "My goodness!" I thought, "I wonder what this is all pointing to," but continued on undiscouraged.

Soon after I had an intense desire to take Anna to church. Because of my religious background, I felt infants must be in church. I shared my feelings with Paul. As he and I were from very different backgrounds, we decided not to attend either of our former churches. We began to visit various churches that were new to us.

One had a minister who wore a robe and I felt at home. Having been raised in a ritualistic church, I found it almost impossible to listen to a minister if he wasn't wearing one. Yet I wasn't interested in listening to a preacher the night

I first tuned in to Billy Graham. I'm sure that if he had been wearing a robe he would never have caught me!

In time Paul and I moved into our first real home, and the Lord provided a Christian friend in my new neighborhood. Jan had a strong influence in my life. When I did not understand a verse in Scripture, she would patiently explain each word.

I was still reading from my giant Bible. I just drank it in. Some nights I propped myself up on my elbows in bed and read until 2 or 3 A.M. One evening Paul said, "Momma, you're going to need a smaller Bible." The very next day he bought me a small white one at the dime store. I was so proud of it.

Realizing what Bible study meant to me, I approached Jan with a new idea. "Stanley parties, Tupperware parties," I said, "why can't we have a party for the Lord? Let's get together and all of us will bring our Bibles and we'll sing and read the Bible together."

It turned out to be one of the sweetest times of fellowship, and I grew in my knowledge of God's Word. Those "parties for the Lord" continued for three years.

Our next-door neighbor, Ginny, attended our Bible study, and one evening after a visit I offered to walk home with her because her husband was away. She appreciated my company while she checked out her lonely house.

As we entered the hall, she said, "Renate, don't go until I get my gun out." Her husband had given her a revolver to make her feel safer. Reaching for the gun, her hand knocked it off the closet shelf and it hit the floor with an explosive crack! Pain ripped through my stomach and I sank to the floor. I grasped at the wound as blood flowed, and Ginny screamed, "Oh, my God, no!" She ran out of the house to get Paul. Soon the door flew open and Paul rushed in, pale but in control. He carried me to the car and raced for Piedmont Hospital.

As the car wheels whined over the pavement, Psalm 23 ran through my mind over and over almost as if the Lord had turned on a record for my heart. I knew I could die, but I had the sweetest peace; there was no fear at all.

I realized at this moment that Christ was the most important person in my life. Through the past three years this relationship had become more and more important, but I am strong-willed and I still had areas of my life in which I felt quite self-sufficient. Now, recognizing my desperate dependence on the Lord, my will was broken and I acknowledged that "all things do work together for good."

The doctors were frank with Paul. "She has a fifty-fifty chance. We just want you to be prepared."

Many prayers went up in my behalf during the crisis, and the Lord spared me.

When I was well enough to go out again, a friend took me to a neighborhood Bible class meeting in her area of Atlanta. The teacher was Darien Cooper. I wasn't at all sure I liked her authoritative approach. But she taught God's Word with a depth and conviction that I'd never heard. Her personal knowledge of Christ was reflected in everything she said.

I returned week after week, finding freedom from many ignorant hang-ups I'd acquired. She taught Ephesians in a thrilling way, and I first understood the Spirit-filled life as she taught from Romans. She opened so many doors of understanding that I have continued through the years to bring other women to her classes. I knew nothing about God's role for a wife until I heard Darien teaching it.

Paul was a Christian and always gentle with me. Because he disliked arguments, I usually got my way. In our earlier years I made the decisions on where we went and what we did. If Paul's suggestions didn't suit me, I'd persist until we agreed on my choice.

Our biggest area of disagreement was always Anna. When she was disobedient and needed a whipping, I'd beg, "Please, Paul, don't whip her, please."

"But she needs to be spanked," he'd say.

"No, you might hurt her."

"Renate, don't you know I wouldn't actually hurt her?"

I thought he'd spank her so hard he'd knock her kidneys loose or something—silly, real to me. I'd object until Paul gave up. Time after time it happened, and I thought I was protecting Anna.

Since I'd assumed the position of authority, Anna came to me when she got out of line and asked me to talk to her daddy. She knew that if she got her way with me I would handle Paul.

The few times I allowed Paul to spank Anna, she'd scream and scream so I'd feel her suffering. I'd go out in the backyard and stick my fingers in my ears; I just couldn't stand her crying.

When our arguments over Anna's disobedience got hot, Paul would say, "You'll be sorry one of these days," and walk out. He would sit in the yard, go to the basement, or just disapppear for ten or fifteen minutes. In time he'd return and say, "How about a cup of coffee, Momma?" I'd say, "OK." This coffee offering became our peace-making ritual. We never discussed our problems—we just poured coffee on them!

When Anna was 13, she began to develop a rebellious spirit. Boys, parties, and popularity became the prime interests in her life. One evening she supposedly left for a party at a girlfriend's house. About ten o'clock the phone rang and Paul answered. The blood drained from his face as he hung up the receiver.

"Who was it?" I asked.

"The police," he said in a quavering voice.

"What's happened?'

"I'll tell you on the way. Get your coat," he said. But a cold silence filled the car as we drove downtown.

Speaking to the police officer in charge, we found that Anna had been to a party, but her friend's parents weren't home. Drinking had begun early, and as the night progressed the house was completely torn apart. Neighbors had called the police because of the loud music. There was two thousand dollars worth of damage done to the house—but our concern was that Anna was safe.

Tears trickled down Anna's cheeks as we drove her home. The ordeal had been so frightening that I felt she had suffered enough.

I recognized that Anna had serious problems, and my solution was to nag at her. I'd demand changes and threaten punishment but never follow through. Like my mother before me, I was all talk and no action. Anna knew this and continued her rebellious ways.

It was a few years later that I heard from Darien about God's plan for me as a wife and mother. My heart broke as I realized how wrong my interference in Anna's discipline had been. Under Darien's teachings I began to adopt the principles set forth in God's Word. I stored each and every truth, not imagining how much I'd need them.

The situation with Anna continued to deteriorate. She cut classes at school and her honor roll grades dropped until she was hardly passing. She no longer looked lovely and feminine. Taking a bath became a traumatic experience for her.

There were symptoms all along the way, but I didn't know the danger signals. When Paul tried to intervene, I'd assure him: "She's in a different generation;" or, "She's only trying to impresss her friends." I really believed it.

Anna's slender figure all of a sudden began to fill out with unbecoming fat. She became moody, cheerful one day and down the next. She'd eat everything in the house and then not eat for days. Or lie in bed sleeping her life away, then spend periods of sleepless nights. I didn't know then that marijuana was making her very hungry, accounting for her weight gain, nor that she had begun to take amphetamines, accounting for her sleepless nights.

At 17, Anna had been dating a boy that Paul and I very much disapproved of. He was from a "good family" and attended one of Atlanta's outstanding private schools, but his affluent background was not apparent in his sloppy dress, rude manners, and lack of respect for his parents. He and

Anna left one evening for a movie. I wasn't to see her again for four days!

She was supposed to be home at midnight. When the clock struck one, fear began to swell inside me. The minutes and hours crept by . . . two . . . three . . . four o'clock . . . and an icy chill ran through me as the ringing of the phone broke into my quandary.

It was Anna. "Momma, let me talk to Daddy," she cried.

I called Paul to the phone and I listened to the conversation on the bedroom extension. She had been charged with possession of marijuana and accessory to car theft, she said. It seemed like hours passed as Anna begged for assistance and Paul talked.

I heard him say, "Anna, this is the very thing we tried to keep you from. This is why your Momma and I have counseled so with you. You didn't want to listen. You wanted your own way. You said you were going to do your own thing. Well, darling, you have arrived at the end of the road we tried to keep you from traveling. I'm sorry, but you'll just have to stay there . . . or call some of those friends you've been hanging around with. Baby, I'm sorry. We love you, but we won't bail you out of this one."

Thoughts and Bible principles kept flying through my mind. "Obey your husband, obey your husband," God said. "Don't let emotions run your life," echoed from my lessons with Darien Cooper.

When Paul hung up he slumped into a chair with a heavy sadness. My own heart was breaking for my child. Frightening thoughts and pictures whirled through my thoughts. I had heard about horrid jail conditions. I envisioned Anna coming in contact with hardened criminals or perverts.

I prayed: "Father, in James 1:5 You say 'If any of you lacks wisdom, he should ask God . . . and it will be given to him.' Dear Father, I claim that promise for Paul and me right now. Give us the wisdom to handle this situation for Your glory and Anna's benefit. I ask that you make me willing to accept this decision Paul has made. Father, I'm trusting Anna to You. You protect her. You draw her to Yourself. In Christ's name, Amen."

As each new day came, Anna would call for help, and each time Daddy would say, "No."

During this time the Lord so beautifully kept His Word and His promises before us. Our home was calm, with a "peace that passes understanding."

Four days later as Paul and Anna talked, I heard him say, "I'll see what I can do."

When he hung up, he said simply, "She's broken."

A few hours later, a tired but calm girl reentered our home. I took Anna in my arms and we both wept with blessed relief.

"Momma," she said, "you know when Daddy refused to come get me, I got so scared. There was a pain of loneliness shooting through my whole body. But, Momma, last night something happened. I realized the mess I was in; I knew I had gotten here all on my own. I thought back to the talks you and Daddy had with me. How you'd told me about Jesus and His love. I thought that by becoming a Christian I'd lose all my freedom, all my individuality. Sitting in that jail cell, I knew that grass had been warping my view. Amphetamines were twisting my decisions. Pressure from my friends motivated my actions. And sitting behind bars was far from being free. I hadn't been in control at all—I saw it. You know what I did, Momma?"

"No; what did you do, Baby?"

"I got down on my knees before God and all the women in my cell and prayed. I said, 'Lord, it's just You and me now. You're the only One who can help me. Momma and Daddy told me about You, so right now, Lord Jesus, I'm trusting You for me.' After that, a real peace settled. I'm so sorry I've hurt you and Daddy, but with Jesus I know things will be different."

It was time for my confession. "Anna," I said, "I want to apologize to you, too. I so wanted you to be happy that I often interfered with your daddy's discipline. I'm sure you could have learned this lesson much younger and in a much less devastating way if I hadn't been so out of line."

We stood there, silently facing each other and holding hands. There were no more words, but an inner "Thank You, Lord." At that moment the Lord broke through our generation gap.

Each day Christ molds and shapes Anna into the beautiful woman He is creating. His presence has touched every part of her life. The rebellious will is broken. Through an undrugged mind, she is again making good grades.

The old group is gone. Anna learned the truth of Proverbs 13:20: "He who walks [as a companion] with wise men shall be wise, but he who associates with [self-confident] fools will [be a fool himself and] shall smart for it" (AMP).

Before I learned my position as a Christian wife, before I understood Christ's chain of authority, I would have reacted much differently to a crisis with Anna—possibly sentencing our precious daughter to disaster. Christ has been so patient with each of us.

Each time Darien begins a new session of her course, Paul joins me in inviting women to attend. My car is always loaded with a new group, and secretly I anticipate how beautiful those faces will be when they see what Christ has waiting for them.

I know there will be times when I stumble, but I know, too, that Christ will always have "the same heart" of love toward me.

Reminiscing with Darien:

God was gracious in giving me such a precious friend as Renate. Initially I was captivated by her radiant love for Jesus Christ and her unreserved care for others. She literally glows with excitement for the Christian life; boredom isn't in her vocabulary. At almost every Bible class she joyfully shared a fresh truth or insight she'd gained from God's Word. Her simple, straight-forward way of presenting these truths could cut deep into one's heart and at the same time stir praise to God.

Even as a new Christian, Renate seemed to sense that the way to grow spiritually was to know and trust God's Word, not others' experiences. An emotion or experience can change with one's physical health, emotional state, or spiritual condition. "Good" experiences can even be counterfeited by Satan! Spiritual guidelines should never be based on them. God has provided knowledge of His will through passages, principles, and doctrines in His Word. The Holy Spirit enables the receptive spirit to understand and apply these truths in daily life.

For real stability in life, it is essential that God's way of thinking becomes ours. This is accomplished by transferring God's truths from His printed Word to our minds. Without this personal knowledge of God's Word, our thoughts and actions will be conformed to this world's flawed ways. (Romans 12:1, 2)

Renate had interfered with God's most gentle form of leading a child: the father's authority in the home. Therefore God used a harsher authority, civil law, to break Anna's rebellious will. When one learns to submit to human authority, it is much easier to be obedient to Christ's authority in our spiritual life. Anna missed this privilege in her early years.

Through her mother's new obedience to Paul, Anna is helped to be obedient to her parents. Renate realizes that Anna's attitude toward authority is more important than the particular issue being discussed. Isn't it sobering to realize that children learn important attitudes from their parents!

Should you meet Renate, you'll recognize her by her love for God's Word. She's walking evidence that "man shall not live by bread alone, but on every word that proceeds out of the mouth of God" (Matt. 4:4).

Thinking Through with You:

Question: *What is a big clue—to you and God—as to the real person you are?*
Answer: "As he thinks within himself, so he is" (Proverbs 23:7, NASB).

Q.: *How explicitly has God provided so that His thoughts and ways may become ours?*
A.: "All Scripture is inspired by God and profitable for teaching, for reproof, for correction, for training in righteousness; that the man of God may be adequate, equipped for every good work" (2 Tim. 3:16-17, NASB).

Q.: *Why should you study God's Word?*
A.: "Your Word have I laid up in my heart, that I might not sin against You" (Ps. 119:11, AMP.).

Q.: *How may we gain a greater appetite for the spiritual food of God's Word?*
A.: "Taste and see that the Lord is good; blessed is the man who trusts in Him" (Ps. 34:8 BERK).

5
View Through A Bottle

Doanne Freig

The waves were draped in hues of gold, orange, and pink as the sun dipped below the horizon. Jon and I had spent many evenings like this, holding hands, walking the beach, talking, and planning. Through the past year of dating we had become soul-mates in the purest sense of the word. But this day was different.

The beach was the same, the waves still beat rhythmically against the shore, but anguish brimmed in our hearts. Jon was going away to Duke University, and it seemed so far from Miami. He'd become such a part of my life that the idea of being separated was almost more than I could bear. We left the beach that day knowing that months would separate our next moments together.

With Jon in North Carolina, my senior year in high school crept by. Our letters challenged the capacity of the U.S. Postal Service. Even at long distance, we decided we wanted a spring wedding. Jon's parents, however, felt Jon should complete his education before marriage, and we reluctantly agreed to wait.

For graduation, my parents gave me a trip to North Carolina. I would stay with Jon's sister, who lived near the university. As the bus whizzed over the flat openness of north Florida, past the tall buildings in Atlanta, and into the rolling hills of North Carolina, my thoughts were constantly on Jon.

We had a beautiful reunion—there was so much to talk about, so many things to share, and so much love to express! As we discussed our loneliness, the promises we'd made to delay marriage began to evaporate.

Jon suddenly ruffled my hair and said, "Sweetheart, let's stop all this talking and get married!"

"Married?" I said.

"Yes, some of the guys told me about a justice of the peace not far from here. There's no reason to wait; I love you and I want you for my wife. There is no point in upsetting our parents, so we'll just keep it our secret."

"Oh, Jon, yes, yes," I exclaimed.

This day was to be a mixture of joy and regret. In front of a business-like justice of the peace, Jon and I became husband and wife. I was full of love for him, but my heart ached for the beautiful wedding I had dreamed of, which now I would never have.

A few weeks after I returned home, I found that rising each morning was a chore. Waves of nausea greeted me each new day. I didn't need a doctor to tell me that I was carrying Jon's child. As soon as I shared the news with Jon, he returned to Miami.

A few days later, I stood in front of my parents' house waving goodbye to Jon as he drove off in his blue sports car for Montgomery, Alabama, to tell his parents about our marriage.

Jon's parents, Bill and Edith, had made a new life for themselves in this country. They had left Belgium when Hitler's armies invaded. His father had established a thriving restaurant business, and his mother devoted herself to the family.

Jon's father wasn't home when he arrived. Jon told his mother about our marriage, and she took the news well, but she convinced Jon it would be better if she told Bill. Jon's father drank heavily and had high blood pressure, and she wasn't sure how he would react. She was afraid, and her fear kept her from breaking the news. Jon finally told his dad in a letter—not the best way to start out with one's in-laws!

Jon left Duke and took a job in Miami with a large engineering firm. We found a darling apartment near Haulover Beach, and for the next two years we lived contentedly. Our baby's birth completed the circle of our happiness.

The first time we visited Jon's parents after our marriage, Bill welcomed me with genuine warmth. Unfortunately, there was a strain between Edith and me from the beginning.

Our ethnic backgrounds made a great difference in our ideas and opinions. I found that one doesn't marry just a man; one truly marries into a family, for better or for worse!

Yet my disagreements with Edith seemed minor compared with the arguments Jon had with his father on subsequent visits.

Bill felt that we should move to Montgomery. He wanted to pass his restaurant business on to his son, and he expected Jon to respect his wishes. Jon didn't want to change jobs, and Bill was determined to make him. After a few drinks and Jon's continued refusal, Bill would storm: "How come you don't care about me? If you had any decency you'd take over the place I've prepared for you!"

One day Jon received a call from Bill. He wanted us to move to Montgomery so Jon could work in the newest restaurant he wanted to buy. Bill said he needed Jon to help carry the work load.

After discussing it, we decided to give it a try. But we decided that Jon would take a regular job and help Bill in his spare time until we knew if "restauranting" was what we really wanted.

I was enthralled by the beauty of southern Alabama. The tall oaks and cedars draped in Spanish moss made me feel a part of the graceful past.

We had hardly unpacked our suitcases when Jon informed me he wouldn't seek other employment. His father had persuaded him to go directly into the restaurant business full-time.

Our original understanding was shattered and I was deeply hurt. I felt Jon had betrayed my trust and I very much resented the influence of his father. I felt Jon had no right to make this decision without consulting me.

Almost overnight, the strained relationship between Jon and Bill changed. They found a new friendship through socializing. Drinking and staying out late seemed to be a part of every business deal!

My fascination with the spreading oaks, Spanish moss, and graceful mansions wore off. This beautiful country had become a threat. I complained to Jon, telling him that I wanted to go home. Our arguments became frequent. I'd tell Jon I was sorry we'd ever moved, that since our move our marriage was going down the drain.

Material gains weren't worth what was happening to us, I tried to explain. I was lonely, I felt isolated in the unfamiliar surroundings, and I didn't like him to be away from home night after night.

When Jon was drinking—which seemed to be most of the time—he'd blame me. "You're never satisfied! You're always complaining," he'd shout. When sober, he would see things as they were and tell me, "I know I treat you bad, but things are going to be different." But they weren't, and I saw Jon starting down the same road his father had gone. I felt miserable and trapped, and my anguished complaints just seemed to drive Jon out more and more.

I shared my fears with the only person I was close to, Jon's mother. She had compensated for lonely hours and lack of love through her daughter and grandchildren. I knew that could never provide a substitute for me.

Jon and Bill would get together with business friends for lunch, have a few drinks, and add a few more until the afternoon was gone. They'd move from the Diplomat to the Embers and on and on. It was a time of high living for Jon.

Many midnights passed while I waited up for Jon, and

usually he would come in drunk. I had never known anyone with an alcohol problem and I was incapable of coping with it. Our late-night arguments followed a pattern:

"Where have you been? Why didn't you call?"

"I've been out getting drunk and I'm stoned."

"Jon, I want a divorce. I simply can't live this way."

"Get one. I don't care. Get one; just walk out and leave."

It wasn't any use fighting. Nothing ever changed. He wouldn't leave and I felt that I couldn't leave because of the children. I know he wanted me to stay but to allow him to behave as he pleased.

Many times I felt like calling Mom and Dad and asking them if I could come home. Then I'd realize they had no idea we were having problems. As far as they knew, we were blissfully happy, and deep down I hated for them to think badly of Jon. It was hell on earth for me; I didn't know whom to turn to or what to do.

I needed Jon so much, his love, his attention, the talks we used to have. As his drinking increased, our sex life almost came to a halt. When Jon did make attempts at physical love, half of me would be thrilled but the other half would be so bitter that I couldn't respond to him.

One evening we attended a glittering party given by one of Jon's business associates. It was held in a back yard, and Chinese lanterns swung gracefully from huge oaks. The reflections danced on the ripples of a pool. It was the same old crowd with the same old problems, but something was different.

Jon had wandered off, talking, drink in hand, leaving me sitting alone. I watched the people like actors in a play, and felt absolutely isolated. The lilting voice of Dionne Warwick whispered the words of "A House is Not a Home," and the message cut deep.

"Doanne," a voice said. I looked up and saw a tall, quite attractive man, some years my senior. We'd met briefly once before. It was common knowledge that he had long-standing marital problems.

He said, "You are looking even more attractive than the last time I saw you." My heart leaped. I was hungry for masculine compliments and attention; it had been so long since Jon had given me any. I thanked him for the compliment, and he called me "adorable" and invited me to lunch. We sat and talked for a long time. The conversation was liberally seasoned with flattering, flirting overtones. The evening was going to my head.

I never gave him a clear answer on the lunch offer. I think I wanted to go—but I was afraid. Only my inbred morality stopped me. The right part of me thought "No," but the wrong part of me was saying, "Why not? What else is left for you? You're young. You're attractive. What are you going to do—wait all your life for Jon?"

Before my wrong side could win, I discovered I was expecting our third child. I considered this the worst thing that could happen. Our youngest was just 18 months old, and the thought of having two babies devastated me. When I shared the news with Jon, he was jolted too. But he never knew how the pregnancy shattered my morale. I had just gotten my weight down and was feeling I looked attractive when the bad news shredded my struggling pride.

Jon's drinking and staying out became worse. The pregnancy plus our problems continually drained me. I'd stay up until three or four o'clock in the morning waiting for Jon, dying inside night by night. The mental torment was almost more than I could bear.

When our daughter was born, she was ill and the doctors feared she had spinal meningitis and wouldn't live. At this point I made a weak attempt at prayer, but I didn't know God. It was one of those, "God, help me; I've got in over my head" prayers. It turned out that the baby wasn't as seriously ill as the doctors thought.

I felt guilty because I hadn't wanted the baby, but in my need seeds were planted in my heart which would take root later. My doctor tried to calm me during the crisis with the baby, but instead of tranquilizers he prescribed: "Try prayer,

Doanne; God can do much more for you than drugs ever can." I was impressed because I respected Dr. Lawrence, and I'd never heard a doctor talk like that. I thought long about this, and the words became implanted in the inner reaches of my mind.

After our daughter's recovery, things began to fall into the same old disorder. But God had begun to draw me to Himself.

Six weeks later, my sister's illness was to make me realize how temporal this life is. It was a comparatively quiet Sunday afternoon when the telephone rang. Jon answered and when he hung up he told me that my sister was in the hospital. She had cancer and they had already removed her right breast.

I screamed, "O God, no," and collapsed in tears. Everything inside of me cried out for God's help. I knew there had to be more. For the first time in my life, my eyes turned from my wretched situation to God alone, and the best I knew how, I asked Him into my life.

I began to going to a nearby church. I had been born into a family that taught the moral "rights and wrongs," but there was no earnest discussion or personal knowledge of Jesus Christ. Hungrily I began to read my Bible, to seek God's will, and to pray.

One woman who attended this church, Linda, obviously knew Jesus Christ personally. She stood out in the crowd of once-a-week church attenders. I sought her out and shared with her the fact that I'd just turned my life over to God and I wanted to grow.

Linda introduced me to her friend Sara who was also a Christian. Through these friends, I found growth, instruction, and a new church where God's Word was taught faithfully.

I first noticed a change in myself one day when I spilled boiling water on my foot. The old Doanne would have cussed a blue streak. But I just thought, "Gee, does that hurt!" I found myself hurrying through my housework so that I could read my Bible and spend a quiet time with God.

One afternoon I was reading in Matthew and pondering

the meaning of chapter 10, verse 36. It said, "And a man's foes shall be they of his own household." I puzzled at this because I felt close to my family and couldn't understand how they could ever be against me for becoming a Christian. I was soon to learn its meaning.

In my new role as a Christian, I had begun caring for my husband's needs rather than nurturing my own disappointments. Jon questioned me about the change in attitude. "Doanne, you look different," he said, "what's happened to you?"

I felt that now was the time to tell him. "Jon, I've found Christ. I've repented of my sins. I'm not afraid of death. There's something more, Jon!"

He got terribly angry. I could see it swelling up in his eyes. Sullenly he answered, "We're different. We're growing apart."

I wondered how much further apart we could possibly get, but still his words hurt. I then recalled what I had read in Matthew that morning and I knew God had been preparing me for Jon's reaction. As I focused my thoughts and faith in Christ, I was flooded with the peace and assurance that He had our marriage well in hand.

From that evening on Jon got worse. His drinking increased. Before, he'd come home drunk and I would do the hollering; now he'd yell and curse me.

The more the battle raged in Jon, the more peace the Lord seemed to give me. During this time I could take anything he could dish out and still be happy because for the first time my happiness wasn't dependent on Jon's actions and moods. But my faith was tested more severely as I heard Jon say things and watched him do things I never dreamed would come from him.

Jon came in one morning, dead drunk, with flames of hostility blazing in his heart. Using the phone downstairs, he asked the operator to ring our number. When I answered on the bedroom phone, he said, "Listen you——, come down here and make my dinner." I thought, "Lord, help me do this." It was 4 A.M. and I had to grit my teeth to remain composed, but I went down and fixed his dinner.

My calm attitude angered him more. He was feeling guilty and he wanted me to lash back and justify his own rotten actions.

He tried to provoke me with crude conversation, but I was rejoicing inside because I could see the conviction of the Lord showering down on him. I knew that as long as I could behave in obedience to the Lord, *He* would deal with Jon. I prayed, "Lord, help me learn this lesson now. I don't want to wander in the wilderness for 40 years like the Israelites did." It was hard at times to respond lovingly to Jon's outbursts, but each time that I held my tongue the next time was easier. It is difficult to describe what Christ did during this time except to say He provided a "peace that passes all understanding."

It was truly a troubled, puzzling time. One moment Jon would curse me and in the next he would say, "You're really wonderful and I'm glad for the peace you've found. Maybe someday it will happen to me—just not right now. I'm not ready." Tears would well up in his eyes and there would be aching silence.

Over a period of ten months, the conflict inside Jon raged on. There were times when my immature knowledge of Christianity put more strain on our relationship. Soon after coming to know Christ, I began to change overt things that I felt weren't the "Christian" thing to do. I lost my desire to go to cocktail parties, so I refused to accompany Jon to them. Jon reacted strongly to this "holier-than-thou" attitude. Without words, I was telling him, "What you are doing is wrong. I don't approve of you or your actions." He couldn't comprehend what was happening to me, and I spoiled my mute testimony by giving him the idea that Christianity was a collection of no-no's.

I was so hungry for God's Word that I read my Bible often. In the evening when I went to bed I read. The picture of me sitting in bed reading my Bible stirred more anger and recrimination in Jon. He struck out verbally because I was making the difference between us more pronounced. I had decided to do what I thought was Christian whether Jon liked it or not.

At a series of neighborhood Bible studies I began to realize that my dogmatic approach was wrong. Friends lent me helpful books, and I listened to teaching tapes. I learned it was my place to submit to my husband. I found that I didn't know anything about the role of a Christian wife.

Christ honored my struggling attempts and immature faith by continual encouragement. He gave me the willingness and love to obey my husband in whatever he asked. It seemed that the Lord cut down the flow of party invitations, but when we did go the Lord provided opportunities for me to share my faith. While Jon was socializing, the Lord often brought someone my way who was hungry to find the same answers I had found.

As the Lord slowly changed my attitudes and responses and gave me a deeper love for my husband, Jon revolted more and more. He knew how to interact with the old Doanne, but the new Doanne upset all his calculations. He retaliated with fiendish ingenuity, and his tactics would have conquered me if Christ had not been recasting my life. Because of Him, there was love instead of manipulation, stability instead of fragility. But I didn't have complete victory yet.

One morning Jon left for work and I didn't see him until the next evening. He had left the office with his friend, Joe; they had gotten drunk and hopped a plane to California. He bought a round-trip ticket for both of them. This foolishness came to well over $600.

As the hours crept by that night, Joe's wife began calling, terribly upset, looking for him. I was praying, trying to keep my thoughts on the Lord and asking Him to keep my husband safe wherever he was. Jon later told me that they began to sober up during the flight and decided they'd better go home. So they had spent all that money and hadn't even got off the plane!

When they returned to Montgomery, Jon got drunk again before returning home. He had Joe call me to come to the airport and pick them up. Weary of trusting Christ to handle our problems, I exploded: "I don't care if you two hop the next plane out!" and I hung up.

I guess I was thinking, "Well, Lord, I appreciate all You've done up to this point, but at the moment I've had it, and thank You very much, but I'll handle this one." I felt that such a financial loss was too much to bear.

The tension and pressure of the night's events overwhelmed me and my old self-pity returned. I told my friends, Jon's parents, the neighbors, the preacher, and anyone who would listen what Jon had done to me. They consoled me with comments like, "You poor girl, you have really gone through it." I knew I was fast slipping away from the spiritual walk I'd known, but I couldn't and wouldn't give up this martyred feeling. I got such gratification from the self-pity that I continued to slide.

Hoping to help, my friend Sue invited me to church for prayer. I recall telling her on the way that God ought to give me a good chastening because I had allowed myself to sink into such indulgence and despair.

When we arrived at the church, people were quietly praying in various pews. I sat down in one of the pews, bowed my head and closed my eyes . . . but that was it. I felt spiritually blank. I thought, "I am wasting my time sitting here. My prayers aren't getting through." I just felt terribly apathetic.

Then during the worship service, a missionary sitting beside me turned, looked me directly in the face and began speaking. "God is all you need, but you are drinking from other fountains and your capacity to receive from God is very small." I had never seen him before, nor have I seen him since, but I knew that God was directing this to me and my needs. In that moment I turned from the frustrations and self-pity I had been indulging in and claimed God's forgiveness. My rebellion drained out as if someone had pulled a plug.

When I got home I picked up my Bible and opened it to Hebrews 12:6, which says, "For the Lord corrects and disciplines everyone whom He loves, and He punishes, even scourges, every son whom He accepts and welcomes to His heart and cherishes" (AMP). I felt that verse was for me personally. I cried and cried and thanked God for bringing me back. I began to prepare myself and my home for Jon's return from work.

The California escapade, which had seemed to be such a curse, was the beginning of a turning point for us. Later when Jon and I talked he said that it had shocked him into some sense of reality. He said that for the first time he realized he wasn't controlling the drinking!

Up-down-up, the roller coaster went on. But now during Jon's sober periods we would have long, quiet talks as we did in our earlier years. Yet coming off the bottle was desperately hard, and in a matter of days he was failing again.

At a family get-together, Jon was criticized by his parents for neglecting his family and his job. During the argument that followed, Jon jumped up and shouted that he wanted all of us to get off his back.

He slammed the door behind him and set out walking the 12 miles home. I got in the car and drove alongside, begging him to let me drive him home. Through sobs he said, "Just go away. I want to be left alone." I tried to reason with him. "Jon, please get in the car. Let's talk." He answered that he needed time to think. "Just leave me alone," he demanded.

A part of me feared that Jon was having an emotional breakdown. He was trembling and walking rapidly, with a disturbed look in his eyes.

I stopped the car and prayed, "Lord, what should I do?" Then I thought, "Well, Lord, maybe he does need to be alone."

I went home, calmed the children and put them to bed. I got out my Bible and began reading and talking to the Lord: "Just take care of Jon. Whatever happens, just take care of him." As I sat there a real peace came over me. At that moment I heard the key turn in the door. I felt the presence and warmth of the Lord, and I continued to pray as Jon came in. "Lord, give me the right words to say. Please, dear God, I love him so much."

Jon came in and slumped into a chair. His body was wringing wet with perspiration. His expression was blank, almost lifeless. I grasped his hand and it went limp. I said, "Please, Jon, talk to me. Let me know you're all right." We sat there for a very long time. He finally said, "All the way home, all sorts of confused things ran through my head, like 'Man, you're really cracking up.' Then I'd tell myself, 'No, no, you're just tired,' and on and on."

We sat up the whole night talking about our marriage, his drinking, and God. It was a time of renewal for us. For the first time Jon responded positively about Christ. He wanted to hear. It was beautiful. What seemed at first to be a disaster turned out to be a precious, sweet time, a real sharing of our selves.

Not long after that night I noticed a change in my husband. He began attending church with me occasionally. God began to tenderly deal with Jon as he heard the Word. He began taking more interest in our home and the children. He began to stay home more, and as his desire to take care of us increased he decided he wanted to take the children to church every Sunday.

A peace slowly began to settle over our home and over Jon. He became more responsible, and although he was still drinking I watched his drinking gradually decrease.

As Jon's eyes and mind began to clear, he began to see himself and his "friends" as they really were. He saw how their drinking was destroying most of them physically, and destroying their homes.

Only a few months passed before Jon personally asked Jesus Christ into his life.

God not only restored our marriage, but He matured us and made our relationship better than it ever was before. Christ has made our in-law relationship more pleasant, more loving, by our letting Him love them through us. Although our relationship with Jesus Christ hasn't yet been shared by our parents, we are praying that it will be and that we will all be united in heaven with our Lord.

About one year ago while attending a neighborhood Bible study I began to listen to Darien Cooper's tape series on God's role for a woman entitled, "Will the Real Woman Please Stand Up?" As we listened to a tape a week, we also used her book, *You Can Be the Wife of a Happy Husband,* as reference material. I felt like shouting with glee that such a book was available for women. I was excited because only through trial and error had I found the principles she shares so clearly in the tapes and the book. I thought how wonderful it was that other women wouldn't have to travel the same treacherous road I had. Here are the principles directly from God's Word for every woman, and I know from experience that they work!

Our quiet talks and long walks together have become a reality once again. Occasionally we visit my folks and again stroll along those Miami beaches hand in hand. Everything is so different now.

We sit silently watching the sun set over the restless sea. So many tides have rolled in and returned, so many storms have lashed the sea . . . and some ships have been swamped by turbulent waves while others returned to port safely—like ours.

Our voyage was launched at one port, has battled the storms of life, and now rests in the harbor with treasures from afar. God has repaired and deepened our love. As I relaxed in the tranquil strength of Jon's arms, I felt the last ray of sunlight on my face and I thanked God for giving us another precious day. And yet our real voyage has just begun.

Reminiscing with Darien:

Wednesday morning was here! My mind touched on the fact that my Tuesday class was over and my Thursday class was a day ahead. Today would be free to tie up some loose ends around my home.

About 10:30 I'd just cut shelf paper and gotten all the cans out of the kitchen cabinets when the phone rang. My heart sank as a voice said, "Mrs. Cooper, weren't you supposed to hold a question-and-answer session for our Bible class at ten o'clock today?"

Oh, no! How could I have made such a mistake? There was no excuse. I simply had not consulted my calendar in several days and this engagement had slipped my mind.

The class had just concluded its ten-week tape course on "The Real Woman." Fortunately, there were two tapes on child training they still hadn't heard, and they graciously agreed to put on a tape while I dressed and rushed over.

God, in His marvelous grace, once again used my blundering for good. As I apologized to the group for my mistake, one woman said she wouldn't have been there had I not been late as her car had broken down. Another confided how comforting it was to know that I made mistakes just like everyone else. I was tempted to take several hours and comfort her some more!

Often when I've failed I think, "Lord, I'll never teach women again. I'm still too big of a mess myself." Then I am reminded that it's God's truths which are life-changing and perfect, not me. None of us will be perfect until Jesus takes us to be with Him.

As we ate lunch, a woman asked me if I had any experience counseling women whose husbands were alcoholics. When I explained that my contact with such situations had been limited, Doanne began to share what God had done in her marriage.

Through a friend Doanne had learned that I would be in Newnan for this session and she had driven from Montgomery,

Alabama. I was so impressed by Doanne's testimony that I asked her to prepare it for this book.

Doanne emphasized that the key ingredient to living successfully with an alcoholic husband was to accept him as he is and to consistently manifest Christ's love. She had tried complaining, nagging, and threatening, to no avail. Obviously Jon had a dual conflict: problems for which he had found no answers, and situations that facilitated his drinking. The liquor bottle became Jon's pleasant diversion and his route of escape.

Doanne's criticism only added to the problem. God reminds us how painful it is to live with a complaining wife: "It is better to dwell in a corner of the housetop [on the flat oriental roof, exposed to all kinds of weather] than in a house shared with a nagging, quarrelsome *and* faultfinding woman" (Prov. 21:9, AMP).

Before Doanne became a Christian, she did not have the power within her to cope with such problems. Even as a new Christian, she complicated the problem by not understanding the message in 1 Peter 3:1-2, where God reminds a Christian wife that her non-Christian husband may be won to Christ through her chaste and respectful behavior. When Doanne refused to go certain places with Jon, he felt he had been abandoned in preference for a stranger. Had she looked at the situation from Jon's viewpoint, she would have realized that he felt threatened, rejected, and afraid that he was losing her. Lacking spiritual insight, Jon could not understand Doanne's actions (1 Cor. 2:14).

Doanne finally realized that being an understanding, confident wife was the real way to share Jesus with Jon. Rather than "falling apart" over this or being fearful of that, she needed to evidence calm strength and quenchless love stemming from assurance that her future was in God's control. The beauty of a peaceful spirit, together with Doanne's praise for Jon's good traits and her response to his leadership, set the stage for God to draw Jon to Himself. She helped also.

Doanne learned not to take Jon's ugly behavior personally

when she was not at fault. She was regularly studying God's Word and correcting areas that He showed her needed changing. That was all God expected of her. Jon's irritability could be explained by unresolved conflicts in other areas of his life. Her response to Jon was to comfort and encourage him, rather than adding to the problem by being offended.

Today Jon is a Christian. Doanne had the opportunity to share biblical truths with him when he began to seek answers. She was careful, however, to answer only what he asked about and not to turn him off by sharing too much. She would share with any Christian that the way to contentment and victory in any need is in doing everything "as unto the Lord" (Col. 3:17, 23). It's not easy, but it's glorious.

Thinking Through with You:

Question: *What encouragement and guidance does God give for winning a non-Christian husband to the Lord?*
Answer: "Wives, be submissive to your own husbands so that even if any of them are disobedient to the Word, they may be won without a word by the behavior of their wives, as they observe your chaste and respectful behavior" (1 Peter 3:1–2, NASB).

Q.: *How can you be a relaxed wife when marital storms swirl around you?*
A.: "Let Him have all your worries and cares, for He is always thinking about you and watching everything that concerns you" (1 Peter 5:7, LB).

Q.: *What is the power of temperate, kind speech?*
A.: "A soft answer turns away wrath; but grievous words stir up anger" (Prov. 15:1, AMP). "By long forbearing and calmness of spirit, a judge or ruler is persuaded, and soft speech breaks down the most bonelike resistance" (Prov. 25:15, AMP.).

6
Depression Doesn't Live Here Anymore

April Harrell

Blackness hung like an immovable veil over me. I struggled to open my eyes, to reach into the conscious world. *Where am I?* My eyes opened to an unfamiliar room. Sterile white walls surrounded me. I fought desperately to clear the confusion, the gaze engulfing my mind.

The pills. I had taken the whole bottle.

What am I doing here? I'm supposed to be dead! "Dear God," I cried, "can't I even kill myself?" Tears of anguish washed down my face. Living or dying, both seemed impossible tasks for me. As my thoughts shrank back behind the black veil, the "whys," the events that had brought me to today, flashed through my recollections like a high-speed movie. Where had it all begun?

I recalled high school, 1956, a lifetime away. My world then had been filled with school, parties, and dates. Being elected homecoming queen had been the culmination of my junior year.

I had learned early the road to popularity: I was a "people-pleaser," par excellence. Even at that point in my life, my real self was torn between the sweet, apple-pie April whom everyone knew, and the swinging, rebellious April that few people met. The two irreconcilable presonalities, "Good April" and "Bad April," already had begun their separate lives.

During my senior year a boy named Keith joined my math class. I sat for an entire period gazing at him, mentally bidding him to turn around and look at me. He didn't.

At home that afternoon I stared into the mirror. My tall, slender frame had filled out well. My honey blonde hair hung down in soft waves around my shoulders. I tried on this dress and that, finally deciding on a white sweater and matching tight skirt.

"That ought to get his attention," I thought. It did.

Keith was tall and handsome, with flashing green eyes, set off by a silhouette of light-brown hair. His spirited personality had won him instant admiration and helped him to be voted "most popular" boy in our senior class.

Keith was everything I dreamed I had ever wanted, and I meant to have him. With graduation behind us, visions of marriage loomed immediately ahead on my horizon. With Keith in agreement, I called our church minister to discuss our wedding plans.

He began to explain the sanctity of marriage, but I didn't hear much—I was thinking of the fun of marriage. He spoke of a lasting commitment to each other, and I answered with exaggerated respect: "Dr. Howell, I really understand that."

In reality, I understood hardly anything. I wanted Keith exclusively. I wanted him right away. What else was important?

White carnations and green ivy adorned the church in Green Bay that warm September day. The beautiful notes of "Because" drifted through the church as Mama put the finishing touches on my gown.

As I stepped into the aisle, I saw Keith waiting for me at the altar, a confident, loving smile lighting his face. Excitement so filled my heart that it seemed like someone else repeating those vows. I knew there could never be another day so beautiful as this.

As the routine of marriage settled in, the starry glamor of first love began to fade into normalcy. Honeymoons were supposed to last forever, I thought. I wasn't prepared for reality.

I did my best to be a good wife. I loved Keith very much. To me, he was everything good and perfect in this world, and deep inside I knew he was everything I wasn't.

Keith spent the next few years working hard to get a foothold in the bridge-building industry. In time he was made a supervisor. I became aware there were rivers all over the world, and it seemed that Keith was building bridges over all of them! He traveled extensively and for long periods of time.

Left at home, an aching syndrome of loneliness beset me. I wasn't the kind of woman to exist without male companionship and attention, and a fire began to burn in my soul. Love Keith as I did, "Bad April" responded more and more to the attraction of other men.

I tried to relieve my frustrations with housework, reading and neighborhood activities—bridge with the girls, lunch at the country club. I managed to control the war inside during the day, but at night the demons of loneliness and sensuality reared their ugly heads.

I didn't know how to handle these desires. They seemed as much a part of the real me as my love for Keith. Though I had professed faith in Christ in my early teens, I considered Christianity more as a way to get into heaven than a way of living. Torn by fervent longings with my husband far away, I surrendered to illicit relationships. Keith never knew.

The years passed and Keith was successful in business. We had three healthy children, but I was getting sick. Never able to appease the counterparts of my inner self, I became frustrated, depressed and neurotic.

My mind played tricks on me. Reality became an illusion. Details of my carnal relationships burned in my eyes, and at times I wasn't sure whether I had sinned against God or was deluded by fantasy. Ordinary mistakes swelled to horrid crimes which tormented my soul.

Soon dressing myself each morning became a major accomplishment. One day began to melt into the next. Activities around me faded in and out of existence. Fatigue hung heavy but I couldn't relax. I couldn't sleep. "Bad April," "Good April," sins, sex, confusion. Finally I couldn't stand another day.

In a flight of desperation I entered a sanitarium in Madison. As I walked up the steps, I reached out for the last help I could think of. Hoping He'd hear, I prayed, "Dear God, please give me a Christian counselor."

The Lord answered my prayer. He provided a dear Christian woman for counseling. She visited me almost every day, but my twisted mind couldn't comprehend the real answers to my problems.

My small room at the sanitarium, with its locked door, kept the fears and pressures of life outside. A sense of security came like a warm blanket to my days. Every moment of my day was arranged; personal decisions were not necessary. Like a child I followed orders, and obedience brought special privileges.

Daily counseling plus group therapy was the basis of my treatment. "Group" problems, like so much garbage, were spewed out while 15 people who couldn't figure their way out of paper bags offered their in-depth thoughts and advice!

No solutions were found to my deep inner turmoil. No major problems were solved. Yet, rested and tranquilized, I began to cope with life. Three months passed, and the doctors decided it was time for my release. The thought of home panicked me. The hospital was my haven. They couldn't take me away from the only peace I'd found!

Only through being deceived did I agree to leave. I was told I'd have to take a month's outside leave and then I could return. In retrospect, I realize I copped out in running to the hospital—a "breakdown" was socially acceptable when one couldn't cope with life.

Keith picked me up and took me home. After a few weeks, family obligations outweighed my need to run, so life went on as before: one step forward, two steps back; two steps forward, one step back.

So the next six years went. There were times when I'd yearn

for spiritual fulfillment. I read the Bible and prayed. I'd try to trust God, but my flimsy faith never allowed me to entrust myself to Him rather than to pills.

By 1972 my precarious grip on life was slipping. I was losing hope. Depression streaked my days. Destructive self-pity ate at my resolves.

Keith decided it would be more profitable for him to move south. Atlanta seemed like the logical choice since Keith's company had a large office there.

Our relationship had become more and more strained, though I couldn't discern the reason. I realized how mixed up I was, but Keith's edgy restlessness was a mystery.

He called one evening and said, "April, let's just forget it. You do your thing, and I'll do mine. I'm going ahead with my move to Atlanta."

Hysterically I yelled, "Not on your life! I'm moving out of this town. I don't care what happens to you and me, but I'm getting these kids out of here and we will have to see how it goes from there."

I associated Green Bay, my home for 33 years, with my problems. I wanted to get away from the small town where I felt everyone knew everyone else's business. I wanted to run again.

Ice floated in the Fox River and snow lay on the ground when we left Green Bay. When we arrived in Atlanta, the dogwoods were just beginning to blossom. For a short time I thought that perhaps our lives also would bloom again.

There were days when, after a hard day of housecleaning, Keith would deliver a sharp criticism and I would collapse in despair. I was so dependent on Keith's words of approval. Everything I did was to please him. What he thought and said could make or destroy my day.

The pressure drove me down and down. Our conflicts came to a head shortly after we moved to Atlanta and Keith packed up and left home. He moved in with an assistant who lived in Decatur.

A few weeks passed, then because of a myriad of circumstances and the illness of our children, I had to call Keith. During the conversation he asked me, "Are you asking me to come home?" I answered, "Yes, Keith, you belong here."

It was settled, or was it? No problems had been discussed, or solutions found; just a decision made.

Depression seemed my constant companion. The black veil was beginning to fall. I knew what was going on around me: my eyes saw, my ears heard, yet it was rather like watching a play in which I no longer could or cared to participate. Loneliness oppressed me. I was locked behind a door, one I constructed myself.

I tried to tell Keith, and I tried to tell my friends how I felt, what I feared and the needs I had, but I don't think anyone understood. Between my speaking and their hearing, the pain behind the words got lost.

"I don't even care anymore," I thought. "It really doesn't matter. There is no way to undo all the mistakes, all the rottenness; no way to forget the pain; no one to understand . . . I need a pill."

Opening the drawer, I found my lovely collection. Pills, two lovely yellow ones, one sky blue one—each containing sweet peace—quiet, soft, floating peace. They offered me a serene world where pain never entered, nor joy, nor tears—a beautiful world of nothingness.

At times I would scream inside: *"Help me. Oh, please, can't you see? Look at me, I'm dying inside. Look at me!"* But my silent screams went unheard.

At church one night I asked the elders to call a prayer meeting for me. I told them that my marriage was in shambles, that I didn't know what the problem was. "I need your prayers," I told them.

Tears fell on my hands as I stared at the floor and began to ask for divine intervention: "I pray that all human frailties be removed and only God's love be present. My marriage is at an end. I can't take it anymore. I don't even know what it is I can't take; I just can't take any more. I'm a Christian, but I seem to find no answers. Please, please pray for my whole family. I don't know where we're headed, but we need prayer."

I felt a measure of peace as I drove home that night. Perhaps the Lord was strengthening me for the heartbreak ahead, but I continued to rely on myself.

When I got home, Keith told me that an old friend of ours from Green Bay was in town. I called her and we agreed to meet at her hotel.

As Jackie talked, my unsolved problems became the topic of conversation. The pain began to spill out. "Jackie," I said, "my marriage is at an end. I don't know what is wrong. If there is anything you know that would help me, please tell me. I don't even know what I am fighting."

She didn't say much for a while, but in time she told me a story which, had it come from anyone else, I would have called a lie. "April, you might as well know what you are up against. Keith has been having affairs for years," she said.

By the time she told me about woman number eight, I said, "Hush, I don't want to hear any more. I can't grasp what I've heard."

The rest of the night was spent in Jackie's hotel room. I couldn't face Keith.

Keith had been my idol. He was good. He was the only guy in the world I trusted. He had always been first in my life, despite my past unfaithfulness. I suppose I actually worshiped him. My idol had fallen. The pain was overwhelming.

I had felt for a long time that there was a barrier between the Lord and me. At that moment I realized it was Keith: he instead of God had been first in my thoughts, first in my love.

I had prayed for years: "Lord, remove whatever is number one, if it is not You!" Now it was done.

When I returned home I confronted Keith with the truth I had learned. He didn't deny it. In my heart I had longed that he would.

Anger rose in his face and voice. "Why in the world did you have to drag all this out?" he asked. I began to realize that he was only upset because I had changed the status quo in our relationship. Momentarily I wished I hadn't.

I still cared so much for Keith that I was determined not to lose him. Like a "good Christian," I tried to "forgive and forget," but not knowing how to appropriate Christ's power, I failed miserably.

I tried to suppress my true feelings. I kept the bitterness, the hurt, the hatred locked inside me. There were times when emotions got the best of me and "Bad April" took over, making me act like a raving maniac.

"And you're supposed to be a Christian!" Keith would scoff. "Is this how a Christian acts?"

I looked everywhere for answers. I read current self-help books. I searched for someone who understood the agony of my life. Through Christian books on marriage, I learned how to be an attractive woman; I learned some useful directions and ideas, but nothing life-changing. I kept searching for some Christian woman to whom I could relate, but found none.

Things in our home went from bad to worse. Grief and resentment ate at my soul until I could no longer contain it. I had been popping pills like candy for years—Valium was my best friend. One Saturday the pain of life became too much. I consumed half a bottle of the tranquilizer by afternoon, and when I dopily awoke the next morning I groped my way into the kitchen. Holding onto the counter, I reached into the cabinet and took out a glass. Turning the water on, I filled the glass and reached into my pocket for my pills. I poured out a handful and swallowed them.

Sleep. Sweet nothingness . . . that was my goal.

A bottle of another tranquilizer sat in the cabinet, and I reached for it. In my daze I don't know how much I consumed. I almost crawled back to the bedroom—I didn't want the kids to find me passed out on the floor, but I did want Keith to find me and have the shock hit him, hurt him.

What if the pills don't work?" my groggy mind contemplated. Crawling now, I struggled to reach Keith's shotgun in the closet. Clothes fell everywhere until my hand touched metal. I dragged the gun out and pulled myself back to bed . . . .

The hospital's sterile walls greeted me as my mind pushed aside the black veil, and I returned to consciousness. I realized I had been on a flashback trip through years of hell.

I looked around, ran my hands down the rough white sheets and over my body. No bandages, no bullet wounds. I guessed I must have passed out before I could use the gun.

In the next few days I decided my presence at home caused me and everyone else pain and turmoil. I concluded my family would be better off without me. I knew I needed rest, and I needed time to find answers to the problems that beset me.

A doctor at the hospital had told me that I wasn't cut out to be a mother and a wife, that what I wanted was to be a "woman of the world." "Get out," he advised; "it's the best thing you can do for everyone." Still depending on human guidance, I followed his advice. When those hospital doors closed behind me, I walked out on my husband and my children.

I checked into a local motel and looked up a young woman named Manya whom I had met recently, a waitress at a near-by restaurant.

Manya sensed something was wrong, and I spilled my story to her. She had been divorced for a number of years and seemed to understand my confusion.

"You can't stay in a motel forever," she said. "Why don't you come over to my apartment?"

I needed a friend, I needed to feel wanted and I needed someone to talk to, so I accepted Manya's gracious offer.

Keith accepted my absence calmly. He kept in touch by telephone, but I didn't see him or the children. I spent my days job-hunting, without success, until I swallowed my pride and went to work as a waitress with Manya.

I was beginning to find some semblance of peace. I couldn't imagine what my future would be, but I was trying not to think about it too much. One day at a time. I tried to take it slow and easy.

One day I called home to check on the children. My mother-in-law answered, and we chatted for a few minutes about news of the children. She told me that Keith had been taking them to church, an innovation that I found hard to believe. Something troubled me about our conversation. I had intended for Keith to bear the full responsibility for the children's care; I didn't want an outsider running my home.

I was being torn again. What should I do?

Suddenly I felt as if I had committed the ultimate sin: I, the mother, had left my children and my husband.

With a shaking hand, I dialed my home. "Mom," I told her, "I know I have made lots of mistakes. I have failed everyone, but I'm coming home."

When Manya came in that evening, I told her of my decision. "I don't know if what I am doing is any more right than what I have done in the past, but I have to go home," I said. "I'll never forget that you were there when I really needed a friend."

"April," she said, "just remember that my door is always open if you ever need a place to stay or just to talk. You take care when you get home and see if you can't get things off on the right foot this time."

Keith was out of town when I walked back into my home. I picked up where I had left off. No solutions, no new directions were visible. I still leaned on tranquilizers to stabilize my emotions.

One afternoon I was standing in the kitchen when I heard Keith's car in the driveway. Automatically I tightened up inside. I wasn't sure what his reaction to my coming home would be. I soon found out. He opened the door and gently took me in his arms.

Things around our house slowly began to change. Little things: his verbal denunciations stopped, and compliments were more frequent. Apparently, in part, my silent screams for help were finally being answered. And slowly I began to realize that I had always heard only the negative. I had never listened for the good. I had been so strung-out that I had overreacted.

Keith and I began to be more honest with each other. This

took a great effort on my part. I began to let him know, without nagging, when his words hurt. This mutual caring, in place of accusations, was a totally new experience for me.

Life was better, but my problems and confusion were not ended. I knew I must learn to live one day at a time—to handle and confront only today's problems and not to concern myself with the "what ifs" of tomorrow—but it was hard. Not until a few months later would I learn how to have a moment-by-moment relationship with Jesus Christ that enabled me to depend on Him, not on myself. And not until then did I realize that I had been trying to program God, to fit Him into my plans, just as I had done with everyone else. I also discovered that God's ways are not my ways. "There is a way that seems right to a man and appears straight before him, but at the end of it are the ways of death" (Prov. 16:25, AMP.).

While doing volunteer work at my church, I first heard of Darien Cooper from my neighbor, Barbara McIntire. "April, I just know this is what you have been looking for, the answers you need. Won't you please go with me when the seminars begin again?" she pled.

"Well, Barbara, we'll see," I'd say, procrastinating.

Barbara lent the tapes of the classes to me and I listened while I worked. I thought Darien Cooper was crazy! There wasn't a name in the book I didn't call her. "She doesn't understand my situation," I fumed. If she were walking in my shoes, she'd change her story. About halfway through the taped course, I picked up the recorder in frustration and threw it across the room. "Who in the world does she think she is?" I screamed.

The solution was plain to me: "Just remove all these problems," I prayed continually, "and I won't be up-tight." Yet I began to feel as if He were saying, "April, I want to teach you through your problems. I want you to grow, to become strong, to become the woman I created you to be."

As my search continued I joined a prayer group in my neighborhood which turned out to be a Darien Cooper "fan club." I admitted to them that I couldn't accept the things Mrs. Cooper was teaching.

Months later a girl who was new to the group, Reba, brought me a book she said I ought to read. It was *You Can Be The Wife of a Happy Husband,* by Darien Cooper.

I thanked her and reluctantly took the book. I prayed, "Lord, I will read this book, but You're going to have to change my attitude. I'm willing, but it is up to You."

About this time I heard of another Cooper seminar. Members of the prayer group began to pray for a change in my attitude so I would attend.

I wanted my marriage to work. I knew my attitudes and actions at home were still wrong. I knew that real changes had to take place for any lasting improvements. I began to feel that maybe the principles taught by Darien Cooper might be the answers I was looking for.

The day came for the class and I did something totally out of character for me: I went alone. I didn't call anyone; I didn't ask for emotional support.

Even though our lives were different, I identified with Anne Carroll the moment she began to speak to the class. I had never seen such complete transformation in a woman. I had never met anyone who had made the transition from the "swinging life" to real-life Christanity. It was Anne who convinced me that a whole new life was possible, even for me. It took both Anne and Darien to make the seminar complete for me.

I knew that I could talk with these women, that they would understand. There would be no criticism, only love, through Christ.

As I attended the seminar, I realized that I hadn't been rebelling against Darien Cooper's ideas. These were *God's* principles, straight out of the Bible. Darien had just given the time, energy and love to allow God to use her.

When I first heard Darien speak, among my thoughts were: "She really has it all together."

But no one can identify with perfection and slowly I began

to see that she too was human. She revealed her mistakes to us. I was fascinated that she was still learning. She made me feel so much better about myself.

After class one morning, I told Darien how Keith's infidelity had almost destroyed me. Nothing had seemed to help, and I kept asking my prayer group to pray that I would completely forget Keith's sin.

"In that act alone, April," Darien said, "it is obvious that you have not really forgiven Keith. You haven't been willing to forget, so obviously you haven't really forgiven. You have kept the memories alive by constantly keeping the subject before you, by constantly discussing it with the prayer group and others."

Darien continued: "The way to forget is not to recall the act to your offender, not to tell it to others, and not to allow yourself to dwell upon it. April, the moment it comes to your mind, you should thank God that He has taken care of it, and respond rightly to Keith, letting God remove it from your mind."

She shared with me many Scriptures to reinforce the solution she had given.

The love that Keith and I once knew had not returned. But as I learned what true love is, I began to take my rightful place as Keith's helpmate. He became the head of our household. In giving myself to him, I realized that love acts for the happiness of others, not for its own. And like a seed, the old love that I had known began to grow again in my heart. Now I could more fully comprehend the words: "For where your treasure is, there your heart will be also" (Matt 6:21, NIV).

I am enjoying so many little things I never cared for in the past. I have canned 200 jars of vegetables for my family. Just the act of washing the corn and scraping the carrots became an act of love. My bonus came when Keith proudly arranged the jars on a display shelf in our basement den and said, "You are something else; I am so very proud of you. It is really a pleasure to come home now."

I glowed all over. What a difference! "Thank you; you have

no idea how much fulfillment I'm getting from so many small things."

I have learned how to take one day at a time. After years of popping pills, I have kicked the habit through the power of Jesus Christ. I don't mean that I have conquered all my problems, And when I get my eyes off the Lord and decide that a problem is one I can handle, I fall flat on my face.

At a drug clinic, a doctor explained that one of the drugs I had been taking was physically addictive. Though I had experienced withdrawal symptoms, I had not considered my pills "drugs." I had been much more aware of the sins and weaknesses of hard-drug users than my own.

Now I know the truth about the pills, the truth about myself and truth about Christ. As Jesus said, "So if the Son liberates you . . . then you are really and unquestionably free" (John 8:36, AMP).

The beautiful music of laughter now rings in our home; honest laughter. Love has been renewed. The children are growing in our love and the love of the Lord. When I place dishes in the dishwasher, I thank the Lord and remember the time when I didn't have one. When I wash the clothes, I think of the child who will be wearing them. When I make our bed, I thank God for the love He restored and the good times in that bed.

Someone once gave me a quote by D. L. Moody which has been especially meaningful to me. I make it personal by inserting my name. It goes like this:

"The world has yet to see what God will do with April, for April, and through April, and in April, by April, when she is fully consecrated to Him; I, April, will try my utmost to be that woman."

I thought long and hard about sharing my story with Anne so she could write it. I prayed and discussed it with Keith. It hurt. It isn't easy for me, even now, to admit how sinful my life had been. Exposing the mistakes and the stupidity to the world is difficult.

God reminded me how I had searched Christan books for

someone to identify with, some woman who had come through the depths of depression caused by sin and enabled to walk with Christ. I thought: "Maybe some other woman needs to identify, needs to know that there is hope, that there are answers." Keith said to go ahead with our story, so I did.

My prayer is:

"Dear God, please use these words, the pain, the sin and the solutions to help others. Impress readers' hearts with the truth that there is no sin, no problem, no failure which You can't forgive. Touch the heart of that woman whose only way of survival is to meet each day, each problem with a pill or a drink. Truly let her know how wonderful it is to be "free" and that Christ can do it if only she will let Him.

"Speak to the heart of that woman who thinks, because the feeling of love has faded from her marriage, that divorce is the answer. Show her what real love is and how You can so gloriously restore a love thought dead. For the woman lost behind the black veil of depression, encourage her. May Your Spirit witness to her. And may this story let her know that truly Christ can remove that veil forever. This is my prayer in Jesus Christ's name, Amen."

Reminiscing with Darien:

April's eyes sparkled as I explained that Anne and I were searching for women who would share their testimonies for this book. She blurted out almost before I finished talking that she had been waiting for an opportunity to tell the world what Christ had done in her life. As time passed, April wasn't sure that she would be able to write her testimony. Going into the dark recesses of her mind was painful and frustrating. I reassured her that God would not ask her to do anything unless He provided the necessary strength. When the time came, she and Anne were able to work together to present her story. I appreciate her willingness to share her successes and failures in order that others may be encouraged to trust Christ.

April's turmoil-filled life could be summarized by the Apostle Paul's words: "I don't understand myself at all, for I really want to do what is right, but I can't. I do what I don't want to—what I hate. . . . I love to do God's will so far as my new nature is concerned; but there is something else deep within me, in my lower nature, that is at war with my mind and wins the fight and makes me a slave to the sin that is still within me. In my mind I want to be God's willing servant, but instead I find myself still enslaved to sin. So you see how it is: my new life tells me to do right, but the old nature that is still inside me loves to sin. Oh, what a terrible predicament I'm in! Who will free me from my slavery to this deadly lower nature? Thank God! It has been done by Jesus Christ, our Lord. He has set me free" (Rom. 7:15, 22-25, LB).

For many years April was enslaved to her old nature because she did not know to confess her sins and to allow Christ to control her life as she established right patterns of living.

April slowly began to see that her wrong responses to the pressures and responsibilities of life had led her deeper and deeper into the endless spiral of depression. She had tried to make Keith meet needs in her life that only Jesus Christ could meet. When he couldn't fill this impossible role, she responded with resentment and bitterness. She reacted with jealousy toward Keith's freedom from the home responsibilities that were so burdensome for her. She tried to fill her loneliness and need for companionship with illicit relations. April's sinful reaction to her initial problems had violated the principles in God's Word that were designed to protect her. God described through Jeremiah the inevitable results: "Your ways and your doings have brought these things down upon you; this is your calamity and doom; surely it is bitter, for surely it reaches your very heart" (Jer. 4:18, AMP.).

The only way April knew to deal with her problems was to increase the amount of drugs she was taking. But drugs could not suppress the anguish caused by Keith's infidelity. Her attempted suicide, as well as her walking out on her children and husband, was an act of vengeance toward them.

When April confided the nasty names she had called me, I remembered how I had rebelled when I first heard the truths I later shared with others. I know how painful it is to see one's rottenness. Yet God shows us our actual condition so we will trust Him to make the necessary changes in our lives.

Because April's depression was a result of sin in her life, there was hope for her. She learned to reverse the cycle that had plunged her into depression by the following steps:

1. Admit your wrong response or action is sin against God.
2. Confess your sin to God, according to 1 John 1:9.
3. Accept God's promised forgiveness.
4. Focus your thoughts on Christ's sufficiency for your particular situation.
5. Take appropriate steps to avoid repeating the same failures.
6. Thank God that He will give you strength to trust Him throughout your struggle.

These steps will work for any woman who truly wants her life to be new and fulfilling.

Thinking Through with You:

Question: *How can Christians overcome the sinful influence of the continuing "old nature" within us?*
Answer: "Walk by the Spirit, and you will not carry out the desire of the flesh. For the flesh sets its desire against the Spirit, and the Spirit against the flesh, for these are in opposition to one another, so that you may not do the things that you please. . . . Now the deeds of the flesh are evident, which are immorality . . . idolatry . . . outbursts of anger . . . drunkenness . . . But the fruit of the Spirit is love, joy, peace, patience, kindness, goodness, faithfulness, gentleness, self-control. . . ." (Gal. 5:16-17, 19-23, NASB).

Q.: *After his own failures and acceptance of forgiveness, how did the Apostle Peter affirm God's faithfulness?*
A.: "He who believes in Him—who adheres to, trusts in and relies on Him—shall never be disappointed or put to shame" (1 Peter 2:6, AMP.).

Q.: *How far is our forgiveness of others to reach?*
A.: "As those who have been chosen of God . . . put on a heart of compassion . . . bearing with one another, and forgiving each other . . . just as the Lord forgave you, so also should you" (Col. 3:12-13, NASB).

Q.: *How do we know that good feelings are to be a product rather than the source of right actions?*
A.: "Joy fills hearts that are planning for good!" (Prov. 12:20, LB).

7
"Keep Those Trucks Coming, Mack!"

Janice Bruner

There was a rainbow touching the earth on our way home. I looked at it hopefully: this was the first sign of color in our whole honeymoon!

I was bewildered—how could anyone be so disappointed with a honeymoon?

All my life I had considered myself a colorful person. I had always felt the admiration of friends my own age and older people as well. In high school, I was Miss This and Miss That. I had skipped hardly any of the bright lights.

My long, dark hair, blue eyes and outgoing personality fascinated my steady boyfriend, Rod, to a point where he would do anything to please me. I'd complain, "Rod always asks me where we should go and what we should do. I just wish he'd make the decisions and tell me where we're going."

Later at college and during my nursing career, I continued to reap attention. When I met Brad, the tables were turned as I found myself caring more for him than he cared for me! All too often he made decisions that ignored me. I didn't like that either!

My unrest dissolved when I met Mack. He was my idea of a knight in shining armor, six-foot-two, dark and handsome, and altogether different from Rod, Brad, or any other fellow I had dated. Mack became all I ever wanted, and it was like a story in a book when he told me that he wanted me too. Our beautiful wedding followed—and then the disappointing honeymoon.

I tried not to think about it. Instead I forced myself to think of the dream house where we would live and have a perfect marriage. The house, which Mack's father had given us, would make everything turn out right, I thought.

Then we arrived! And I could not believe my eyes! Was this old house what Mack had described in glowing terms? Or had my romantic heart just heard it that way?

In my dreams rainbows arched over honeymoon cottages that had groceries in clean cabinets, gingham at the windows, geraniums in window boxes and warm rugs to dig your toes into. But, oh, the reality: cracked walls, accumulated junk, roaches, and a toilet that couldn't be repaired and had to be thrown out the second-story window!

For three years our "dream house" remained bare, unremodeled, and stale. The little improvements I made were hardly noticeable as the house was in need of such major repairs. I would come home from my nursing job, walk numbly through the door, and drop my savings alongside my husband's in our next dream-house fund.

Talking about the problems didn't solve anything for me. Mack loved to discuss our situation, always optimistically. I dreaded the encounters because it's very difficult for me to discuss my feelings. Things will be different, he'd say, if I only met his needs. "What needs?" I'd ask. I wanted desperately to please, but all he ever asked was things like, "Go to the lumber yard and buy some nails"; "Bring me the hammer"; or "Mend my pants." Big deal!

When I'd forget to run one of his errands, he'd be impatient. "Why don't you make a list," he suggested. "Make a list," became fighting words to me. Why should I start each day making a list of things to do for him when my needs were not being met? I wanted Mack to be proud of me—to think I was extra-special—and I felt like I was drowning in trivia—all five-foot-three of me.

Our frustrations faded into the background when we moved into the grand house we had schemed and saved to build. We had designed "just what we always wanted," we thought. I didn't get window boxes, but I did manage custom-made shutters, wallpaper, a lush lawn, one rose bush, doorbells—and heartaches. The roaches didn't accompany us to our new house, but the bugs in my old self did.

They showed up in various places. There was the drapery rod that came out of the wall and hung from one end for a year. Some women might have called a repairman, but I didn't need to because my talented husband could fix anything (if he wanted to).

After going around the mulberry bush with him, nagging, pleading, coaxing and loving, then back to nagging again, I finally became bitter about dangling curtain rods and other loose ends. If Mack really loved me, he'd see how much these things meant to me and fix them!

After months of turmoil, he fixed the defect. Just like that, but it didn't mean anything to me. By then I'd struggled so long that I was emotionally exhausted. A new house had not met my needs. What was the answer?

As Darien Cooper's sister, I had grown up eight years her junior. I'd always viewed Darien as an ideal sister, smart and logical. She was more aggressive than I, and openly derived pleasure from mastering her problems. I labeled myself as "passive" and "just different" because I didn't like to talk through my problems. That always got too personal and took too much time; I kept my problems to myself—until the pressure valve exploded in a crying session.

Living in Orlando, we visited Darien and her family about every three months. As my marital problems became more baffling, I began to view our visits as my pressure-valve release. With Darien prodding, I would tearfully divulge the woe engulfing at least one major problem. We would talk it through and I'd go home, red-eyed, with a new-found principle from the Bible to put into practice. My soul would seem sore for about two weeks after each visit—I'm sure I was using certain spiritual muscles for the first time!

Slowly, from God's Word, I began to see my real self: ugly. I didn't like that. The brilliant colors of my "self-portrait" went glimmering and the true, cloudy outlines revealed my impatient, proud, and bitter profile.

I began to see that Mack needed a helpmate who was available; he needed my participation in the "little things." I should consider his needs when planning my day, and be available for what he liked to do when he came home from work.

Working this out wasn't always what I would have planned. Mack would invite me out to the cold garage, infested with mosquitoes that tortured my legs, to watch him work. Interesting things, like grinding valves or scraping up oil off the concrete floor! Sometimes I'd respond with a nod and bored, "Really?" Other times I was able to put my whole self into my participation.

As the months rolled along, I realized that as I gave myself willingly to my husband, he abundantly gave of himself back to me. If I had to leave the dishes to be with him, he'd help me with them later. A closeness grew that wouldn't have been possible any other way.

It was a new adventure learning that God has designed specific principles for the marriage relationship and that they work. God designed me to respond to Mack in certain ways because He had my best interests at heart. And Jesus Christ was coming alive to me in a new way. I had accepted him as my personal Saviour as a child, but now I was seeing Him as a way of life.

The days that I'd willingly surrender my free time to pick up nuts and bolts, recaps, roofing shingles and lumber in town, I'd invariably have a need of my own met. One day as I ran errands for Mack, I found a much-needed pair of red sandals for two dollars that lasted for three years. Apparently God wanted me to have a long-term reminder of His faithfulness. Another day, when I was riding around town with

Mack, he suggested that we stop at a garage sale—that in itself was phenomenal! We picked up articles that we needed at a fraction of their cost. And we'd enjoyed it together.

I even woke up less grumpy and more agreeable in the mornings. That, definitely, was not the old me! Little did I realize how much chipping and sanding from the old me had to be done to allow the real, new me to emerge.

Darien suggested that God works and leads in our lives through our husbands, and that God was trying to develop patience in my life. I knew I was very impatient and could see the merit in this lesson, but she went on to suggest that my attitude toward Mack revealed my spiritual relationship with Christ. This I couldn't believe. Everything was great between Christ and me; Mack simply was impossible at times.

Shortly afterward I was pulling weeds from my rose bush when Mack asked me to stop and drag the garden hose to a different area of the yard for him. I refused. Why, I reasoned, should I stop my work and do that piddling job for him?

The next day as I was walking to the mailbox, I saw my next-door neighbor working in her yard. The Lord quickened my heart with the thought, "Go talk with Mrs. Jones. Share with her how she can know Me personally." I spontaneously reacted: "I don't want to stop what I'm doing to share with her. Some other time." While returning to the house, I realized that my rejection of Christ's leading was identical to my refusal of my husband's request the day before. I was indeed rebellious toward authority.

God used our first child 'Chelle to teach me more about obedience and trust toward God through my husband.

Mack and I dearly loved 'Chelle. She looked like a little Oriental doll at birth, with jet-black hair and dark eyes. As she grew and developed, sometimes we'd reflect that she had brought us so much joy already that if God took her to heaven we could still be grateful. I was soon to realize that saying those words was much easier than living them.

One day when 'Chelle was a year and a half, we prepared for a trip to town. I would drive the car and Mack was taking the truck to pick up some building supplies. Imagine my horror when Mack put 'Chelle in the back of the pickup truck! Knowing the freedom that Mack had as a child, I was sure he was going to let her ride there alone the eight miles into town along a four-lane highway.

Impetuously I grabbed her up and put in my car. Muscular Mack, in turn, grabbed her back, placed her in the back of the truck and left!

I was sure I'd never see her alive again. I knew I'd been wrong in defying my husband, and I could someday ask his forgiveness, but I didn't want to pay for his bad judgment with the death of our daughter!

I ached so badly inside I couldn't cry hard enough to relieve the pain as I gripped the back door. I felt like I'd been hit by one of those large trucks on the highway, yes, a "Mack truck."

The sofa soaked up my tears, but it didn't help. It was probably only moments, but it seemed an eternity until I looked up and saw Mack at my side, with 'Chelle in his arms. He had never intended for her to ride in the back on the highway—he meant to transfer her to the cab down the road.

Why hadn't I trusted Mack? Why hadn't I trusted God? Why my violent reaction?

The truth resounded in my mind, embarrassingly clear! I did not trust my husband with our daughter; I did not trust God with our daughter. I'd previously experienced fear as I'd watched Mack toss 'Chelle into the air, catching her in play, and his bicycle rides with her had frightened me.

I labeled my worry "motherly concern." It was sin. My masquerade gradually ended over these next four years as God taught me to let 'Chelle go.

One evening when Mack was working late, I heard something outside. My fear swung into full gear, and I fed it until it was robust. I was completely miserable until Mack breezed into the driveway. By that time I was petrified with fear, my stomach ached and my jaws were tight.

The next night I decided I didn't want to go that route

again. I decided to be logical—to think through my problem. "Now, if Mack were here with me I wouldn't be afraid." I reasoned. As clearly as if I'd heard it for the first time, I knew: Either God is here with you or He isn't. Which is it? Does God care for you as carefully as Mack does? You trust Mack—but let's face it, if you really trusted God you wouldn't be afraid. I'd put a limit on God, saying in effect, "You can go pretty far, but not that far."

Then I admitted:

The way I trust my husband is the way I trust the Lord.

The way I respond to my husband is the way I whisper to God.

The way I seek the leadership of my husband is the way I follow my Lord.

The way I plan for my husband is the way I entrust tomorrow to my God.

The way I shout to my husband is the way I scream out at God!

The way I bridle my tongue toward my husband is the way I harness my power from God.

The way I relate to my husband is the way I relate to God.

I was to face other tests as Mack and I put our energies into being good parents.

One day, out of the blue, 'Chelle began stuttering. I had quit work when 'Chelle was born, but I researched my nursing notes and concluded this would pass. Neither of us said much about it at first. Then her stuttering got worse; she stammered with almost every word.

Mack and I had been studying God's Word from Proverbs on raising children. With the help of an able teacher, we began to see the importance of scriptural training. We saw that conquering a child's will in love and consistency was the overall issue confronting us.

Mack decided to put the principle into practice. "We'll discipline her," he said, "because this is simply a bad habit she has developed. Every time she consistently stutters, we'll spank her with the rod."

My responder-signals went berserk. Surely that was all wrong! That would seriously damage her character.

"Oh, dear, I believe I hear another Mack truck roaring toward me," I thought.

Mack was consistent in his discipine. I half-heartedly tried to carry out his orders. While he was at work and 'Chelle and I were at home together, I'd frequently pretend not to hear her stuttering. Or I'd say to myself, "Oh, that was just a little one."

One afternoon when Mack was out plowing the garden and I was cooking supper, 'Chelle started the awfullest case of stuttering I ever heard. I was consciously trusting Christ to be my patience and wisdom, but suddenly I didn't think I could stand it anymore. I escaped to the bathroom to pray. But the same old grinding questions came up: "Do you really trust Mack? What if he's wrong?" My fear revealed that I wasn't trusting. I reassured myself, "Either God is limited or He isn't."

When Mack came in, 'Chelle virtually stopped stuttering. I thought, "What goes here? What am I doing wrong?"

Later, while I washed the dishes, Mack volunteered to give 'Chelle her bath. They had a heart-to-heart talk that I hope goes on forever. He asked her why she stuttered.

"Because I want to, Daddy," she said.

In his firm, kind voice he explained to her, "Honey, God made you in a very special way. If you stutter just because you want to, some day when you get older and bigger you won't want to stutter—but you won't be able to stop."

He told 'Chelle that we wanted her to be a happy girl, and that's why we were spanking her so that she could break her bad habit.

She said, "I understand, Daddy."

After I finished the dishes she and I played in the hallway while Mack bathed. She began stuttering. Through the door, Mack told me to spank her.

Just a few days earlier Mack and I had disagreed and I had not been submissive about something. Mack told me to obey and that night while 'Chelle prayed she thanked Jesus that she wanted to obey and to help Mommie obey Daddy, too! I almost toppled off of my knees. But, back to the hallway.

With the greatest feeling of victory I've ever had, I joyfully said, " 'Chelle, come on, let's obey Daddy." We walked hand in hand to her room. As I got the rod she pertly said, "Mommie, I'll lie across your knees." She offered no resistance when I spanked her. She didn't cry loudly as she usually did, but sobbed afterward on my shoulder for a moment. Then as quickly as a summer shower starts and stops, she smiled and started to play. With my mouth hanging open and tears filling my eyes, I felt that we should talk like we always did after discipline. But I realized there was no need; I had said all I had needed to say when I urged, "Let's obey Daddy." I think my attitude toward Mack triggered her response. She turned to me, and speaking slowly and clearly, said, "See, I'm not stuttering." We all laughed, clapped our hands, and thanked Jesus.

All the next day I swung the rod in love when she stuttered, saying, "We will obey Daddy." I thought to myself, "You're not responsible. He's responsible. He's responsible." 'Chelle responded beautifully and did not stutter the rest of the week. To this day she has never stuttered again.

I still cringe in relating this experience to anyone, and I seldom do. I do not offer it as a remedy for stuttering; I describe it merely as a prescription for responding to one's husband and leaving the results to God.

Through this experience I began to see that God meant even the devastating Mack trucks in my life to deliver only good to me. In that perspective I could truthfully say, "Keep those trucks coming!"

Throughout our six years of marriage and 'Chelle's three years of life, God was chiseling away more and more at the rough edges of my life. Had He cut away the whole imperfection at once, I would have crumbled under the impact.

Probably the most regular conflict in my life those six years occurred at Christmas. I had had a "normal" childhood at Christmas, I thought, with gifts, Christmas trees, blinking lights, Santa Claus and surprises. Mother would usually get us everything on our lists, with a few extras thrown in as a bonus. She thought we would be disappointed if all our wishes weren't granted. It was her way of saying, "I love you and want you to be happy." I adopted that same policy for 'Chelle.

Mack grew up with a different set of values. When he made out his list, he seldom got anything on it. He logically concluded that it was too painful to expect anything.

With two such opposite ideas, you can imagine how peaceful our Christmases were. Sometimes Mack would surprise me with a gift, and other times he exuded as much enthusiasm for the holiday as a turtle at a track meet. One year I bought my own gift, wrapped it, and opened it with delight. I got what I wanted—but not really. I was searching for the real Christmas spirit and didn't know it. Mack was searching too.

After 'Chelle was born, Mack had announced that our child would never be lied to in any regard—starting with Christmas and Santa Claus. His orders were easy to obey the first couple of Christmases. The year that 'Chelle was three, I felt unsure and threatened. After all, her little friends would be talking and pretending and sitting on Santa's knee. What could anyone put in the place of those merry traditions? My whole Christmas season would crumble.

By March I knew that I had to trust God with the problem area or else I'd be crazy by December. I wanted so much to trust Him with all the details of my life, but I was afraid He would take too much away from me. So from March to September I prayed, "O God, if You can straighten out my Christmases You can do anything!

By October I realized that I could no more tell 'Chelle a lie about Santa Claus and make it a part of our family way of life, than I could lie to her about anything else. As I focused on this truth, God provided peace for each day. It was a peace that "passed all understanding" because by November I had not even bought the first gift.

Then December came and again I went quickly to my knees. I almost felt like a reformed alcoholic wanting to reach for the bottle. Each day I asked myself, "Is God big enough to handle this day?" Each day He proved that He could as I patiently kept my eyes on His sufficiency as promised in 2 Corinthians 12:9.

Ways of celebrating Christmas which would be fun and still maintain the truth of the season began to formulate in my mind. We put together a birthday party for Jesus, with 'Chelle and I making Christmas cookies. Her friends gathered with all the party trimmings, and we sang "Happy Birthday" to Jesus.

While 'Chelle and her little friends were playing, Mack and I planned a treasure hunt around the house with notes from here to there for each one. Each ended her search with a small gift found in the dryer, drawer, or some corner. We all had such a good time searching that we laughed till we almost cried.

On Christmas Eve Mack took 'Chelle and me for a wheelbarrow ride around the neighborhood, singing carols. When we got home, Mack and 'Chelle lay down in front of the fireplace, and I brought out a sack full of gifts for 'Chelle. We watched as she opened the items I had carefully chosen from the grocery store. There was a package of flower seeds, a box of muffin mix that she mixed herself for our Christmas breakfast, and her favorite candy. She unforgettably lifted her arms to me and said, "Oh, those were such good gifts, Mommie—let me hug your neck." Tears came to my eyes. Such little things—but they meant a great deal to her.

'Chelle also learned the true spirit of Christmas in another way. I had bought an advent calendar with little doors to open each day before Christmas. Behind each door was a Scripture verse, and it was amazing how many of those verses she learned by heart.

On Christmas morning at one o'clock I woke up. I wasn't sleepy. I wasn't worried—just saturated with peace. So I got up, made a lemon pie, sliced oranges for the ambrosia, listened to a Bible study tape and finished the handwork on a new dress. Two hours' work. During part of that time, I heard some of the most beautiful Christmas music over the radio that I have ever heard. God and I shared a very special few hours; He was reassuring my trembling heart that He would work out the minutest detail of our Christmases.

Our Christmas presents to family and friends brought special joy to all of us. We wrote each person's name and the amount we usually spent on them, then we filled a mission envelope for each one, placed them in a small box tied with red ribbon, and let 'Chelle put "Jesus' birthday gift" in the offering plate. That anonymous red-bowed gift caused no small stir in the congregation. It was like we three had a wonderful secret shared with our heavenly Father. Shopping had been a breeze. Mack had sent me out for a box of cards which announced that our gift to our loved ones this year was helping to spread the Gospel around the world.

The change of seasons, winter to summer, offered new unconquered horizons for me. One good thing I could say about our honeymoon was that we went to the mountains instead of the beach—not only could I not swim, I was deathly afraid of water. Mack loved the water; he had grown up in Florida. I had grown up in eastern Tennessee, surrounded by mountains and seeing few lakes and fewer swimming pools.

Not until after we were married did Mack learn I couldn't swim, and it actually was no big deal to him. He accepted that along with the rest of his surprise package, but he began gently and gradually to condition me to the water. It took me two years to stick my head under water, the next three years to swim in shallow water, and finally I learned to swim all over the pool.

One day Mack and I were at a beach motel swimming pool, and I swam alongside him, back and forth, the length of the pool. I could do well with my body—it was my mind that kept wanting to sink! As I'd get to the eight-foot marker, I'd be tempted to panic. Then I'd ask myself, "You mean your God isn't as big as eight feet." I'd literally laugh up at the clouds. I memorized well and drilled myself on Romans 8:38-39—"For I am persuaded that neither death, nor life . . . nor height, nor depth, nor any other creature, shall be able to separate us from the love of God, which is in Christ Jesus our Lord."

My fear of swimming floated away that day. I realized how fortunate I was as I sat by the pool with a group of friends and Sandy dolefully commented, "I'm afraid of the water and I always will be!" And I said to myself: "That's a cozy place to be—all cuddled up in your fear with no one to drag you out into the cold world!"

Then I realized that my release from fear must have compared in some remote way to the joy of forgiveness Mary Magdalene felt as she stood before Jesus. Since salvation, I had never felt such gratitude to God for my newfound freedom. I was likewise grateful for a husband who cared enough to help draw me out of my fear.

Although I was released from my fear of swimming, it wasn't long until I had to face another challenge. Shortly after our son Michael was born, Mack announced that he had been pondering about an investment for our family entertainment. He had sorted out all the facts—an instinctive trait with him—and decided we needed a sailboat.

Physically I froze. Inside I was screaming, "God, I can't take another Mack truck. I thought I was going to get a rest from trusting You for major things for awhile. Now Mack comes up with this! I've just come through major surgery with my fear of swimming, and now you ask me to go right back to the operating table. Surely this is too much! I can't do it."

Mack stood before me, eagerly waiting for my response. "Mack Bruner," I said, "the only other worse thing I could possibly imagine is sky diving. And I expect any day now for God to ask me to trust Him for that one."

As usual, God worked slowly and gently in my life. Mack dismissed the subject for awhile, but he was "sailing in his mind." He rented a day sailer and took 'Chelle along. She cried the first time, but with Mack's encouragement she learned to relax and trust him. It became obvious that "Mommie was the one who would be a problem."

It made my stomach ache to think of myself and the children out on that big lake, rolling from side to side. For two hours one evening I poured out my apprehensions to Mack as I had never done before. He was so gentle and tolerant that though he never said, "No, I'll forget it," I was comforted. I even consented to sailing with him and 'Chelle.

Out in the breeze, tilting from side to side in a small boat, I softly cried with each gentle gust. I would have bawled if 'Chelle had not kept saying, "It's OK, Mommie. Don't be afraid. I'm not. "

After a few more times of bawling in the wind and stomping back on shore with vows I'd never go again, I began to see a glimmer of a chance that it might work.

Then all of a sudden Mack's "someday sailboat" became a reality. It was a stable boat, large enough for six adults, with a small cabin, and self-righting leaded ballast. That spelled security to me. Then, after a few times of struggling with Michael in life jackets, pulling ropes and manning the jib sail, lowering the centerboard and counterbalancing, I kept so busy and mad that I almost forgot to be afraid. As long as I didn't look up at that giant sail or see how far we dipped to the side, Mommie was OK.

My real security came as I realized one day that I had done everything I could do—and if we capsized, well, Mack was going to have his hands full. After all, the children and I were entirely his responsibility. That was a very stable horizon for me to focus on. To this day I am secure in sailing with God's provision for me and my children—and sailing isn't bad at all.

Sharing adventures on a sailboat and sharing everyday experiences at home have strengthened our life together. Matter of fact, I'm becoming "liberated" and loving every minute. Just recently, after a busy day, I sat feeding Michael his evening meal and Mack opened the refrigerator. "Sure needs cleaning out," he remarked. Because I've learned not to take his remarks as a personal attack when I've done the best job possible that day ("as unto the Lord"), I responded, "It sure does. It's really a mess. Why don't you clean it out if you have time?"

Mack put his arms around me and said, "Honey, that reaction sure is a change from what it used to be. I'm glad."

Another day, we realized at lunch that almost everything on our plates had been given to us. There was fresh speckled perch from Jack, corn on the cob from Tom, cole slaw—cabbage grown by the man down the street—and fresh homemade bread baked by this "happy wife." You better believe we bowed our heads for thanks! Yes, our country is in a recession-depression. Evidently God is not. I was reminded once again that God takes care of his own.

Yes, I am happy and I am the wife of a happy husband, too. Not long ago I received a compliment from my husband which makes every painful growing experience worth it all. We were on our way home from a friend's house. It was a brand-new house, with grand furnishings to match. Mack had been talking about how talented our hostess was in decorating her home—and fearfully I asked him if he would like our house to be "elegant."

"O, Jan, no," he said. "Never. I couldn't live like that. That's fine for them, but that is just not us. I love the simplicity of our home. I love the way you've made it. In fact," he said, "tonight as I sat there among those guests I watched you. Jan, you radiate a loveliness that no one else had. A peacefulness. An inner joy. I was very proud that you belonged to me. Thank you for being like that."

In his own way my husband had praised me as God says the loving husband will commend the good wife. "Her husband . . . praises her. Many daughters have done virtuously, but thou excellest them all. Favor is deceitful, and beauty is vain but a woman that feareth the Lord, she shall be praised" (Prov. 31:28-30). My Mack is definitely more than a truck.

Reminiscing with Darien

As a young child, I frequently longed for a sister. So when Jan was born, eight years my junior, I considered her God's special gift to me. Even though I dearly loved her, the age difference kept us from having much in common until we were both married.

Once we had common interests to share, I discovered God had not only given me a wonderful sister but a dear friend. Our totally opposite personalities, temperaments, and talents haven't divided us but have contributed to both our maturing. As I really get to know my sister, I can appreciate a perspective opposite from mine, and see how we can wonderfully complement and learn from each other. A husband and wife's differences as well as their strengths and weaknesses should be used likewise to complement each other.

In December 1967 I poured out my heart to God in prayer requesting that He show me how to enjoy life to the fullest and how to share this faith with others. I could hardly contain my excitement soon afterward when Jan brought two vital booklets to me: "The Four Spiritual Laws" and "Have You Made the Wonderful Discovery of the Spirit-Filled Life?" These Campus Crusade booklets were just what I needed, though Jan was barely acquainted with them.

In my enthusiasm over the thirst-quenching truths I was learning, I let them bubble out and splash over anyone who come close to me. Later Jan and Mack revealed that my exuberance over these spiritual insights had been like a grain of sand in an oyster's shell to them. I am so thankful that God used my excitement over His Word to develop a spiritual pearl rather than an ugly sore in my sister. Today I realize that spiritual insights should be shared as others feel the need and are ready to receive them.

As Jan and I studied God's Word, she began to discover that true fulfillment is not based on such things as where she went, what kind of house she lived in, or her husband's temperament. Instead, her identity, stability and inner peace are based on her relationship with God and to her husband according to God's design. Properly related to her husband, she is fulfilled and the climate is set to encourage her husband to be the man God intended him to be.

Jan, as well as the majority of women I know, finds it very difficult to accept the fact that a wife's response to her husband's leadership reveals her spiritual condition. God's plan is summarized in 1 Corinthians 11:3. "Christ is the Head of every man; the head of a woman is her husband, and the Head of Christ is God" (AMP). Notice that the woman is not the only one under authority. The man is under Christ's authority, and Christ is under the Father's authority. Christ was willing to assume this position while on earth for our blessing, and wives must assume this position to obtain the protection and blessing God has for us.

Your position under authority never means that you are inferior or that you are to be treated as a slave or a doormat. Instead, it means that God has assigned you and your husband complementary roles in order that you may receive His protection, blessing, and happiness. The husband's role as leader or the head gives the home direction; your role as responder could be compared to a heart that gives life—the pulse of the family. Each role, equal in importance, demands each partner's all—100 percent of our talents and dedication.

Many wives fear that their individuality will be suppressed by being under their husband's authority. Actually, the opposite is true. It's been wonderful to see Jan's unique creativity, talents, and resources develop as she stays under her husband's leadership. She had been freed from fears, impatience and pressures that were a deterrent to individuality. I, too, have seen how God develops my individuality beyond my highest dreams, as I have responded positively to God's leadership through my husband DeWitt. The only way you and I can be free individuals is to be obedient to God's plan for our lives. Otherwise we are in bondage to our sin-nature within.

"But what if Mack is wrong?" Jan had thought when she disagreed with Mack about 'Chelle's stuttering problem. Jan shared her opinion with Mack according to her medical knowledge and her motherly intuition. That was her responsibility, and she did it with love rather than an authoritarian manner. Then she left the final decision to Mack. God honored her obedience and worked it out for the benefit of all concerned. He can do that because His plan is perfect—not His people or their decisions.

Putting into practice the principle of trusting God by obeying your husband can be very painful. Whether your obedience involves a deep hurt, doing something you don't want to, or not doing something you wanted to, may be a process of trying, failing, and trying again in order to break wrong ways of responding and developing new ones. When you see the pain ushering in greater happiness, your purpose is strengthened for the next time.

The better you know Christ and understand His perfect love for you, the easier it is to obey and trust His plan for you as a wife. He wouldn't die to make you a part of God's forever-family and then design a miserable plan for your marriage! His plan is for your happiness by obeying Him and letting Him work out the results under your husband's authority.

Thinking Through with You:

Question: *What role did God assign the husband and wife in the marriage relationship?*
Answer: "Wives, be subject—be submissive and adapt yourselves—to your own husbands as [a service] to the Lord. For the husband is head of the wife as Christ is the Head of the church" (Eph. 5:22-23, AMP).

Q.: *How do you know that God's position for you in the marriage relationship does not lower your worth or importance as a person?*
A.: "There is neither male and female; for you are all one in Christ Jesus" (Gal. 3:28, NASB).

Q.: *Why is a wife to obey her husband even if he is not a Christian?*
A.: "In the same way, you wives, be submissive to your own husbands so that even if any of them are disobedient to the Word, they may be won without a word by the behavior of their wives" (1 Peter 3:1, NASB).

Q.: *How do I know that my advice, insights, perspective and abilities are needed by my husband?*
A.: "The Lord God said, 'It is not good for the man to be alone; I will make him a helper suitable for him' " (Gen. 2:18, NASB).

8
It's Never Too Late

Mildred Brown

I watched in horror that windy April day at the sight of flames lapping through the roof of our store. It seemed like minutes before I could drop my clothes basket and run, screaming the warning: "George, George, the store is on fire!"

Moments before, I had stoked my woodstove to boil water for my last load of wash, and the crumbling chimney was unable to confine the flames. The attic of the frame building was crammed with flammable objects, and in ten minutes everything was destroyed except for the cash drawer and account books that George had the presence of mind to rescue.

As my nostrils burned with the stench of smoke, I numbly recalled that only minutes before I had walked through the store that shelved a special bolt of material which would make a new dress for five-year-old Darien. Now, soot-covered, I stood hand in hand with my husband and silently prayed: *Surely Lord, this doesn't mean we have to return to tenant farming!* We had grown so weary of moving from farm to farm.

George and I were married in the middle '30s during the economic depression. In the South at that time there was very little industry and few jobs except farming. But George loved farming.

I had become a Christian when Darien was three months old, after searching for inner peace with God for years. One night I fell to my knees and prayed, "God, I've tried everything I know to become a Christian. I'm at the end of myself; I'm hopeless and helpless. The rest is up to You." I quit trying to find salvation through my efforts, put it all in His hands, and accepted what Christ had done for me on the cross. I experienced immediate peace, and I walked around for several days with a sense of His presence surrounding me. Though I knew little about the Bible and its principles for Christian living, I trusted Christ as completely as I knew how.

When Darien was three years old, the federal government offered to help Southern tenant farmers with long-term loans at low interest rates. Horses and equipment were main requirements for the loans.

We began eagerly to search for a farm and located one 30 miles away. The agent commented that I seemed reluctant to move that distance and asked, "Would you get homesick?"

I fretted. I'd always felt dependent on my mother after my father died when I was 16 and we moved from Colorado's prairies to Tennessee's rolling hills to be near Mother's parents. We decided not to buy the farm.

My mother had proved to be a shrewd business woman when she was forced to support her three daughters. For years she had successfully managed a country store. I thought she was much wiser than either George or me. During my regular weekly visits, I always told her all about our plans and decisions.

These visits became a source of irritation between George and me. I'd casually say at breakfast, "George, I'd like to go to Mother's and spend the day." And he'd groan, "Why do you want to go there all the time? You went there last week. Don't you have anything to do around here?"

"You know that's the only place I ever go," I'd protest. "Do you expect me to stay home all the time? You go anywhere, anytime you please, and you begrudge me going to Mother's once a week!" By the time we finished arguing, the coffee would be cold, and I'd be even colder. Who could be warm, I thought, toward a selfish, domineering man who would not let his wife visit her mother?

Soon, however, we had an opportunity to manage a store of our own, and I asked my mother's advice. "Do you think George and I could make a success of it?"

"Well, I don't know if you could or not," she said, "but I'll be glad to help. It's a big job, you know."

"Mother thinks we could make a go of it," I told George. "What do you think?"

"Well, if nothing else will do you, I guess we can try," he said, "although I'm not sure it's the best thing to do."

Anything seemed better to me than farming. The crops and weather were always uncertain, and, at best, money was scarce.

After all, I rationalized, George loved to talk with his friends after a hard day's work, and the local store was the central gathering place. He would feel right at home with the daily yarns and woes of farming—the milking, harvesting, and butchering of hogs.

Renting a store spelled security to me. But the fire turned my security and dreams to ashes. Just as dramatically, however, the dream was reconstructed. Within two weeks we were back in business as friends and relatives built a store and living quarters board by board, nail by nail, on a half-acre of land nearby. Their rallying around us was remarkable.

About two years later we had a chance to buy some land adjoining our store. I was very excited about George's opportunity to stop renting a farm and own one.

"George, we have enough for the down payment, and I'm sure we could borrow the rest," I said. "Now is the time to get the land you've always wanted."

He was uneasy. "Do you think we could pay for it?"

"I know we can," I assured him. "Look how well we have been doing in the store, and with what you would make off the land, we could do it easily."

Of course, I had consulted my mother. She agreed with me. We borrowed the money, and the land was ours.

George then voiced his opinion that we should build a house and sell the store.

I thought to myself, "That will never happen. It just can't! I need the store. I like to have money without asking George for it; he probably won't have money to give me, anyway. We couldn't send our children to college or have the things I've always wanted."

To George I said: "You're never satisfied. We are doing great here. I don't believe you know what you want." He looked at me steadily from behind his rimless glasses, "I've never wanted anything but a farm of my own," he said.

We left it at that—my way.

I did most of the buying, stocking, waiting on customers, and pumping gas. I also shuffled our daily groceries from our stock to my pantry with no bookkeeping. In addition, I liberally withdrew money for clothing for Darien and Janice or for household items—with no voucher in return. George, I reasoned, didn't need to know how expensive little girls' dresses were, and though I wasn't extravagant I thought our girls should have the best available. Besides, he would probably fuss.

George had been reared about 10 miles from where we lived. At the age of 16 he was rudely thrust out on his own by the death of both parents. His family of 11 brothers and sisters, most of whom were grown, went their individual ways. It was after this blow that George had become a Christian. He went to live with a nearby farm family and helped with the work. I learned that he fashioned his idea of a perfect couple from the married son living on the farm. She seemed to live to make her husband happy, she was an immaculate housewife, and a good cook. They seemed very devoted to each other.

That was fine for them, but I wanted more out of life than what appeared a humdrum existence. I wanted to do something important that made a contribution to society—and something that made me happy!

Since the beginning of our marriage George had dropped by

the nearest country store after supper and chatted with others for his "recreation." He invited me to accompany him, but I'd much rather read a good book at home. "I really don't care who sold a cow or calf or got their tobacco plowed or set out, or how many pigs Tom Jones' old sow had, or the latest gossip that's going around."

And George had no patience with my reading. "How you can sit around with your nose in a book all the time is more than I can understand. Why do you want to read about all those things that are make-believe?"

"The characters are a lot more interesting and do lots more wonderful things than anyone I know!" I'd retort.

Mother's house had always been so neat, and she kept herself neat, too. She allowed me to cuddle up and read for hours at a time, and so now it seemed much more important to finish the last chapter than do anything else. I could sit right down beside dirty dishes, dirty clothes, unswept floor, and mounds of ironing, and it never bothered me one bit.

Sometimes between novels, I'd sew or crochet, or do an oil painting. I liked to have the house spotless when I was expecting company, but to work for that every day seemed like wasting time.

George didn't agree. He liked well-planned meals on time, not merely something whipped up at the last minute. We had many quarrels over this. When Darien got older, she helped with many meals. I did have to tend the store, but it was more of an excuse than a reason for late, hasty meals.

One night when George came home from milking, I was sitting in the store reading a magazine. He didn't even wait to see if I had supper ready. He just grabbed my magazine and threw it in the stove. I couldn't believe anyone would do anything so terrible. I only lacked a few paragraphs of finishing the story, and now I would never know how it turned out. Besides, I was humiliated in front of several customers.

I went fuming to the kitchen to conjure up supper. I had never liked scenes in front of others. I was completely crushed, and I waited until everyone had left that night before I unbridled my anger at George. A neighbor once said of us, "You think George can fuss. You should hear Mildred lash back when no one's around."

George forgot his anger quickly. Not so with me. Mine came to a more gradual boil and also took much longer to cool. By the time I would get "back to normal" another boiler was heating up, and off we'd go again.

During the long winter months, most of the men in the community would sit and loaf in our store. Many would come early in the morning, buy crackers and cheese or bologna, chew their tobacco, and spit into or at the boxes of ashes in front of the huge pot-bellied stove. On these long days, George was always working in the barn or just doing anything—it seemed to me—to keep himself occupied outside the store.

By evening, weary with work, I'd complain: "George, how come you are the only man in the neighborhood who has any work to do? If we didn't have a store, I bet anything you would be in someone else's store just like the rest of them. Tonight I'm staying in the living room, and I'm not coming into the store at all, not for anything!"

"To hell with the store," he said. "I have work to do and I'm going to do it, tomorrow and the next day and the next!" Then he'd meander into the store to mingle with the customers.

I had become indifferent to George and his needs. He had hurt my feelings so many times that I had built a shell of protection to keep from being hurt more.

I believed Jesus Christ loved me, but He seemed far away in heaven. Then I began to read some books by a well-known preacher. I found out that Jesus was ever-present. I could imagine Him sitting beside my bed at night. I could imagine laying all my problems, cares, and heartaches in His lap and going to sleep with His hand holding mine. I began learning a few Bible verses and specific promises that I quoted when I felt the need for comfort.

Meanwhile I lavished attention on the girls; I wanted them to be happy and have all the things they wanted. I found happiness in their happiness, their friends, and the future. I also tried to protect them from George's "temper tantrums," as I called them. I never told him about our expenses unless I had to, and I bought what I wanted when I wanted it.

As World War II ended and money became more available, our customers went more frequently to town to shop in the supermarkets. We couldn't compete with their prices, and my financial security started to crumble. George began talking about building a house on the farm, and the dread of that lonely life and financial uncertainty brought me close to a nervous breakdown.

Then my mother's health began to decline and she needed help in her store. She convinced George to buy a half-interest in it and move next door to her. We sold our store, and George commuted three miles to his farm each day.

It took us two years to grow weary of this arrangement—it was senseless for George to drive back and forth to work. Besides, I eventually got tired of being told how to do every little thing by my mother. George and I agreed to sell our interest in the store and to move as far away as necessary. "The farther, the better," I said.

So we bought a house near our farm. I was slowly but surely coming untied from Mother's apron strings.

By this time Darien was in college and planned soon to be married. And with Jan growing up fast, I began to panic. Soon Jan would be leaving too. I began a frantic search to bring fulfillment into my life.

I tried everything I could do in our church. I taught a Sunday School class, held Training Union office and served in the Women's Missionary Union. I was there every time the doors opened. I also took part in the PTA, attended Jan's school ball games, and in my "spare time" became a Girl Scout leader and directed day camp.

George began to fuss about all my activities. "You are gone all the time! I'm tired of you running all over the countryside fiddling with a bunch of kids. How do you expect me to farm without any help? You're interested in helping everybody but me," he complained. "It's got to stop!"

"But I like doing something worthwhile," I told him. "I'd go crazy just staying at home all the time. I told you that you wouldn't like living on a farm. We can't make a living here. You aren't satisfied with anything."

That's how it went. We squabbled all the time about money. It cost much more to live than he had thought it would. Darien, going to college, needed as many nice things as her friends had, I thought. That cost too much, too, George said. Soon Darien was married and moved 300 miles away.

At this point in my life, I had a longing to be of definite usefulness in the world. Through our pastor I learned of an opening for houseparents in a children's home. "How beneficial," I thought.

I talked George into applying, and shortly afterward we rented out the farm and moved to the home, just 100 miles from Darien. I was sure God had planned it that way.

George wasn't certain. He didn't like the idea much, but we needed more money, and since neither of us was happy he consented.

I liked it from the beginning. I had my own income and could again buy things for Janice and myself without asking George. I loved the children. The work was hard and many things were not pleasant, but I kept hoping they would improve.

During this time I began to turn more and more to the Lord for comfort and the sense of acceptance that I was not finding in my relationship with George.

George tried to do his work well, but at best the working conditions were bad. After struggling two years, he gave me an ultimatum: "I'm going home, Mildred. If you don't want to go, you can just stay here!"

Darien had confided that George felt I cared nothing for him anymore. She reproved me: "He shows much more affection for you than you show in return. You don't put him first in your life, or prove your love for him."

I shrugged off her comments. I felt Darien didn't understand what I had to put up with. Instead, I prayed that God would make something happen to change George's mind. I thought of my job as "missionary work and very worthwhile."

I expected a miracle—right up until the morning the moving truck arrived. I went along, but not happily. I thought George was leading us out of God's will for our lives, and I saw myself as God's number-one agent to make George suitably remorseful.

Expenses back on the farm piled up. I laughed while recounting each new calamity to my friends. The refrigerator quit running, the well pump had to be replaced, and on and on. "They just don't appreciate God's sense of humor," I thought smugly. I was trusting and praying, "Lord, I know that if things get bad enough George will be glad to go back."

I took a full-time job and George was back to cooking his makeshift meals again. I usually drove home late at night, tearful with unhappiness, and found George already asleep.

Janice, caught in the middle of our turmoil, developed a peptic ulcer. But in the midst of all this trouble, George emphatically assured me that he "never wanted to see the children's home again."

"God," I prayed, "You sure have a problem."

Then George was hospitalized and I knew that *I* had a problem.

We both thought he might die. I saw very clearly at last that he was the most important part of my life. I felt that I could not stand to live without him.

"George, you've just got to get well," I said. "I would be completely lost without you. Life would not be worth living."

"I don't know if I'm going to make it or not," he answered, "but one thing I know, I'm ready to go home if that is the Lord's will."

I stayed day and night until the critical time was past. Then I worked all day on my job and drove the 60 miles to the hospital afterwards to spend the night with him. He couldn't bear for me not to come, and I couldn't stand not to go. Work, money, nothing else seemed important anymore.

All day long I prayed, "Lord, please just spare him to me

this time. I want another chance to show him how much I love him. I know I've never been a good wife to him, but, Lord, please give me one more chance."

The Lord gave me my chance.

George returned home to convalesce. I kept on working. With no hospital insurance, the bills were very high. I tried my best to show my love for him, but I felt as though we were fighting a losing battle financially. Janice had gone off to college for nurses' training, and I thought of all the "nice things" she was needing.

George was so discouraged that he was close to agreeing with me when I suggested that working together in a children's home might be better than the way we were living.

Darien put us in touch with a children's home near her. George consented to an interview, and we were offered a position. But he was in a quandary.

Finally I said, "George, forget the whole thing. There is nothing you want to do but farm, so farm! We'll make it some way, so let's stay here." That was that, as far as I was concerned.

But before long, George was saying, "We really ought to try the job. We couldn't be much worse off than we are now. Let's try it, and if and when I decide to come back, you won't try to change my mind but come willingly."

I agreed, and we journeyed to Georgia—me with a song in my heart and an almost absolute assurance that the Lord wouldn't ask me to return.

George had been raised in an era when parental authority was respected. Although he worked outside during the day, our evenings with the children in the cottage were vexing to him. As acting housemother, I didn't always know how to handle the lack of respect for authority as George thought it should be handled. He looked forward to "better days."

I enjoyed feeling useful now that our girls were grown. Darien had her family, and Jan had married and moved to Florida. Then on one of her visits, Jan told Darien and me about some wonderful seminars they had been attending at their church. We became excited about the ""new" truths they were teaching: how to confess your sins, claiming First John 1:9; the filling of the Spirit; and walking moment by moment under Jesus Christ's control. We realized there was to be an abundant life for Christians as mentioned in John 10:10.

Darien, Jan, and I agreed to have a period of Bible reading and prayer early in the mornings in our separate homes. We exchanged prayer requests. And things began to happen in our lives that showed the Lord was at work. We began to study doctrinal tapes from an experienced Bible teacher, and stability began to shape our lives.

Darien began teaching a neighborhood Bible class for women. I attended several of them and was happy and proud that the Lord was using her. My greatest desire had always been that my girls would be used of the Lord.

One day George came in from working outside and noticed the obvious disobedience and rude language being directed at me by one of the children. This was not unusual. Many of the youngsters behaved this way. George decided this behavior had to stop, and he took over the discipline of this child by giving her a much-deserved spanking.

She was furious. "I'll get even with you," she screamed and ran from the room.

The next day at school she painted a lurid picture of cruelty to a sympathetic teacher, and the teacher pressured the superintendent.

The official was apologetic when he came to see us. "My hands are tied," he said. "In the six years you've worked here, you've been among the best houseparents I've ever had but the lack of understanding by outsiders involving problems with the children forces my decision. I feel it's best for all concerned to let you go."

I answered calmly, "Although all things are not good, I'm sure God means this for good in our lives."

"Yes," he agreed. "Probably this will work out for your good after all."

By this time Darien had begun to study the marriage relationship and was developing a class to teach scriptural principles of marriage. I was very interested in her teaching, but I did not immediately apply the principles to my own life. Listening to her in classes of "Will The Real Woman Please Stand Up?" I marveled at my daughter's being used of God to help young women. "How wonderful for them," I thought. The principles didn't seem all that important in my case—George would just have to be satisfied with me after all these years.

Darien didn't seem to agree. She suggested certain principles that would help me, and I was convicted of some wrong attitudes.

I saw that our last job had been obtained mostly because I wanted it, rather than its being George's choice. I still thought, however, the Lord should give both of us work that we could enjoy and feel useful in doing. For the next year, though, circumstances caused me to rely solely on George for our financial support. Since I wasn't working I had to be quiet and to think. I was convicted of my actual unwillingness to return to the farm if George decided on that, and prayed in the words of Psalm 37:4, "Lord, I'm claiming Your promise to change my heart's desires if I commit my way to You—I'm willing for you to do that if you want us back on the farm."

George had taken a temporary job. The hours were long and the work was hard. For the first time, I sat at home alone, waiting for George to return. Then one day, through no efforts of mine, George was offered a good-paying outdoor job. The salary was more than he and I combined had ever earned! Included were a lovely apartment, paid utilities, and many conveniences. God and George had done it all!

I began practicing certain principles in Darien's course: I learned to genuinely praise my husband, and I tried not to nag to get my own way. George was generous with his money, but, oh, how I hated to *ask* for it! In the deep recesses of my mind, I still believed I needed to help make a living. So once again I tried to make my own money.

I did babysitting in the evenings, and sold cosmetics door-to-door in the daytime. I did not earn much—in fact, a good deal less than George thought I grossed. He began to ask me to buy groceries and other items with my money. He also stopped my writing checks.

When I told Darien about George's growing unpleasantness over money, she said, "Don't you see, Mother? You're doing the same thing all over again. Daddy is supposed to make the living. You are depriving him of this privilege, and now you are having to pay for it. God made the man with the ability to support his family and enjoy it, instead of it being a burden. You need to stop working for money altogether, and just go back to depending on him for everything."

And so I did. One night I said, "George, I've stopped all my outside jobs. I've always hated selling, and other people can take care of their own children. Besides, this is your responsibility, and you are a capable provider. I've been wrong all these years. Will you forgive me?"

Forgive he did. "I never wanted you to work anyway," he said. And with that step, I thought I had arrived. Surely, I was doing *everything* right now!

At first I felt very awkward asking for money, thinking I had to convince George of the merit of the expenditure. Then I learned to relax and simply state my need. He never refused me, though I was ready to accept his decision.

One day at the grocery story I filled my cart only to discover as I stood in line that a twenty dollar bill had disappeared from my purse! "Oh, God. Please, this can't be happening to me," I pleaded. I'd have to write a check and that was forbidden. There seemed to be no other logical solution.

Afterwards I wandered out into the drizzling rain trying to think of some way I could replace the twenty dollars before George knew it was gone. Then I remembered a Bible principle. I'd simply tell the truth.

I braced myself for an explosion at home, but George seemed to sense my dependence on him. "Don't worry," he said, "Forget about the check. Maybe you'd better straighten out your purse."

I felt a warm and comforting fellowship with him that I'd never known before. I began to have a new love and respect for him that I had always wanted.

Our future seemed laid out pretty clearly. George and I would never have many things in common, so I had planned a cozy compromise with as few conflicts as possible. We had been married 39 years, and in two more years George would retire and we would go back to the farm. He could do what he wanted to do there without me, and I would stay home and listen to Bible tapes, visit my friends and relatives, or just be a hermit if that struck my fancy. Surely, that was all the Lord and I could expect. I had long ago given up my dreams of complete fulfillment in marriage.

Then, in one night, my world changed. As quickly as lightning flashes and just as intensely, pain struck my knee. The pain was almost unbearable. For the first time in my life, I thought I was dying. The pain was gone by morning. But the next night it struck in my other knee. Again it was gone by morning. This continued each night, striking first one joint and than another all over my body.

At first, my doctor thought it was a virus. But during his examination, he discovered a thickening in my breasts, and I was scheduled for immediate surgery.

I was sure that cancer had spread all over my body. I would probably die, I thought. I wasn't afraid. In fact, with all my pain, death seemed quite welcome, "My work is done anyway," I thought. "My girls are grown, married, and doing well. I'm not needed anymore. I'll be glad to go home, Lord, where there is no more pain, no more sorrow."

Then I thought of George. What would happen to him if I were gone?

I knew he would be unhappy without me, and I became very sad. I knew that his dream had always been to live on a farm with a wife who enjoyed it and was satisfied with the life he provided. Now what would hapen? I began to think about what would make him happy.

Then the thought came to me: "Maybe he'll go back home

if I die, find a woman who likes the same things he does, marry her, and live the kind of life he's always wanted."

The thought cut me to the heart.

"O Lord," I prayed, "if only I have the chance, I'll be that woman. I'd love to go back home to our farm and live the kind of life George has always wanted." In that moment, as I lay on my hospital bed awaiting the results of the tests, *the desires of my heart were changed.* I longed to go home with George and make him happy.

While I was in the hospital the Lord used my daughters to point out that I still had a lot of unfinished business. Jan, who had always felt that I neglected her father, asked Darien to talk to me.

Darien called me at the hospital. "Mother," she said, "you know Jan and I love you dearly and would never do anything to hurt you. Knowing the pain you are already having and not knowing your prognosis, it's especially difficult to share with you what is on my heart. But Jan and I know that if pain in your soul is needed for God's will to be done in your life, you would want it that way.

"We know that you have made some changes toward Daddy, but we wonder if he is the center of your life as he should be. Jan wonders if you realize the importance of spending time with Daddy, doing the things he enjoys such as gardening, visiting people, or just listening to him.

"Please don't take our opinions as from the Lord," Darien said, "but go to Him in His Word and ask God to reveal if this is true. Again, remember we love you dearly."

I reread my daughter's book, *You Can Be the Wife of Happy Husband.* In Bible quotes I saw God, not my daughters, commanding submission to my husband in all things (Eph. 5:22-24; Col. 3:18; I Peter 3:1-6). Not to some newlywed, but to *me,* who had lived nearly a lifetime doing it all wrong!

I read the pertinent Scriptures and a veil was lifted from my eyes; I got a new look at me and the truth really hurt. I realized I had lived a totally selfish life.

My attitude had been, "George will adjust, he'll get along all right," and then I had lived for my children's happiness, which was just an extension of myself. I was trying to live my life through them. Not only had I deprived George of his rightful place in my life, but I had deprived him of his place as a father by making all the decisions regarding our children. I'd left him out.

I had satisfied myself that I had a good and desirable relationship with the Lord. I thought I was obeying Him in everything. I had hoped in the beginning for a close relationship with George, but had given that up as impossible.

Now as I studied His Word, He drove home to my heart the indisputable fact: I did not have the right relationship with Him if there were any of His commands I ignored or refused to obey.

I had ignored and disobeyed His command to be under George's authority and leadership. The command wasn't dependent on whether George was the kind of husband I thought he should be. It wasn't based on how he acted or reacted. His spiritual condition was not the issue.

I saw that I had the same attitude toward God that I had toward George. I hadn't wanted to be under His authority, either. My personal desires had never been laid aside. I had never trusted Him to supply my needs without my help.

Now I wanted God's best. "Lord," I prayed, "I confess this as sin and accept Your forgiveness. Now, make me the person You want me to be, totally under Your authority by being under George's authority first."

The doctors diagnosed the joint pains as a strain of hepatitis. Although risky, surgery was scheduled for the breast tumor. It was malignant. My breast was removed. Recovery went well, and I convalesced at home. Now I had my dream back: the dream I had when I was first married—that of making my husband happy and being happy myself.

I tried to put some more of the things into practice that I had learned. Instead of talking all the time about things that interested me, I decided to sit quiely and listen to what

George wanted to say. He talked about his childhood—things I had never known. I found him very entertaining and I began learning so many things about him that made me understand him more and appreciate him deeply. I began to find out that he was a much finer, more stable, mature man than I had ever thought. We were becoming acquainted for the first time. I liked him as a person. It was amazing how he began to show respect for my opinions as well.

Recently we moved back to a farm and George and I are both so much happier now, and he is farming as he always wanted to do.

The other day we got a doctor's bill in the mail. Seeing the expression on George's face, I thought, "Oh, this is it! Everything's gone down the drain. There's going to be an old-time explosion."

The lampshade must have rocked on its bulb, and the ivy must have withered in the corner as George blew his top. I felt the old anger and hurt feelings boiling up inside me.

I thought, "Now the truth is coming out! I see how you really feel about me, Mister! You think more of your money than you do of me. If it's going to take all your earnings to save my life and make me well, you'd rather keep your money."

But just in time I remembered the proper way to deal with hurt feelings. "Mildred," I cautioned myself, "confess that sin of anger and bitterness to God. Give your hurt to Him and leave it there. Do not strike out blindly against George. Do not close your heart to him."

So as George continued to rant and rave, I, by the grace of God, kept my mouth shut. What a miracle!

Later as I spoke to the Lord about it, I began to understand George more. Only the day before, he had proudly deposited farm earnings in our savings account. I'm sure it was very satisfying to him, and now he must feel the doctors were conspiring to deplete his savings with that unexpected bill. I remembered his earlier readiness to pay the staggering hospital costs not covered by insurance.

As always, George's temper was quick to flare and quick to cool. A few months earlier I would have carried resentment toward him for several days, but I was learning not to take anger as a personal attack. With my new way of responding to our problems, I felt no resentment toward George.

I don't always feel different from the way I felt in years past, but instead of giving him the cold shoulder that I sometimes feel, I kiss him and by faith act the way I should. Before long God makes my inner feelings match my outer trust. I find that my shell of protection is no longer needed; Jesus Christ is my armor of protection.

It's so difficult to change the habits of a lifetime! Recently I found myself scheming how to divide grocery money to buy our granddaughter a birthday present. I'd buy it, I thought, show it to George, and then ask him to replace the money for groceries.

Then I realized I was trying to get my own way again. I wasn't trusting God to provide as good a present for 'Chelle through my husband as I could purchase. I was also robbing George of the joy of planning and buying our grandchild's gift.

So I talked it over with him and we agreed what she would like. He gave me the money to buy it. He then spent great effort in finding a box, packing the gift, and mailing it. He further suggested that we call Jan long distance on 'Chelle's birthday. What pleasant surprises!

The principle of being under my husband's authority has recently guided me down more new avenues. Since I had not lived under George's authority, I did not trust my daughters to their husbands' authority and care.

It was my pattern, and my duty, I thought, to worry as Mack and Jan traveled the 500 miles from Florida to visit us. I would almost prefer that they not come because of my fear. On one visit Mack said to me, "Mrs. Brown, you surely don't trust me to take care of Jan, or you wouldn't worry so much."

God used Mack's words to pierce deep into my heart, showing me that I was to trust God to care for my girls through their husbands.

The pain of seeing my mistakes is real, but the joy experienced by correcting these attitudes and actions more than compensates me. I'm so glad and grateful that it's never too late to become the wife of a happy husband!

Reminiscing with Darien:

Through my tears, I attempted to explain my emotions to my husband, DeWitt. Mother and I had just returned from the surgeon's office and we both feared that the cancer discovered in one of Mother's breasts had spread throughout her body. Our time together would be short, we felt.

I wasn't frightened of death because I know Mother would be with Jesus in heaven the moment she died. My pain came from knowing that I would no longer enjoy the fellowship of a precious friend, a friend who was always eager to rejoice with me in my joys and empathize with me in my sorrows. She never expressed ridicule or disappointment when my weaknesses or failures were evident. Instead she helped me believe in myself by listening and gently guiding me to see myself and my situation objectively. I could depend on her to understand me when I didn't understand myself. One is truly blessed to have such a friend, and I believe doubly blessed when that friend is also your mother.

As I shared these thoughts with DeWitt, the Lord brought to my mind that He wouldn't take Mother to be with Him unless it was best for both of us. So then and there, I accepted her death. Now that we know her cancer is not terminal, I can truly enjoy our relationship without being dependent on it.

It has been exciting to learn about my role as a wife and be able to share the good news with Mother. We are able to help each other correct mistakes by discussing how God's truths apply in our situation. Growing together in this area has developed a special closeness that we wouldn't have experienced otherwise.

Mother now understands that many unnecessary problems, heartaches, and disappointments developed in her marriage because she did not understand the "job description" of her chosen career. That career was to be Daddy's helpmate, meaning to "leave Father and Mother" and become "one flesh" with her husband, helping him accomplish his goals in life more effectively because he's married to her.

Mother centered her life around *her mother's* advice, direction, and approval rather than her husband's. As a result they didn't buy the farm Daddy dreamed of owning. Instead, they spent years of conflict in a general store, where Mother sought security through money rather than in God through her husband. Daddy's harsh reactions were attempts to gain his rightful place in his wife's life, not to become an over-bearing tyrant.

God doesn't want our individuality to be crushed; He means for it to bloom. It's not our responsibility to change our personalities or to pretend we like things we do not. God wants us to express our ideas and desires. Once a wife has shared her views and feelings, the final decision rests with her husband. If your ideas are overruled, you can relax and follow your husband's guidance, knowing that this doesn't carry either your approval or disapproval.

I've discovered that if I play the role of "go-between" for DeWitt and our boys, their relationships deteriorate rather than improve. I believe my Daddy would have had a closer relationship with his daughters if Mother hadn't tried to work out every situation. Mother, as the great "go-between," was actually a barrier.

Mother now understands that a wife has the freedom to participate in as many outside activities as she desires as long as they do not interfere with her career of marriage. She now has ample time to paint, listen to study tapes, read, and give her time to benevolent services.

The traits Mother wanted to change in my father's life are a mold in God's hand for reshaping her own features. For instance, spending time with Daddy has kept her from becoming the recluse she was edging toward. His desire to have meals on time and the house in order has encouraged the discipline she needed for self-respect. His thriftiness has counteracted her impulsive, excessive spending. His explosive nature has prodded her closer to Christ as her shell of protection.

Mother was reluctant to share her testimony in this book

because she was ashamed of the many mistakes she had made. Then she realized that others might be encouraged by seeing how God has used even her mistakes for all of our good as we have trusted Christ. Anyone who has met my mother need fear no longer that it's too late to make two people one in marriage.

Thinking Through with You:

Question: *What can I learn from God's Word as to how my home should be kept?*
Answer: "All things should be done with regard to decency and propriety and in an orderly fashion" (1 Cor. 14:40, AMP.).

Q.: *How important is financial security to you, and what does God's Word teach about this?*
A.: "He who trusts in his riches will fall, but the righteous will flourish like the green leaf" (Prov. 11:28, NASB).

Q.: *How is God and His truth affected by a Christian wife not in subjection to her husband?*
A.: "Encourage the young women to love their husbands, to love their children, to be sensible, pure, workers at home, kind, being subject to their own husbands, that the Word of God may not be dishonored" (Titus 2:4-5, NASB).

Q.: *Who is the only one who can enable you to unselfishly serve your husband?*
A.: "I can do everything through Christ who strengthens me" (Phil. 4:13, NIV).

Q.: *How does a married woman know that her husband is to be first in her earthly relationships and activities?*
A.: "The married woman has her cares [centered] in earthly affairs, how she may please her husband" (1 Cor. 7:34, AMP.).

9
Sex Is God's Gift

Charlene Dale

"F-I-G-H-T! You've got to F-I-G-H-T! Fight, Panthers, Fight!" The yells filled the air as I walked into the stadium for the first high school football game of the season. Girls decked out in gold mums with blue ribbons led the cheers for the home team in the bleachers on our side.

In early 1951 my family had moved to Norcross from Atlanta. At Grady High School I'd been a little fish in a big pond, but here in Norcross I was the "city" fish in a small pond. Almost immediately Margaret, a tall, blonde, Swedish girl, had become my best friend. As we found our seats for the game, my eyes checked out the football players who filled the bench below us.

"Average, average" and so on down the bench, I calculated in my head. And then, "WOW!" The most attractive guy my 16-year-old eyes had ever beheld: tall, with jet black hair. I turned to Margaret and asked, "Golly, who is that number 12?"

"You would spot him," she replied. "That's Alex Dale, only the most popular boy in school. Listen, Charlene, he's a junior and already a four-letter man!"

"Tell me more," I said.

"There's not much more to say. He's a loner, and you'd better forget it."

The game was fantastic. Norcross won 21-0. Alex made two touchdowns, and the crowd went wild.

Afterward everyone went to the gym for a victory dance. As I entered my eyes scanned the crowd, but he was nowhere to be seen.

Records played as I danced with this boy and that. Right in the middle of Eddie Fisher's "Many Times" I saw *him.*

He made his entrance, all decked out in blue jeans and white sweater with a big gold "N" on the front. He walked boldly through the crowd, tapped my partner on the shoulder, and cut in.

"I'm Alex," he said.

"Yes, I know," I answered. "I'm Charlene."

"You're new at Norcross, aren't you?" he asked.

"Yes." And the conversation continued. I felt like the queen of the hop. Alex asked me for every dance, and as we said our "good-byes," I knew I'd really captured the "big man on campus."

I got up early that following Monday. When I saw Alex that day, I wanted to look just right. I had even polished my penny loafers the night before.

I thought, "Well, if I'm going to be Alex's girl, I'd best look the part."

Between first and second periods we met in the hall—and passed in the hall. *Blam;* reality hit me. I wasn't going to be Alex's girl after all. He was nice, friendly, but yet he was distant.

For almost a year, thoughts of Alex took a back seat to cruelty jokes, 3-D movies, and my current steady, Roger.

Then my parents broke the news that we'd be moving back to Atlanta. Roger and I had broken up a few weeks before, and thoughts of Alex had again filled my head. Now we were leaving. I had to make my move.

With my friend Margaret, I plotted and maneuvered. Margaret had been going steady with Jerry, one of Alex's best friends. Margaret and I arranged with Jerry to have Alex ask me for a date.

Poor Alex, he thought the whole evening had been his idea. He called and asked if I'd like to go to a movie with Margaret and Jerry. I faked surprise at hearing from him and answered an excited "Yes."

This was my chance. I dressed ever so carefully. I wore a blue felt skirt, navy cinch belt, baby blue angora sweater and, for good measure, I put on extra crinolines. To top it off, I had my red hair cut into the newest "poodle" style.

When Alex picked me up, he looked adorable: pink shirt, black slacks and a pink-and-white belt . . . Wow! I secretly thought we had to be the best-looking couple around.

We picked up Margaret and Jerry and headed for the Fox Theater. After the movie we stopped for hamburgers and shakes. Later, holding hands at my doorstep, Alex asked if he could call me again!

Though Mother, Daddy, and I moved back to Atlanta where I enrolled in North Fulton High, Alex and I continued to date. For the next year we were inseparable. What a marvelous year! Football games, parties, and the ultimate: Alex's senior prom.

My parents went out of town the first few weeks of the following summer. I convinced Mother that leaving me with my grandmother would give her and daddy the opportunity for a lovely trip alone. In reality, my motives weren't that honorable. I simply didn't want to be away from Alex.

Spectator sports were one of the many interests Alex and I had in common. One warm summer's evening we had gone to see the Atlanta Crackers play. When we left the ballpark, we stopped at my house to watch television as Grandmother didn't have one at her house.

After a few minutes of "The Cisco Kid," we completely forgot the gunfire and thundering horses on the screen. A private house, a year of dating, and our surging emotions were more than either of us could or cared to control.

I was shattered by our intimacy. "How could things have

gone so far?" I thought. I felt that to give myself physically before marriage was unforgiveable. A "nice" girl just didn't do it!

But I believed that in giving myself to Alex, I'd formed an eternal bond between us. I knew without asking that Alex didn't feel this way. And however enjoyable those moments of ecstasy had been, they weren't worth the massive weight of guilt I began to carry.

Between my parents there was no touching or physical expression of affection shown in my presence. At the time when I needed to have serious, open talks with my mother, she completely avoided the subject. In my mind, the reason for this taboo had to be that sex was tainted, not completely honorable even for married people.

Conversations in the gym with some of the older girls became a source of sex information. I graduated from "gym talk" to salacious books that were then kept in an out-of-the-way rack at the corner drugstore. Other bits of knowledge were added from dirty jokes and movies. I felt that sex somehow verged on sin and degradation.

When Alex and I left my house that night, I swore to myself that the intimacy we shared would never happen again. But intimacy once begun is difficult, if not impossible, to end. We learned that we couldn't go from an intimate relationship back to hand-holding. One affectionate situation would lead to another: our lingering kisses led to petting, and the rising passion became so urgent we succumbed completely.

Each time we'd vow it would never happen again. Once, overwhelmed with guilt, I told Alex, "Let's pray; maybe that will keep this from happening again." But we forgot prayer and God the next time our passions were aroused.

Three years after we'd begun dating, I maneuvered us into marriage. Alex was perfectly willing, but I think he was not fully aware how he arrived there. A few nights before our wedding, Alex shared with me his ideals and expectations for a wife. His model was his grandmother, whom he admired deeply. The ideals sounded beautiful that night, but in a short time I found I couldn't or wouldn't live up to them.

We were most compatible during our first year of marriage, enjoying many mutual interests. In retrospect, I see how we ran from one activity to another in a relentless quest for happiness, excitement, and fulfillment.

Our children, two boys, came a year apart. All of a sudden I was hit by fatigue, boredom, and jealousy. Seeds of discontent took root and manifested themselves in resentment of Alex's freedom from home cares.

One by one, the interests we shared began to disappear. We both became very aware of the growing chasm.

Alex felt that if our sex life could be revitalized, the other breaks in our relationship would heal. He introduced new techniques of sexual stimulation that pleased my body but tortured my mind.

I enjoyed the innovations, yet many times waves of guilt would wash over me after Alex fell asleep. Nausea would overcome me as recollection of our love-making raced through my mind. That kind of sex reminded me of the "dirty" books in the drugstore. I was horrified to think what kind of woman I must have been to have enjoyed such pleasures. "Oh, if I could just bathe away the filth!" I agonized.

In time Alex bought us a beautiful new home in the Dunwoody area of Atlanta, and we began to attend a lovely church nearby. At this point in my life God began to move. He made me aware that even with a new home and a good husband there was still something missing. Through the church services I realized that I believed in the existence of a man named Jesus Christ, but I certainly wasn't a Christian. As I heard the Gospel, I pictured myself someday standing before the Lord and saying, "Lord, Lord, have I not done many good deeds in Your name?" Then He would say to me, "Depart from Me; I never knew you!" I was crushed by the recognition that I was spiritually lost.

Not knowing how to deal with this cruel reality, I kept up a Christian facade. I was able to fake out most people with my Scofield Bible and Strong's concordance.

But the planted seed of truth began to grow. Fortunately, my Sunday School teacher was evangelistic-minded and she recognized my Christianity as an act. As we talked one day, I broke down and told her: "Mrs. Sullivan, I don't know what's wrong with me. I just feel completely dead inside."

She answered by explaining simply why Christ came to earth and why He died and rose again. She told me of His deep love and concern for me personally. I learned how I could accept Christ's sacrifice for me. I left her that day with the *real* peace and life of Jesus Christ within me.

I practically lived at the church, after discovering true Christianity. I was starved for spiritual food. During this time I completely ignored Alex and his needs. I lost interest in home, old friends, and family. I only wanted to be with Christians. I recounted to anyone who would listen my story of finding life in Christ. I also did my best to push and preach Alex into conversion.

The drastic changes in my life made Alex quite uncomfortable. He felt left out, separated from the world I had joined. I am sure he must have tried to communicate in many ways, but I wasn't listening. I was running high on Christianity. Alex reacted by making himself scarce. I blamed Alex's lack of Christianity for the continual friction in our relationship.

Our sex life had almost died. I felt now more than ever that Alex's new style in our physical relationship was not only indecent but was evil for a Christian. Through words and action, I conveyed these opinions to Alex.

Of course, I was a lovely Christian wife while witnessing to the unsaved or visiting with other Christians. But at home I was irritable and high-strung, and I continually suffered from tension-headaches.

The ugly discrepancy between my private and my public Christianity finally became clear to me. I decided that if Christianity didn't work at home, it wasn't of much use to me in this life. How could this tension and strain be the "abundant life" Christ had promised?

Then, as if to match my resignation as wife, mother, and

homemaker, Alex quit his job. He spent afternoons drinking coffee and shooting the breeze with some of his friends. In the evenings they'd hop from one northside bar to another. Golf and fishing filled his weekends, drawing him away from home and from me.

I began to spend much time in prayer. "Dear Lord, please help me. I really want Your will. Please lead me to someone, something, which will teach me, show me how to mend the rifts in our home."

In answer to my prayer, the Lord led me to a seminar that taught me many helpful principles. The mood in our home began to brighten, but we still had a long way to go. As I faithfully studied God's Word and put into practice the principles I learned, He began to show me His deliverance.

I learned that a woman is to be submissive "even as Sarah obeyed Abraham." I began to understand that God would work through my husband for my benefit, even though he wasn't yet a Christian.

Richard, a friend of Alex's, owned two airplanes. When Richard had to have both planes in Las Vegas for an antique plane show, he asked Alex to fly one out for him.

Alex told me about the trip: "Charlene, since we would be getting our way paid, I want you to go along with me. There are some terrific shows out there with big-name stars, so be sure you pack some snazzy clothes. We'll make the rounds of the clubs."

"Oh, no, Lord," I thought. But He helped me to keep my big mouth shut, and I prepared to go.

Richard was a heavy drinker, and I had dreadful visions of what was ahead. I was afraid Alex and Richard would take me to vulgar shows and drown the evenings in alcohol. But I recalled the biblical admonition "Cast all your anxiety on Him, because He cares for you" (1 Peter 5:7, NIV). Little by little I turned my worries over to the Lord in prayer.

The Lord did so many little things that first night in Las Vegas to protect me. After arriving, we rented a car and drove toward town. Only a mile from the airport we had a flat tire.

Rain was falling, so by the time Alex and Richard had changed the tire they were muddy from head to foot.

We drove directly to the motel so Alex and Richard could clean up, and after a hot shower Alex lay down on the bed and fell asleep.

I thought, "Oh, thank You, Lord. Now we won't have to go out tonight." No sooner had the prayer left my heart than the phone rang and woke Alex up. It was Richard asking us to come down to the motel lounge.

"Charlene, get your clothes changed," Alex said. "We're going down to the bar!" I prayed silently, "Father, You promised to deliver or protect me, and I'm counting on You."

We walked into a dimly lit bar and stumbled our way past empty tables to where Richard was waiting. There we sat near a phone on which our waitress tearfully begged her boyfriend not to go out with someone else. The piano player seemed to know only one song: "I Can't Live If Livin' Is Without You." The melancholy atmosphere turned Alex off. He stood up and said peevishly, "Let's get out of this place; I can't stand all this depression."

The rain had stopped as we stepped out into the night. The lights of Las Vegas blinked alluringly up and down the street, but hunger pangs overtook all of us, and Richard suggested we dine in the Bacchanal Room at Caesar's Palace. We had a marvelous dinner in a room decorated with a Roman motif. I had never seen such beautiful appointments, nor enjoyed such gracious service.

Dinner and the Lord seemed to dilute Alex's bar-hopping desires. Instead he dropped Richard off at the Frontier Hotel and we began to tour the electrical fantasies. We walked past many dazzling casinos and some of the most luxurious hotels in the world, and just watched other people going about their night lives. The Lord spared me uncomfortable and embarrassing situations and yet let us see the interesting part of the city without upsetting my husband.

Yet the strain in our personal lives remained. I really didn't enjoy Alex's company, nor he mine. We had so few things in common. We still loved each other, but we were so far apart I wondered if there were any way to bridge the gap.

On my knees I asked the Lord to open other doors of instruction. The seminiar I had attended had taught me much, but it didn't satisfy my deeper needs as a woman and a wife. In a few days a friend of mine told me about a seminar called "Will The Real Woman Please Stand Up?" She said she had attended the previous seminar and it dealt directly with God's principles for womanhood. I thought that was exactly what I needed.

As I attended the course, I learned in depth of God's appointed role for a wife. Until then, I had understood "submission" as a response to force. I thought that only if my husband had threatened me was I compelled to obey him.

Darien Cooper taught me from God's Word of a different kind of "submission," of love, of graciousness, of contented willingness. It was an entirely different world.

After each class I went home and began to apply the assignments that Darien gave at the end of each lesson. She explained that we must allow Christ to produce these attitudes and actions in us. As we open ourselves to Him, she said, He will begin making the necessary changes.

I had already tired to do similar things without Christ's help and had failed miserably. But as I became receptive to Christ. He began to change my heart, my attitudes, and my life. The spirit of love began to grow in the garden of our home.

The Lord began to make me aware of many areas of my life in which He had much work to do. In the past, Alex had made cutting remarks about my church attendance. He said, "You spend so much time at that church, maybe you ought to move down there." I never had an answer for that statement.

As I began to apply the principles from God's Word that Darien taught, I realized I indeed had my priorities out of order. The words of Paul passed through my mind: "The married woman has her cares [centered] in earthly affairs, how she please her husband" (1 Cor 7:34, AMP). So I could spend more time with Alex, I quit going to church on Wednesday and Sunday nights. Alex's jealousy of my Christian activities began to fade.

One night I sat down and had a heart-to-heart talk with the man I had married. "Alex, I have just come to understand how wrong my dominance of our home has been," I said. "I know I have copped out in my duties as your wife and the children's mother. You know, honey, it was frightening to realize I wasn't even pleasing the Lord."

Alex sat silently with an "I-can't-believe-this" expression on his face.

"Darling, I apologize for taking control of our marriage, and from this day forward I am backing away. The control of our home, our lives, the whole ball of wax is yours," I said.

Alex, being the dominant type, was astounded by my turnaround, and he seemed in no time to grow in stature with the responsibility I had returned to him.

After much prayer about it, I felt the Lord wanted me to stop my Sunday morning church attendance also. It was obvious that Alex still thought I preferred church and Christians to being with him. I was so afraid to stop going to church altogether that I delayed more than a month after I knew the Lord wanted me to stay home. I feared I would falter in adhering to Christian principles if I weren't reminded regularly by that church service.

Through intense studying and praying, I saw that whatever was in God's will, including pleasing my husband, would not cause me to fall. It was amazing how I was spiritually fed during this period.

I attended a weekly Bible class when it wouldn't interfere with my being with Alex. I read books and listened to teaching tapes. I had the opportunity to hear some unusual speakers on television, such as Corrie ten Boom. I prayed more, and deliberately followed the Lord's Word.

After three months Alex and I were out driving one evening when he asked, "Why in the world did you stop going to church?"

"Well, I learned that it pleased God for me to please

you," I answered. "And I know how opposed you are to my going to church, so I quit. I love you and want your happiness."

He pondered a few minutes and then said words I never expected to hear: "I want you to go back to church and take the boys with you. The church has been good for the boys, and I want them and you to go back."

Miracle!

Alex's attitude has changed greatly, but I still go to church only on Sunday mornings. I know there will be a time when I can resume normal attendance, when it doesn't affect Alex and our relationship. When there is a special program, I ask if he minds if I attend. I try to use better judgment in considering participation in church activities.

Tension lingered on in our bedroom. My fear that Alex's ideas of sex were perverted continued to plague my mind and our relations. One night he said, "You know, I might as well be going to bed with a nun."

The words cut me deeply, but I couldn't cope with my feelings of shame. Alex almost became impotent and I struggled constantly against frigidity.

Eventually I talked with a close friend who was also experiencing sexual problems. I had never been able to discuss my feelings, thoughts, and problems on the subject with anyone, but Sharon was so open that together we learned, read the Scriptures, and discussed what I had heard at Darien's seminar.

Darien said the physical union in marriage was ordained by God for our blessing. "God has designed our desires for the marriage relationship so that when we come together as husband and wife we can share in a physical way what has already happened in our souls," she said.

She talked about the closeness developed in marriage by giving ourselves one to the other. Fulfilling each other's desires and giving each other pleasure is part of the joy of marriage, she said.

I first realized that sex was God's idea as I read Genesis

1:27. "He created him; male and female He created them." God created man and woman, then "saw everything that He had made, and behold, it was very good" (Gen. 1:31, AMP). I had never thought of sex as being fully right and good, and from God.

All of a sudden it was as if someone had turned on the light in a dark room. Since there had been no display of affection in my home and the information I had obtained came from disreputable sources, I felt the whole subject was something that nice people could not revel in.

As the inner light became brighter, I realized that I should satisfy my husband's sexual appetite as a fountain satisfies a thirsty person. I learned that there are no sexual perversions when a wife is satisfying her husband's sexual desires and needs. (Of course, Charlene was not referring to acts of sadism.) The writer to the Hebrews said, "Marriage is honorable in all, and the bed undefiled" (Heb. 13:4).

I also learned that I could be a stumbling block if I didn't satisfy my husband's desires. "Do not refuse and deprive each other [of your due marital rights] . . . lest Satan tempt you [to sin] through your lack of restraint of sexual desires" (1 Cor. 7:5, AMP).

Of course, my concepts and feelings didn't change instantly. But I constantly kept 1 Corinthians 7:4 before me as I needed to be reminded that "the wife's body does not belong to her alone but also to her husband" (NIV).

Viewing our relationship according to God's Word made a complete difference in my response to Alex. Realizing how beautiful this oneness is, I can fully express my love for Alex. I praise God that I am liberated now from the world's tawdry view of sex and living in Christ's freedom of pure love.

Alex is not a Christian yet. But I heard him tell the boys the other day, "God has made me responsible for you, and therefore I expect you to do as I say." I have learned through mistakes that I am not to do the work of the Holy Spirit. I need not preach at Alex; I am going to do my best to make Alex happy, and let God make him holy.

Reminiscing with Darien:

I was eager to meet Charlene because reports I was hearing indicated she was not a "secret-service Christian." Not only did she bring women to hear my lectures, but she encouraged them on the way to class that God's principles really do work. After class they would meet for coffee or lunch and talk about how the truths applied to their individual situations. Charlene was an answer to my prayer that the large class size would not prevent individual needs from being met.

Charlene entered her marriage with "two strikes" against her. She had absorbed distorted views about sex as a young person, and she bore guilt because of premarital relations. Both of these conditions adversely affected her personality and emotions, which are vital elements in sexual compatibility.

Charlene learned that God forbids sex outside of marriage because He wants to protect our happiness. Illicit sex not only damages one's personality, it can destroy the body. The Bible directs: "Flee immorality. Every other sin that a man commits is outside the body, but the immoral man sins agsinst his own body (1 Cor. 6:18, NASB). The deeper, spiritual harm is cited in Proverbs 6:32, "Whoso committeth adultery with a woman lacketh understanding; he that doeth it destroyeth his own soul." Distrust, jealousy, and disintegration of identity may stem from sexual immorality.

Charlene's guilt and frigidity were corrected when she confessed her sin of immorality and began looking at sex from God's perspective.

Charlene's other valuable lesson was that it is not *where* you are that's important but *why* you are there. She was willing to accompany her husband to a night club to please him, but God intervened in such a way that Alex did not blame her. Other women have found that when God didn't prevent them from going to questionable places, He used their uncondemning spirits later to draw their husbands to the Lord.

Charlene understood that she must temporarily stop attending church in order to correct Alex's erroneous idea that she preferred the church and Christians to being with him.

Because Charlene knew that the spiritual food and strength customarily gained at church must be replaced with personal Bible study and other help, she was not "neglecting the assembling" of Christians cautioned by God's Word. She refrained for a time for a godly purpose. And God honored her obedience.

As Charlene concentrates on fulfilling *her* role, God will fulfill His purpose for Alex in His time.

Thinking Through with You:

Question: *What kinds of sex does God condemn?*
Answer: "Don't be under any illusion—neither the impure, the idolator or the adulterer; neither the effeminate, the pervert . . . shall have any share in the kingdom of God. And such men, remember, were some of you! But you have cleansed yourselves from all that; you have been made whole in spirit; you have been justified in the name of the Lord Jesus and in His very Spirit" (1 Cor. 6:9-11, PH).

Q.: *How did Jesus combine compassion and correction toward the woman caught in adultery?*
A.: "Neither do I condemn you; go your way; from now on sin no more" (John 8:11, NASB).

Q.: *How may sins of sexual immorality be forgiven?*
A.: "If we confess our sins, He is faithful and righteous to forgive us our sins and to cleanse us from all unrighteousness" (1 John 1:9, NASB).

Q.: *How does God commend the pleasures of marital union?*
A.: "Let your fountain—of human life—be blessed [with the rewards of fidelity], and rejoice with the wife of your youth. Let her be as the loving hind and pleasant doe [tender, gentle, attractive]; let her bosom satisfy you at all times; and always be transported with delight in her love" (Prov. 5:18-19, AMP).

Do remember: when the principles of God's Word become a part of your life:

You will find fulfillment in your personal life and your marriage;

You will have a closer relationship to God who ordained marriage;

You will discover that you are a real woman—the wife of a happy husband!

Also Available
Cassette tape recordings relating to the ministry of Darien Cooper.

Carousel Slide Presentation based on the book, *You Can Be the Wife of a Happy Husband.*

Video Tape Series based on *You Can Be the Wife of a Happy Husband* (eight 55-minute seminar presentations).

For complete details, write:

HIS WAY LIBRARY
P.O. Box 630
Buchanan, GA 30113
Phone: 404/646-3858

For materials by Anne Kristin Carroll, write:

LOVE'S OUTREACH
P.O. Box 888312
Atlanta, GA 30338

Recommended Reading

(These authors and their books have influenced the life of Darien Cooper.)

Andelin, Helen B., *Fascinating Womanhood.* Santa Barbara, Calif.: Pacific Press.

Bright, Bill, *Revolution Now.* San Bernardino, Calif.: Campus Crusade for Christ, Inc.

Christenson, Larry, *The Christian Family.* Minneapolis, Minn.: Bethany Fellowship, Inc.

Hallesby, O., *Prayer.* Minneapolis, Minn.: Augsburg Publishing House.

Handford, Elizabeth Rice, *Me? Obey Him?* Murfreesboro, Tenn.: Sword of the Lord Publishers.

LaHaye, Tim, *Spirit-Controlled Temperament, How To Be Happy Though Married,* and *Transformed Temperaments.* Wheaton, Ill.: Tyndale House Publishers.

Miles, Hubert J., *Sexual Happiness in Marriage.* Grand Rapids, Mich.: Zondervan Publishing House.

Narramore, Clyde M., *A Woman's World.* Grand Rapids, Mich.: Zondervan Publishing House.

Price, Eugenia, *God Speaks to Women Today.* Grand Rapids, Mich.: Zondervan Publishing House.

Rice, Shirley, *The Christian Home.* Norfolk, Va.: Norfolk Christian Schools.

Smith, Hannah Whithall, *The Christian's Secret of a Happy Life.* Westwood, N.J.: Fleming H. Revell Company.

Stanford, Miles J., *The Principle of Position, The Green Letters,* and *The Reckoning that Counts.* Colorado Springs, Colorado: Christian Correspondence.

Stuart, W. David, *A Gracious Woman.* Warr Acres, Okla.: The Warr Foundation.

Thomas, Major W. Ian, *The Saving Life of Christ.* Grand Rapids, Mich.: Zondervan Publishing House.

Tournier, Paul, *To Understand Each Other.* Richmond, Va.: John Knox Press.

Wilcox, Ethel Jones, *Power for Christian Living.* Glendale, Calif.: G/L Publications.

BOOKS SUGGESTED BY THE PUBLISHER

Baker, Elizabeth, *Love Around the House*. Wheaton, Ill.: Victor Books—**6-2603/$1.95.**

Christenson, Evelyn, *Lord, Change Me*. Wheaton, Ill.: Victor Books—**6-2756/$2.95.**

Christenson, Evelyn, *What Happens When Women Pray*. Wheaton, Ill.: Victor Books—**6-2715/$2.50.**

Florio, Anthony, *Two to Get Ready,* Wheaton, Ill.: Victor Books—**6-2635/$3.50.**

Hendricks, Howard G., *Heaven Help the Home*. Wheaton, Ill.: Victor Books—**6-2240/$3.25.**

Hess, Ruth, *Love Knows No Barriers*. Wheaton, Ill.: Victor Books—**6-2780/$2.25.**

Johnson, Rex, *At Home with Sex*. Wheaton, Ill.: Victor Books—**6-2639/$3.50.**

Landorf, Joyce, *The Fragrance of Beauty*. Wheaton, Ill.: Victor Books—**6-2231/$2.25.**

Mallory, James D., *The Kink and I—a Psychiatrist's Guide to Untwisted Living*. Wheaton, Ill.: Victor Books—**6-2237/$2.95.**

Myra, Harold, *Love Notes to Jeanette*. Wheaton, Ill.: Victor Books—**6-2638/$3.50.**

Neff, Miriam, *Discover Your Worth*. Wheaton, Ill.: Victor Books—**6-2783/$1.95.**

Petersen, J. Allan, *Conquering Family Stress*. Wheaton, Ill.: Victor Books—**6-2632/$3.50.**

Stroud, Marion, *I Love God & My Husband*. Wheaton, Ill.: Victor Books—**6-2734/$1.95.**

Wright, Norman, *The Family That Listens*. Wheaton, Ill.: Victor Books—**6-2633/$3.50.**